MW00824371

"To make true Mexican cuisine, you must start with heart and soul. In this book, Rogelio bares his soul and displays his love through cooking."

—**VAL CANTÚ**, chef and owner of Californios, the first US restaurant serving Mexican cuisine to earn two Michelin stars

"*Convivir* is the antidote for those who don't see the grandeur of Mexican cuisine married with a love of America's best wine belt; it sits at the intersection of wine and good communal eating, with roots in traditions millennia old stretching across oceans and continents. This is a beautiful, fresh take meant to make you rush into the kitchen."

—**MICHAEL TWITTY**, author of James Beard Award–winning *The Cooking Gene*

"In *Convivir*, Chef Rogelio Garcia uses creative and sumptuous food to share his compelling and improbable personal journey. Gratefully, this beautifully photographed and well-written cookbook inventively expands the narrow conceptions that so many hold about Mexican cuisine."

—**ADRIAN MILLER**, culinary historian, author, and two-time James Beard Award winner

"I've had the privilege of watching Rogelio mature and grow throughout his journey from a young cook at the French Laundry to the accomplished, Michelin-starred chef he is today. *Convivir* provides an inspirational view of this journey, capturing his authentic hospitality, fueled by his love for cuisine, culture, and the people that have helped shape him as a chef, both past and present. The recipes, stories, and photos in these pages are sure to resonate with both aspiring young chefs following a similar journey and anyone, like me, looking for the keys to unlock the secrets behind amazing Mexican cuisine!"

—**PHILIP TESSIER**, Michelin-starred chef, 2017 gold medalist and 2015 silver medalist of the Bocuse d'Or, and author of *Chasing Bocuse*

CONVIVIR

Modern Mexican Cuisine in California's Wine Country

CONVIVIR

Modern Mexican Cuisine in California's Wine Country

By Rogelio Garcia

with Andréa Lawson Gray

Photography by John Troxell

CAMERON + COMPANY

Petaluma, California

CONTENTS

PREFACE

"Your Social Security number has been denied, and you need to call the Social Security office."

This is my first memory of being rejected for a job at a high-end restaurant where I really wanted to work. I felt a knot in my stomach. As I walked out, my eyes filled with tears.

This memory, albeit painful, is at the heart of what has inspired me to write this cookbook. At some point, I felt compelled to tell my story and share my immigrant experience through food—the journey of what it means to be born in Mexico and grow up in Northern California.

My mother, Irma Robles, was twenty-six years old when she crossed the border in 1988, a single mother with two small children. I was two and my sister was seven. Much later, I realized the magnitude of what she had done for us, and eventually I found myself wondering, *How bad could Mexico have been for her to leave everything behind?*

My mother came to this country with no money and no way to call home to let her family know how she was. The border crossing is treacherous, and every year, hundreds of migrants die, the relics of their lives strewn across the deserts where northern Mexico meets the southern border of the United States or washed up on the banks of the Rio Grande. Given both the inhospitable landscape and the distance, the reality is that the family you leave in Mexico may never see you again. I've long asked myself how my mother did this and what drove her. Irma, you are a brave woman.

The realization that my mother left her homeland and every family member, friend, and relationship so her children had a chance to chase the American dream created a fire that burns deep inside of me. I feel that my mother passed me a torch, and I hope and pray that my two sons, Daniel and Christian, understand this so that I can pass the torch on to them.

Fortunately, my children have not grown up with the uncertainty that is the hallmark of the life of the undocumented. They will never truly grasp how it feels to drive in fear of getting pulled over, to be unable to get a job the *right* way, to always keep their heads down, to try to take up as little space as possible, to try to be invisible.

To some of my friends, this may sound incongruous with the Rogelio they know. They may not understand that the very basic opportunities that most Americans enjoy are the same ones I have been seeking and can never take for granted. When I was younger, I was ashamed to talk about my immigration situation. Today, I want to share the deep pain I feel about being unable to truly be part of this country. America is the golden cage that we can never leave.

President Barack Obama gave the undocumented an opportunity in 2012, the year the Deferred Action for Childhood Arrivals (DACA) passed, and I applied for and received DACA status. It was the opportunity I had been looking for since 1988, and I am thankful for it every single day. It allowed me to walk without fear—or so I thought. But without a path to citizenship, we can never truly feel secure in our adopted country. This became a painful truth for me early in 2023 when my DACA renewal application was delayed due to a governmental backlog. I had been employed as the executive chef of a new fine-dining restaurant for less than two months when I was forced to take an "administrative leave." While the leave lasted for only three weeks, it seemed like an eternity. I felt the panic and the uncertainty all over again. Even though I still had my legal status and could move freely, I once again felt like that sixteen-year-old kid who was denied a job because he didn't have a Social Security number—that kid who was afraid that one driving error could result in deportation.

I know that I will not be free from this awful feeling until I have my US citizenship. Nor will I feel secure until we are all secure—until there is a path to citizenship for all DACA recipients and, beyond that, for the many Mexicans and Mexican Americans who make up the labor force that runs this country's restaurant kitchens. I dedicate this book to them.

That's also how I approach food. At the heart of my cuisine is Mexico, but the ingredients, discipline, and techniques are pure California. It is through food that I am able to translate my experiences and tell my story.

When I walked into a restaurant kitchen for the first time at the age of sixteen, it was intimidating mostly because I had no idea that cooking was both an art and a discipline. I didn't understand that food not only had to taste good but also look good—to be exquisitely presented.

Even more daunting were the flavors and many of the ingredients. Something as basic as chives was unfamiliar, and pâtés and truffles were completely foreign to me.

What I knew were the classic flavors of Mexico that my mother cooked. I remember seeing the more experienced line cooks make Mexican "family meals" (when the staff eats together at the end of a shift) like enchiladas, Spanish rice, beans, chilaquiles, and huevos rancheros and thinking that these comidas were better than the European-style dishes we were serving in the restaurant. As it turns out, I spent the next six years or so focused on that Eurocentric cuisine, absorbing everything I could from the chefs I worked with and collecting cookbooks for information and inspiration.

In time, it was my turn to make family meals, which, in all the fine-dining restaurants I worked at, once again meant Mexican food. That's when I started getting creative, using leftovers to make dishes that took the food that I grew up with to the next level.

Once I experienced that burst of inspiration, it was as if a culinary floodgate had opened, and little by little, those flavors started to creep into the restaurant menus I was charged with creating. This book is a way for me to express all that creativity, to share everything I've learned, starting in my mother's kitchen.

Today, my food is a unique mix of my mother's home cooking and my classic French training, garnished with a bit of Spain along the way—all made possible by the amazing ingredients just outside my door here in Northern California.

INTRODUCTION

What Is Convivir?

Translated literally, *convivir* means "to live together." When I speak of convivencia (coexistence), my thoughts turn to living together, commingling, and respecting one another's space, culture, values, and viewpoints—all of which can happen through food. That is what makes this book special. The pandemic, the Black Lives Matter movement, the war in Ukraine, the culture wars—these and countless other current events have changed our world forever. It is my hope that through sharing recipes or a meal, we can find some common ground "on a plate," a renewed respect, and the will to create changes for the better. The dinner table is an almost sacred space, one where we are able to share our life experiences, our knowledge, and the stories that made us who we are today. Being proud of your heritage and culture at this moment in time, when diversity is finally being celebrated, is exciting. It is this pride in my own culture, as a Mexican and as a Californian, that motivates me to share my cuisine with others.

The concept of convivir also speaks to working in harmony with the environment—to appreciating how the food I cook in my kitchen is connected to its sources. This relationship starts in the fields, orchards, and farms of Northern California. There's an energy and joy in sourcing the ingredients, in the smell of the soil and the sea, in my friendships with the ranchers, farmers, and fishers. In our kitchens and at our dining tables, we honor both the ingredients and the labor that brings them to market. Through the recipes in this book, I hope to share that energy and joy—to encourage you to follow my recipes and make the food you cook from them—my food—your own.

The reach of convivir is much greater in Mexico, where the ebb and flow of daily life, especially in the pueblos, revolves more fully around food and food preparation. Traditional kitchen tools, ingredients, techniques, and recipes are preserved and passed down through the generations. This spirit of "connection" is another kind of "coexisting," of convivencia, in which food preparation means "living together with one's ancestors." It is the culinary basis of *mexicanidad*, a word used to describe Mexico's connection to its pre-Hispanic indigenous cultures, a link perhaps best captured by the tamalada, or "tamale party."

Tamales are one of the world's oldest recorded foods, the preparation of which has changed little over the centuries. While the social gathering itself is the end game, the tamalada begins days before the actual party with the coming together of the women who create the meal. First they take the maíz (corn) to the molino (mill) that grinds the masa quebradita (coarse masa for tamales) and then they work together to make the tamales for the big party.

I've included a complete menu for a tamalada along with step-by-step instructions for making tamales (see pages 30–33).

The tamalada gives a glimpse into the role fiestas and their menus play in Mexican life, bringing people together and embracing customs that have changed little since precolonial times. I've also included menus that share the customs and food traditions for three of Mexico's most important fiesta days, Día de los Muertos, Día de la Independencia, and Año Nuevo, as well as menus for other celebratory gatherings. Taken together, they are a sort of cultural culinary immersion that offers a window into another place and even another time.

It is this convivencia, this energy and joy of coming together to cook and chismear (gossip) and then to eat and drink and laugh that is at the heart of what cooking in Mexico is all about. It is also at the heart of this book.

The Story of Mexican Cuisine in California

In California, Mexican cuisine has always been intertwined with California's winemakers, so it is only natural that a cookbook on modern Mexican cuisine would come out of wine country. The story begins more than 240 years ago when Father Junípero Serra, a Franciscan missionary, brought settlers from Mexico to establish Mission San Diego de Alcalá, the first mission in Alta California. They soon planted what would later be recognized as the first vineyard in California, the harvest of which was used for communion wine. As immigrants have always done, these Mexican newcomers carried their techniques, flavors, and even their cooking tools north with them.

The idea of traveling with kitchenware may seem strange, but the practice has historical roots in the adelitas, unsung heroines of the Mexican Revolution. Also known as soldaderas, these female soldiers often carried pots, pans, and griddles around their waists, sometimes along with their children strapped to their backs. When not fighting side-by-side with the men, they prepared meals in the camps. Even today, it is not unusual for someone to have a molcajete (mortar) passed down through generations, each with its own story and hundreds of years of flavors ground into the volcanic stone. Treasured family cooking secrets are sometimes painstakingly handwritten in notebooks, which, like the tools, are handed down through the generations.

Over the next two centuries, Mexican cooking in California evolved, and in the 1970s, it was integral to the birth of California cuisine, which celebrates locavore cooking and dining and embraces the culinary contributions of the myriad immigrants who live in the state. Of course, the early settlers from Mexico were fusing Spanish, Mexican, and Indigenous American cooking, using the locally grown ingredients they found in their new homeland, long before California cuisine made it popular.

Cooking in Mexico is, and always has been, a locavore experience. Outside of Mexico's major urban centers, Mexicans tend to cook what grows around them. Aside from the "three sisters" (squash, corn, and beans), which are found throughout the country, farm-to-table cooking largely accounts for the development of Mexico's seven regional cuisines: Yucatecan, Oaxacan, Poblano (from Puebla), Baja Californian, Veracruzano, Northern Mexican and Western Mexican. Similarly, California cuisine continues to take its inspiration from its local flora and fauna or, as described in the 2019 *Michelin Guide California*, is characterized by an "emphasis on fresh, local ingredients, innovative techniques and an openness to the cultural influences of the state's diverse population."

The term *modern Mexican* when applied to cuisine is almost an oxymoron. Mexican cuisine is ancient, using tradition-bound techniques and nearly sacred ingredients. In fact, some of the ingredients *are* sacred, like corn from which the Aztecs believe the gods formed the first humans, and chocolate that was made into a ceremonial beverage before Catholic missionaries eradicated such rituals. The longevity of techniques like nixtamalization, cooking tortillas on a comal, and grinding spices in a molcajete speak to the ingenuity and mastery that is Mexican cooking. In 2010, UNESCO described traditional Mexican cuisine this way when inscribing it to the Representative List of the Intangible Cultural Heritage of Humanity:

[It is] a comprehensive cultural model comprising farming, ritual practices, age-old skills, culinary techniques and ancestral community customs and manners. It is made possible by collective participation in the entire traditional food chain: from planting and harvesting to cooking and eating. The basis of the system is founded on corn, beans, and chili; unique farming method . . .; and singular utensils including grinding stones and stone mortars. . . . Mexican cuisine is elaborate and symbol-laden, with everyday tortillas and tamales, both made of corn, forming an integral part of Day of the Dead offerings. Collectives of female cooks and other practitioners devoted to raising crops and traditional cuisine are found . . . across Mexico. Their knowledge and techniques express community identity, reinforce social bonds, and build stronger local, regional and national identities.

In this, we can see how Mexican gastronomy is both ancient and modern: a living, evolving cultural legacy passed from generation to generation for centuries. Many cooking techniques and recipes that were in use in pre-Hispanic times are still in use. Modern Mexican cuisine, as represented in this book, looks to the local produce and purveyors of Northern California, adapting and modifying traditional dishes based on what is local in California's wine country.

That openness and those cultural influences are part and parcel of what gave birth to modern Mexican cuisine in Northern California. It is this freedom to be creative while honoring the traditions of one of the world's most respected and complex cuisines that provided the fertile ground for the recipes in *Convivir: Modern Mexican Cooking in California's Wine Country.*

HOW TO USE THIS BOOK

Traditional Mexican food is "slow food": everything is made from scratch, starting with taking corn to the molino to be milled into masa, which is then used in a variety of ways. Traditional preparation for some dishes can take at least several hours or up to several days and is often a communal endeavor, with women (typically) from neighboring households and/or the extended family sharing the tasks. Making tamales is an excellent example.

Modern cooking doesn't look like that. People have busy schedules and limited time in the kitchen, so I've tried to make my recipes user-friendly. For example, I have indicated when parts of a recipe can be prepared in advance. Sometimes an element or two of a recipe can be made ahead and frozen until you're ready to tackle the entire recipe. While I've approached each dish through a made-from-scratch lens, I've also provided store-bought options when they make sense and don't change the dish significantly.

Because I am a chef, my inspiration begins at the source, so most of the recipes are organized by where the main ingredient originates: milpa, a small cultivated field; mar, the sea; and rancho, a livestock farm. There is also a section on masa in which all the recipes are based on corn or wheat flour. In the Milpa section, I have taken the organization one step further, with some recipes grouped according to their main ingredient, such as lavender, stone fruits, corn, or chiles.

Throughout the sections, I have also provided menus for a few popular Mexican holidays, including Día de los Muertos, Día de la Independencia, Día de la Virgen de Guadalupe, and Año Nuevo; a Thanksgiving meal with a Mexican twist; and a dinner celebrating DACA immigrants. For some of these menus, I've added wine pairings for many of the courses in the featured menus and some individual recipes, as well as tequila pairings for one of the menus. For anyone who prefers to access recipes in a more traditional manner, there is an index of recipes by course at the end of book.

Starting on page 259, you'll find useful recipes, techniques, and information, including directions for preparing such commonly used basics as stocks, compound butters, and dressings; a wealth of salsas; a guide to Mexican and Californian chiles; instructions on dry roasting chiles and rendering lard; a glossary that covers both ingredients and tools; and much more. Many of the basic recipes can be prepared in advance and refrigerated or frozen, so they'll be on hand when you need them.

Whether you are planning a dinner for a special occasion with friends and family—in which case one of my featured menus might be just the thing—or want to incorporate new techniques and recipes in your cooking, I hope you will come to share my passion for modern Mexican cuisine and fresh, local ingredients.

MASA

MASA

MASA: A PRIMER

The recipes in this section explore a modern take on the corn masa creations that are best known through Mexico's street food. Masa—literally "dough"—is at the heart of Mexican cuisine, turning up in tacos, tamales, tostadas, sopes, huaraches, tlacoyos, and tetelas. I've also included recipes based on wheat flour, which was introduced to Mexico by Europeans during the Spanish conquest.

There is evidence that maíz (corn), a staple of the Mesoamerican diet, was cultivated as early as 5000 BCE in the valleys of south-central Mexico. Its importance is reflected in the Mayan creation myth, which recounts how the gods formed the first humans from corn masa. The basis for such quintessential Mexican dishes as tamales and tortillas is examined in detail by Jeffrey Pilcher in *¡Que vivan los tamales! Food and the Making of Mexican Identity*, a cultural and political history of Mexican food. In it he notes that "part of the ongoing effort . . . to Europeanize Mexico was an attempt to replace corn with wheat. But native foods and flavors persisted and became an essential part of . . . what it meant to be authentically Mexican."

Of course, the most enduring modern manifestation of Aztec cuisine is the tortilla, which occupies an almost sacred place on the Mexican table. History is blessed with the writings of Spanish conquistador Bernal Díaz del Castillo, known as the "father of food history," who finished his great work, *The True History of the Conquest of New Spain*, in 1568. It recounts in great detail the then decades-old campaigns of the Spanish in Mexico, including an occasion in which Montezuma II was served tortillas that were "very white, and . . . brought to him in plates covered with clean cloths." Little has changed. Tortillas are presented this way even today, in baskets covered with painstakingly embroidered cloths. Also unchanged, even as cornfields have given way to housing tracts in modern Mexico, the "three sisters"—corn, beans, and squash—along with chiles, remain staples of the Mexican diet.

The process for getting the most nutrition from corn, which was first used in the pre-Columbian era and is still practiced today, is called nixtamalization, a form of wet milling. The corn kernels are brought to a boil in an alkaline solution of wood ash or lime (calcium hydroxide, labeled "cal" in Mexican groceries) and water and then left to steep in the solution before hulling. This process softens the kernels, liberating the nutrients that provided the Mayans and Aztecs, and now all of Mexico, with the basis for a balanced diet. Traditionally, the next step was to grind the kernels on a metate (three-legged grinding stone) with a metlapil (stone rolling pin) to produce masa, a laborious task. Although store-bought masa harina (flour) is widely available today, many Mexicans continue to carry their corn to mills where they line up to watch as it is ground into flour.

Masa vs. Masa Harina

Specifically, masa refers to dough made from processed corn flour and is the basis of much of Mexican cuisine. In this case, the term *processing* refers to nixtamalization (see page 21).

According to Masienda founder Jorge Gaviria, masa harina, the powdered basis for tortillas and tamales, was invented at the turn of the twentieth century when Texas-based José Bartolome Martinez "tinkered with intentionally dehydrating freshly milled masa [in order to create something that] could be safely held for months before use" and rehydrated with water as needed. This was a game changer for Mexican women who faced the time-consuming task of preparing nixtamal (limed kernels) each night and grinding fresh masa daily (the first refrigerator for home use was not invented until 1913).

The Case for Handmade Tortillas

The secret to a great tortilla, like anything you create in the kitchen, lies in the ingredients, which are few. If you are not lucky enough to have a local vendor who mills their own fresh masa, all you need to make your own is masa harina, water, and maybe a bit of salt (and in some cases manteca, or lard), so your choice of masa harina is critical.

Commodity vs. Artisanal Masa

Maseca is the dominant masa harina brand. It sells commodity masa harina in that the corn is intensively farmed. The company offers a variety of products, from blue corn masa harina to masa harina specifically for tamales. Bob's Red Mill also offers masa harina, including an organic option, and is definitely a better choice: it is sustainably produced, non-GMO, and stone-ground.

An even better option, and my recommendation, is Masienda-brand masa harina, which is made from heirloom corn. According to Masienda, its corn "comes from farmer-preserved seeds that have been hand-selected for the best flavor and maintained for hundreds (even thousands) of years. Each

generation does its own part to further perfect the corn's flavor and quality before it's passed on to the next generation."

Can I Mill My Own Masa Harina?

For those of you who like everything from scratch and thrive on reproducing traditional techniques in your own kitchen, the answer is a resounding yes. You probably won't grind your nixtamalized corn the traditional way, on a curved grinding stone (though you can purchase metate and metlapil sets on online retailers). The go-to source for all things masa is Masienda founder Jorge Gaviria's cookbook *Masa*, which will walk you through the steps of the nixtamalization process, then offer options for grinding your corn, which include everything from a food processor to a hand mill to your own molino.

What About Store-Bought Tortillas?

The easy way out, of course, is to use store-bought tortillas, and when time is short, this can be a great solution. Fortunately, with the dual drivers of the popularity of cooking Mexican food at home and GMO-free, organic farming, there are probably several brands of pretty good locally produced, ready-made tortillas at your local high-end market (more likely than at your local Mexican market). They should be stocked in the refrigerated section. Always check the label for non-GMO corn flour and no preservatives.

Buying Fresh Masa

Fresh masa is a gift! If you have a local store or other vendor who has a commercial repar (mill) and makes fresh masa from corn, going through the process of nixtamalization on-site, you're in luck. Such purveyors usually offer at least two different kinds of fresh masa and sometimes more.

If you are making tortillas, you will ask for "masa preparada para tortillas" or "masa fina," which is a smooth dough made from freshly nixtamalized corn, water, and salt. It may be available in an array of colors—white, yellow, blue, red—depending on the type of corn used. Sometimes you can find masa verde (green),

which gets its color from the addition of nopales (cactus paddles).

Tortillas taste best when you use fresh masa fina made the same day. The masa will keep well covered at room temperature for up to 12 hours. You can refrigerate tightly covered fresh masa for a day or two, but the resulting tortillas will be a little less light and fluffy. Masa fina used for making huaraches, sopes, or tostadas can be refrigerated for up to 3 days.

If you are making tamales, you will ask for "masa preparada para tamales," or "masa gruesa," which is a coarse dough made from freshly nixtamalized corn, water, and salt. It will keep in an airtight container in the refrigerator for up to 3 days or in the freezer for up to 3 months. After thawing, you may need to add a little masa harina, and maybe even a little lard, to achieve the desired consistency, as masa tends to get a little aguada (watery) because of ice crystals that form in the freezing process.

ABOUT TORTILLAS

Tortillas are almost synonymous with Mexican cuisine. Multifunctional, they are at once eating utensils, comestibles, and even a dinner bell of sorts (when the tortillas are on the comal, it means dinner is ready). Spanish colonizers were quite taken by these masa creations, as noted by Frances Calderón de la Barca, a Spanish aristocrat, in *Life in Mexico*, a collection of her letters home self-published in 1843:

> *Those who are rather particular, roll up two tortillas, and use them as a knife and fork, which, I can assure you from experience, is a great deal better than nothing, when you have learnt how to use them . . . They first cook the grain in water with a little lime, and when it is soft peel off the skin; then grind it on a large block of stone, the metate, or, as the Indians (who know best) call it, the metatl. For the purpose of grinding it, they use a sort of stone roller, with which it is crushed, and rolled into a bowl placed below the stone. They then take some of this paste, and clap it between their hands, till they form it into light round cakes, which are afterwards toasted on a smooth plate, called the comalli (comal they call it in Mexico), and which ought to be eaten as hot as possible.*

BASIC MASA
FROM MASA HARINA

Different brands of masa harina yield slightly different results and require a slightly different ratio of flour to liquid. The flour and water amounts used here are based on working with Masienda-brand masa harina. If using a different brand, refer to the package for the ratio of liquid to flour. Lard can be added, although is not traditional in Mexico. The result will be a more pliable tortilla with a slight flavor boost.

INGREDIENTS

1 cup (120 g) Masienda-brand white, yellow, blue, or red masa harina

¼ teaspoon kosher salt

1 scant cup (230 ml) warm water or stock of choice

1 tablespoon lard, duck fat, or bacon fat (optional)

MAKES 12 OUNCES (340 G) BASIC MASA

In a stand mixer fitted with the paddle attachment (or in a large bowl with a handheld mixer), stir together the masa harina and salt. On low speed, slowly add the water and beat just until evenly incorporated. (You can instead mix the ingredients with your hands in the bowl.) Now, using your hands, knead the masa well in the bowl, making sure the water is fully incorporated and no powdery spots remain. Add the lard, if using, kneading to incorporate. Your masa should be moist to the touch, leave wet bits on your fingers, and have a slightly sticky feel. If your masa is too dry, add a little more warm water. If it is too wet, add a little more masa harina.

Use the masa immediately. If you must wait for several minutes before using, cover your masa with a clean, slightly damp dish towel or wrap in plastic wrap. Depending upon the lapsed time, you will likely need to add a little water to return it to the correct consistency.

HOMEMADE TORTILLAS

MAKES SIX 6- TO 7-INCH (15- TO 17-CM), EIGHT 5- TO 6-INCH (12- TO 15-CM), OR TWELVE 3- TO 4-INCH (7.5- TO 10-CM) TORTILLAS

INGREDIENTS

12 ounces (340 g) store-bought fresh masa for tortillas (page 22) or Basic Masa from Masa Harina (page 24)

1½ teaspoons kosher salt (optional; use only for store-bought fresh masa)

In a bowl, combine the masa and salt, if using, and knead with your hands until evenly mixed. Divide the dough into six 2-ounce (55-g) balls for 6- to 7-inch (15- to 17-cm) tortillas; eight 1½-ounce (40-g) balls for 5- to 6-inch (12- to 15-cm) tortillas; or twelve 1-ounce (28-g) balls for twelve 3- to 4-inch (7.5- to 10-cm) tortillas. The masa does not hold well and dries out easily. Cover the balls with a sheet of parchment paper or a damp dish towel to prevent drying until you are ready to use them. Work quickly so the masa doesn't dry out.

To cook the tortillas:

Heat a comal over high heat until it is extremely hot. If your comal is not hot enough, the tortillas will stick. (If you do not have a comal, a nonstick pan or stovetop griddle can be used.)

Cut two circles (or squares) from a plastic storage bag to the size of the tortilla press. They must not be smaller than the press. It is fine if they are just a bit bigger. If you make tortillas often, you may want to purchase a tortilla press liner.

Place one piece of plastic on the bottom part of the opened press. Place a ball of dough in the center of the plastic liner and lay the second piece of plastic over the dough ball. Close the press. Start by pressing lightly, then open and take a look at the thickness of your tortilla. You are looking for a thickness of approximately ¹⁄₁₆ inch (2 mm). If needed, press again to thin out your tortilla. (If your tortilla is too thick, you'll find it hard to handle; it may tear when you try to move it from the plastic to the comal. If this happens, no worries, just start over.)

Open the press and "peel" the tortilla from the press, allowing it to stick to the upper plastic circle. If your tortilla is not too thin, this should be easy. The goal is to have thin tortillas that don't fall apart. This can take several attempts if you are not experienced at making tortillas by hand. Be patient and you'll get the knack soon enough. If your tortillas are too thick, gently press a second time. If they are hard to work with because they are too thin (they stick to the press or break when you try to put them on the comal), no worries. Simply reform your masa ball and try again.

Next, using your dominant hand, and starting from one side of the tortilla, gently release the tortilla from the plastic directly onto the hot comal, making sure the plastic doesn't touch the comal. Again, if your tortilla is not too thin, this should be easy.

The first tortilla is a test tortilla. Because the comal needs to be very hot, the tortilla should cook quickly. The masa will start to change color slightly from the edges inward within 20 to 30 seconds This is when the tortilla is ready to turn over. Experienced cooks do this by grabbing the tortilla with two fingers, but feel free to use a spatula. Cook for another 20 to 30 seconds on the second side. If the tortilla cracks, the masa was too dry. Add a little water to the masa, repeat the above steps, and test again.

When you are confident the masa is the right consistency and the tortilla is a thickness you are happy with, start your tortilla "production," making only as many as you think you will need for one meal. Wrap your hot tortillas in a clean towel or cloth. A beautiful embroidered napkin is often designated for tortillas in each Mexican household. Serve in a chiquihuite (tortilla basket).

BASIC HUARACHES

Named for their sandal-like shape, these masa creations are filled with refried beans and topped with everything from chorizo to seafood. Two of my favorites are Huaraches with Chorizo and Queso Panela (page 47) and Huaraches with Shrimp and Salsa a la Diabla (page 48). Other great toppings would be carnitas (page 230) with Spicy Carrot Salsa (page 265) or the toppings from California Pambazos with Farmers' Market Vegetables and Queso Panela (page 72).

INGREDIENTS

2 pounds (910 g) store-bought fresh masa for tortillas (page 22) or Basic Masa from Masa Harina (page 24)

1½ teaspoons kosher salt

About ½ cup (8 oz/225 g) refried beans (page 260), depending upon the size of your huaraches

MAKES 8 TO 12 HUARACHES

In a bowl, combine the masa and salt and knead to blend well. Divide the masa into 8 to 12 equal portions, depending on the size you prefer, and shape into balls. Cover the balls with a damp kitchen towel to prevent drying.

Follow the directions for pressing Homemade Tortillas (page 25) to form 8 to 12 tortillas that are 5 to 7 inches (12 to 17 cm) in diameter.

To make the huaraches, add 2 to 3 teaspoons of refried beans to each tortilla (adding more or less depending on the size of the tortilla), spreading it into a thin layer. (1) Form a masa "cigar" by gently rolling up each tortilla, using your fingers to push any of the beans that come out of the ends back into the cigar. (2) Repeat to fill and roll up all of the tortillas. (3) Heat a comal.

Using the lined tortilla press, gently press (see page 25) each masa "cigar" to a ¼ inch (6 mm) thickness, forming a large oval or "sandal" shape. (4) Alternatively, you can place the "cigar" between sheets of plastic on a cutting board and flatten them with a heavy cast-iron skillet. As soon as you press each huarache, quickly transfer it to the hot comal. Cook for about 1 minute on the first side, or until dotted with small light brown spots. (5) Flip and continue to cook for about 3 minutes, or until cooked through; the exterior will be crusty and the center can be a little soft. Transfer to a wire rack or sheet pan to cool. Repeat until all the huaraches are cooked. Now, you are ready to top your huaraches with your topping of choice. (6)

QUICK FIX If you do not want to make stuffed huaraches, make the tortillas and roll the unstuffed tortillas into masa "cigars." Follow steps 4 and 5 to press the huaraches to a ⅛-inch (3-mm) thickness then cook on the comal. The cooled huaraches can now be refrigerated in an airtight container for up to 3 days. When ready to serve, spread a thin layer of refried beans over the top and then top with your favorite toppings.

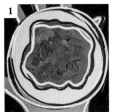 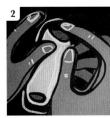 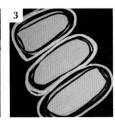  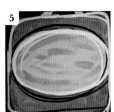 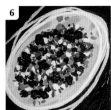

BASIC SOPES

Sopes are like miniature thick-crust pizzas made of masa—small, thick corn tortillas with pinched-up sides. They freeze well and make a great snack topped with refried beans and melted queso Oaxaca and garnished with onions and cilantro. Use these for Sopes with Sonoma Artichokes Three Ways and Verdolagas Salsa Verde (page 51). For a hearty lunch, top sopes with carnitas (page 230) and your favorite salsa, garnished with onions and cilantro.

MAKES 12 SOPES

Divide the masa into 12 portions of about 2 ounces (55 g) each and shape each portion into a ball. Cover the balls with a damp kitchen towel to prevent drying.

Follow the directions for pressing Homemade Tortillas (page 25) to form 12 tortillas that are each about ¼-inch (6-mm) thick.

Heat a comal over medium-hot heat, then reduce the heat to medium. One at a time, quickly transfer a prepared tortilla to the hot comal. Cook for 1 to 2 minutes on the first side, until the masa starts to change color slightly. Flip and cook on the second side for 1 to 2 minutes, or until cooked through. Transfer to a work surface.

Taking care not to burn your fingers, immediately pinch the edges of the hot tortilla to create a rim ¼ to ½ inch (6 to 12 mm) high to hold the toppings. If you are planning to serve the sopes later, you may stop here and keep them covered on a plate at room temperature for a few hours. Or, store cooled sopes in the refrigerator in an airtight container for up to 3 days. Reheat just enough so that they are warm, either quickly on a comal or in a 300°F (150°C) oven, before proceeding to fry them.

When ready to serve, heat a large skillet over medium-high heat. Coat the skillet with oil. Working in batches to avoid crowding, add the sopes and fry until crisp, about 1 minute. While frying, spoon hot oil over the tops of the sopes to crisp the top.

Serve immediately with the toppings you like.

INGREDIENTS

1½ pounds (680 g) store-bought fresh masa for tortillas (page 22) or Basic Masa from Masa Harina (page 24)

Light olive oil, for frying

BASIC CORN TOSTADAS AND TOSTADITAS

Tostadas are flat, crisp tortillas. Tostaditas are mini versions of tostadas, perfect for appetizers. Top tostadas with any of my ceviche recipes. Use the tostaditas for Caviar Tostaditas with Mexican Chorizo and Potato (page 199).

INGREDIENTS

1 pound (455 g) store-bought fresh masa for tortillas (page 22) or Basic Masa from Masa Harina (page 24)

Canola or vegetable oil, for deep-frying

Kosher salt

MAKES 8 TOSTADAS OR 16 TOSTADITAS

For tostadas, divide the masa into 2-ounce (55-g) portions and shape into balls. For tostaditas, divide the masa into 1-ounce (28-g) portions and shape into balls.

Follow the directions for pressing and cooking Homemade Tortillas (page 25), cooking the tortillas for about 30 seconds on each side. Set aside.

Pour the oil to a depth of about 2 inches (5 cm) into a deep sauté pan and heat to 350°F (175°C). Line a sheet pan with paper towels and set it near the stove.

When the oil is hot, add the tortillas one at time and fry, turning once, for 30 to 60 seconds on each side, or until golden brown and crispy. (You may be able to fry the smaller tortillas two at a time, depending on the size of your pan.) Transfer to the paper towels to drain and season immediately with salt. Let cool before using.

Tostadas and tostaditas can be made in advance and stored an airtight container at room temperature for up to 7 days.

ABOUT TAMALES

Tamales are the most ubiquitous of Mexican antojitos and can be filled with almost anything. Traditional fillings in Mexico are rajas y queso (strips of poblano chiles and queso Oaxaca) or pulled pork or chicken in red or green salsa. They are often eaten for desayuno (breakfast) on a bread roll, making a sort of sandwich, especially by those going to work. Tamales are also considered fiesta food and make their appearance at family gatherings, including Día de La Virgencita de Guadalupe, Christmas, and New Year's Eve. You'll find some of my favorite tamale recipes in this book: Pork Rib Carnitas and Carrot Tamales with Spicy Carrot Salsa (page 39), Shrimp Tamales (page 40), and Fig and Goat Cheese Tamales (page 36).

A Historical Look at Tamales

Preparation of tamales, central to Mexican fiestas since pre-Hispanic times, is a complex, time-consuming communal task that traditionally falls to the women. Within a decade of the arrival of the Spanish in what is now Mexico, Franciscan friar Bernardino de Sahagún, widely considered a pioneer of modern anthropology, was traveling through the newly conquered Aztec Empire and recording what he saw. Among his writings, which were later gathered into the twelve-volume *Florentine Codex*, is a description of a tamal seller's offerings:

> *[He has] salted wide tamales, pointed tamales, white tamales, . . . rolled-shaped tamales, tamales with beans forming a seashell on top, [with] grains of maize thrown in; crumbled, pounded tamales; spotted tamales, . . . white fruit tamales, red fruit tamales, turkey egg tamales; turkey eggs with grains of maize; tamales of tender maize, tamales of green maize, abode-shaped tamales, braised ones; unleavened tamales, honey tamales, beeswax tamales, tamales with grains of maize, gourd tamales, crumbled tamales, maize flower tamales. These [latter] were passed around in a basket at banquets, [and custom mandated that they] were held in the left hand.*

The word *tamal* comes from the Nahuatl word *tamalli*, which translates as "carefully wrapped"—best described as masa "pockets" steamed or boiled in a banana leaf or corn husk wrapper. The Aztecs and the Mayans, as well as the Olmecs and Toltecs, fed their armies and hunters tamales, as they are an ideal "traveling" food. Although initially disdained as food of the lower class by the invading Spaniards, who considered native maize "a more convenient food for swine than for men," tamales' universal appeal assured their longevity. Today, traditional tamal fillings include meats, cheeses, and vegetables, especially chiles, which, though not as widely varied as what Sahagún observed in the time of the Aztecs, still makes for a festive tamalada. The stories and rituals around the making of perfect tamales are many. In some pueblos, the locals swear that "los tamales se hacen locos" (the tamales will come out crazy) if there is a fight in the kitchen, with some coming out fine and others raw. In another village, the failure of the cook to drink wine or to dance around the pot can account for a poor outcome. But nearly everyone seems to agree that the cook must tie a couple of strips of corn husk on the pot handle to protect the tamales from absorbing any discord that might prevent them from cooking perfectly.

STORE-BOUGHT FRESH MASA FOR TAMALES

INGREDIENTS

2 pounds (910 g) fresh masa for tamales (page 22)

Water and/or masa harina, as needed (optional)

1 to 2 tablespoons lard, as needed

MAKES 2 POUNDS (910 G) MASA, OR ENOUGH FOR 12 TO 16 TAMALES

Your store-bought fresh masa may be ready to use or may need a little water (if it is too thick) or masa harina (if it is too thin) to achieve the texture you are looking for. Just mix in whatever is needed until thoroughly incorporated. The masa should be the consistency of a medium-thick spread (a little thinner than peanut butter).

To test your masa, form a small ball and drop it into a cup of room temperature or cold tap water. If it drops and then immediately rises and floats, it's ready. If it sinks, it needs more lard. Knead a little lard into the masa until well combined, then retest in the water. Your masa is likely to need more lard if you have frozen and defrosted fresh masa.

If not using immediately, wrap tightly in plastic wrap and store in the refrigerator for up to 1 day.

BASIC MASA FROM MASA HARINA FOR TAMALES

Different brands of masa harina yield slightly different results and require slightly different ratios of masa harina to liquid. I've based my recipe on Masienda-brand masa harina. If you use a different brand, refer to the package for the ratio of liquid to flour.

INGREDIENTS

3½ cups (420 g) Masienda-brand white, yellow, blue, or red masa harina

1½ teaspoons baking powder

2 teaspoons kosher salt

1 cup (240 ml) warm water

1 to 1¼ cups (240 to 300 ml) vegetable, chicken, or beef stock

1⅓ cups (275 g) lard, at room temperature, or vegetable shortening, whipped for a few minutes with an immersion blender or handheld mixer

MAKES 2 POUNDS (910 G) MASA, OR ENOUGH FOR 12 TO 16 TAMALES

In a stand mixer fitted with the paddle attachment (or in a large bowl with a handheld mixer), stir together the masa harina, baking powder, and salt. Add the warm water and beat on low speed until combined. Add 1 cup (240 ml) of the stock and mix on low speed until well combined. Finally, add the lard (or shortening if you prefer a vegetarian version) and beat until well blended. You may want to increase the speed of the mixer slightly to make sure ingredients are well blended, but be careful not to overmix. The masa should have the consistency of a medium-thick spread (a little thinner than peanut butter). If not, add up to ¼ cup (60 ml) of the stock to reach the right consistency.

To test your masa, form a small ball and drop it into a cup of room temperature or cold tap water. If it drops and then immediately rises and floats, it's ready. If it sinks, it needs more lard. Knead a little lard into the masa, 1 tablespoon at a time, until well combined, then retest in the water.

If not using immediately, wrap tightly in plastic wrap and store in the refrigerator for up to 1 day.

FILLING AND COOKING TAMALES

MAKES 12 TO 16 TAMALES

Soak the corn husks in water for 30 to 45 minutes, leaving the corn husks in the water until you need to use them. Before using them, drain them in a colander and pat dry with a paper towel.

To fill each tamal, place 2 husks, smooth side up, in the palm of your nondominant hand, with the wide end near your body and the point facing away from you.

Spread 2 to 3 ounces (55 to 85 g) of the masa (about ¼ cup) on the husks, making sure to leave about a 2-inch (5-cm) border on each side and the pointed end uncovered. (1) (If you have leftover tamale masa, depending upon the size of your tamales, it freezes well for up to 2 months wrapped with plastic wrap.)

Add 2 to 3 tablespoons of the filling mixture of choice, spreading it evenly. (2)

Fold the sides of the husk close to the center. (3)

Fold the pointy end of the husk back toward the front of the tamal. (4) Now your masa-filled and closed corn husk "envelope" is ready to steam. (5) (If you like, you can tie each tamal with a strip of corn husk before steaming.)

Add 2 cups (480 ml) of water to a large steamer pot fitted with a stainless steel vegetable steamer insert. Add the tamales to the steamer insert, arranging them so the folded end of the tamale faces down and they stand upright. Try to arrange the tamales in the insert so they do not fall over and begin to unfold.

Cover the pot and bring the water to a boil over high heat, then reduce the heat to medium-low and cook, covered, for 2 hours. Check the water level several times during cooking as you will need to add water frequently, so it doesn't run dry. In Mexico, it is common to place a few clean coins in the bottom of the pot, as these will rattle when the water level is low.

NOTE You will need 24 to 32 corn husks for the recipes in this book, but it's always a good idea to soak more husks than you will need as some will split and be unusable, which is why I call for 30 to 40 husks in the ingredient lists.

INGREDIENTS

30 to 40 corn husks

2 pounds (680 g) store-bought fresh masa for tamales (page 22) or Basic Masa from Masa Harina for Tamales (page 24)

About 2¼ cups (approximately 440 g) filling of choice

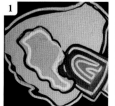 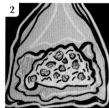 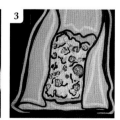 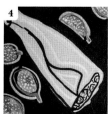 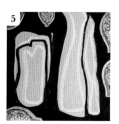

FEATURED MENU:
TAMALADA FOR DÍA DE LA VIRGENCITA DE GUADALUPE

El Día de la Virgen de Guadalupe (the Day of the Virgin of Guadalupe), which falls on December 12, is one of the most important holidays in Mexico, where it is celebrated everywhere, from the biggest cities to the smallest pueblos and most remote ranchos. After the religious ceremonies honoring the Virgen are over, friends and family typically gather together for a tamalada (tamale party).

La Virgencita, Protector of All Mexicans

You'll see the terms *Virgen* and *Virgencita* used interchangeably in Mexico and in Mexican American communities, the diminutive form indicating endearment. Most Mexican homes display the image of La Virgencita in the form of a painting or statue, or both. You'll also find her smiling down on her people in any number of barrios in US cities with large Mexican populations, typically as a mural. Not just a religious figure, the Virgin of Guadalupe is the cement that binds all of Mexico and a source of profound pride in being Mexican, a symbol of nationalism and patriotism.

Despite Mexico boasting the second-largest Catholic population in the world (Brazil is first), most Mexicans consider themselves Guadalupanos first and Catholics second. Well-known writer and Nobel laureate Octavio Paz explains the deep-seated faith in the Virgin of Guadalupe this way: "When Mexicans no longer believe in anything, they will still hold fast to their belief in two things: the national lottery and the Virgin of Guadalupe. In this I think they will do well. For both have been known to work, even for those of us who believe in nothing."

Appearance on the Hill

According to legend, the Virgin of Guadalupe revealed herself to Juan Diego Cuauhtlatoatzin on December 9, 1531, on the hill of Tepeyacac (now Tepeyac), north of Mexico City. Juan Diego, a member of the Chichimeca people who had recently converted to Christianity, was attracted to the spot by the most beautiful chorus of birds he had ever heard. Suddenly, the story goes, the singing stopped and before him stood a "beautiful woman adorned in clothing that shone like the sun wrapped in a cloak bearing an array of stars" who was calling out "Juantzin, Juan Diegotzin" (the diminutive of his name). She appeared to Juan Diego again on December 12, and so he could prove her existence to the local bishop, she imprinted her image on his rustic cactus-fiber cloak. That cloak can be seen today in the Basilica of Our Lady of Guadalupe in Mexico City.

An Epidemic Gives Birth to a Patron

One reason the Virgin of Guadalupe won such widespread devotion may lie in a 1736–37 epidemic that took the lives of forty thousand people in Mexico City and fifty thousand in Puebla over a period of eight months. The Virgin was said to have intervened collectively for "her people" to protect them. Her efficacy was proclaimed when there appeared to be a subsequent cessation of deaths, at which point she became an official emblem of Mexico, embraced even by the reticent upper class.

El Día de la Virgencita de Guadalupe Today

The Basilica of Our Lady of Guadalupe in Mexico City is Christianity's most visited sanctuary, with millions of people making the pilgrimage every year in early December, with the largest gathering—more than a million—on December 12. Tens of thousands arrive from Mexico's pueblos, many of them riding bicycles all night in the cold and dark. Others walk or run—some barefoot—from their villages, often carrying torches and banners as a way to demonstrate their devotion. At the basilica, the most devout ascend the stairs on their knees.

TAMALADA MENU

Brentwood Corn Champurrado 34

Pork Rib Carnitas and Carrot Tamales with Spicy Carrot Salsa 39

Shrimp Tamales 40

Fig and Goat Cheese Tamales 36

BRENTWOOD CORN CHAMPURRADO

Give me a warm mug of thick, rich champurrado on a rainy night and I am home. My mom, a nurse and a single parent, worked as many long shifts as she could to support me and my two siblings. The one time we could all count on being together around the dinner table was on Sunday nights. Serving champurrado and a bolillo (bread roll) or concha (sweet bread) meant Mom didn't have to cook when she was exhausted. Of course, we kids loved this satiating "meal replacement," as it was like having breakfast for dinner. What we didn't know was that since champurrado is made from white, yellow, or purple corn, it is rich in fiber, minerals, and vitamins, so we were getting plenty of nutrients as well!

Champurrado is atole with chocolate added. It is wonderful in place of hot chocolate on a cold winter day. I use corn from the Brentwood area, which lies southeast of the Napa Valley in the Sacramento River delta. Some of the sweetest corn I have ever eaten is grown there, so it makes a particularly delicious version of this warming drink.

INGREDIENTS

Kernels from 4 ears yellow, white, or bicolored corn (see page 271)

2 cups (480 ml) whole milk

¾ cup (170 g) fresh yellow or white corn masa for tortillas, homemade (page 24) or store-bought

6 cups (1.4 l) Corn Stock (page 269), made without salt

4 ounces (115 g) Mexican chocolate, preferably Rancho Gordo brand, or dark chocolate (60 to 70 percent), coarsely chopped

2 tablespoons grated piloncillo (see page 274) or packed light brown sugar, if not using Mexican chocolate

1 cinnamon stick (3 inches/7.5 cm), plus 8 sticks for garnish (optional)

Pinch of kosher salt

MAKES 8 SERVINGS

In a blender, combine the corn kernels, milk, and masa and blend on high speed until smooth.

Pour the corn stock into a large saucepan. Pour the corn-milk mixture through a fine-mesh sieve into the pan with the corn stock. Place over medium heat and bring to a simmer, whisking constantly to prevent lumps from forming. Add the chocolate, the piloncillo, if using dark chocolate, the cinnamon stick, and salt and cook, continuing to whisk constantly, for 10 to 15 minutes, or until thickened to the consistency of gravy.

Ladle into eight mugs and garnish each mug with a cinnamon stick, if desired. Serve at once.

RED CHILE CHAMPURRADO Add 1 ancho or guajillo chile to the pot with the corn-milk and corn stock mixture. Remove before serving.

FIG AND GOAT CHEESE TAMALES

This tamal is a culinary celebration of two traditions: the form—masa and corn husks—was born in Mexico, of course, but the filling is very California. The state boasts the largest fig crop in the United States, with most varieties bearing fruits in two seasons, late spring or early summer and fall. These lusciously sweet, uniquely textured fruits are paired with bright-tasting fresh goat cheese, preferably locally made Laura Chenel brand, which was started in Sonoma County in 1979. If figs are out of season at tamalada time, soak dried figs in water to cover until they plump up, at least a couple of hours or up to overnight.

INGREDIENTS

30 to 40 corn husks (see Note, page 31)

12 ounces (340 g) fresh goat cheese, preferably Laura Chenel brand

3 ounces (85 g) lard or vegetable shortening

3 fluid ounces (90 ml) honey

3 teaspoons baking powder

3 teaspoons kosher salt

2 pounds (910 g) store-bought fresh masa for tamales (page 22) or Basic Masa from Masa Harina for Tamales (page 30)

12 to 16 fresh figs, 1 fig per tamal, stemmed and thinly sliced, lengthwise

MAKES 12 TO 16 TAMALES

Soak the corn husks in water for 30 to 45 minutes, leaving the corn husks in the water until you need to use them. Before using them, drain them in a colander and pat dry with a paper towel. You will need 24 to 32 husks, 2 per tamal.

In a stand mixer fitted with the paddle attachment, beat together the goat cheese and lard on medium speed until fluffy. Add the honey, baking powder, and salt and continue to beat until well mixed.

To fill and cook the tamales, follow the step-by-step instructions on page 31, adding about 3 teaspoons of the goat cheese filling to each tamal, then arranging the thin slices of 1 fig atop the cheese layer for each tamal.

To serve, open the tamales, leaving them in the corn husks or removing the corn husks as you prefer.

PORK RIB CARNITAS AND CARROT TAMALES
WITH SPICY CARROT SALSA

This recipe really is a celebration of the humble carrot, which, with its sweet earthiness, is a perfect foil for the carnitas. Seasoning the pork ribs overnight with a dry rub of Mexican spices means the rich flavors of the rub and marinade have time to develop and the slowly braised meat just melts in your mouth. Mixing the grated carrots into the tamal masa adds a beautiful color and flavor. You can prepare the carrot salsa and the carnitas in advance. That way, everything is ready to go when you get down to tamale making.

MAKES 12 TO 16 TAMALES

Soak the corn husks in water for 30 to 45 minutes, leaving the corn husks in the water until you need to use them. Before using them, drain them in a colander and pat dry with a paper towel. You will need 24 to 32 husks, 2 per tamal.

In a bowl, combine the carnitas and ¾ cup (180 ml) of the salsa and mix well. Ready the masa as directed, mixing the grated carrots into the dough.

To fill and cook the tamales, follow the step-by-step instructions on page 31.

To serve, open the tamales, leaving them in the corn husks or removing the corn husks as you prefer. Top with the remaining salsa and garnish with the queso fresco and onion-cilantro mixture.

INGREDIENTS

30 to 40 corn husks (see Note, page 31)

2 pounds (910 g) Baby Back Rib Carnitas (page 230)

1¼ to 1½ cups (300 to 360 ml) Spicy Carrot Salsa (page 265)

2 pounds (910 g) store-bought fresh masa for tamales (page 22) or Basic Masa from Masa Harina for Tamales (page 30)

2 cups (220 g) peeled and grated carrots

1 pound (455 g) queso fresco, crumbled

½ cup (65 g) minced Spanish white onion mixed with ½ cup (20 g) chopped fresh cilantro

SHRIMP TAMALES

The mild heat of the chiles, tempered by the crema Mexicana, makes the filling for these shrimp tamales palatable for even those who don't enjoy spicy food. To "spice" them up, finish with Salsa Chiles de Árbol Salsa (page 264) or El Californio Fermented Salsa (page 264).

INGREDIENTS

30 to 40 corn husks (see Note, page 31)

4 cascabel chiles or guajillo chiles, dry roasted (see page 271)

10 Roma tomatoes, halved

3 tablespoons olive oil

1 yellow onion, diced

5 cloves garlic, minced

1 jalapeño, minced

2 cups (120 g) sliced cremini mushrooms

1 cup (240 ml) dry white wine

3 tablespoons tomato paste

Kosher salt

1 pound (455 g) large shrimp, peeled and deveined

1 cup (240 ml) Mexican crema or sour cream

¼ cup (10 g) chopped fresh basil leaves

2 pounds (910 g) store-bought fresh masa for tamales (page 22) or Basic Masa from Masa Harina for Tamales (page 30)

Salsa Chiles de Árbol (page 264) or El Californio Fermented Salsa (page 264)

½ cup (65 g) minced Spanish white onion mixed with ½ cup (20 g) chopped fresh cilantro

MAKES 12 TO 16 TAMALES

Soak the corn husks in water for 30 to 45 minutes, leaving the corn husks in the water until you need to use them. Before using them, drain them in a colander and pat dry with a paper towel. You will need 24 to 32 husks, 2 per tamal.

In a bowl of warm water, rehydrate the dry-roasted chiles for about 20 minutes, or until softened. Remove and discard the stems and seeds. Add the chiles and tomatoes to a blender and blend to a smooth purée. Set aside.

To make the filling, in a large frying pan over medium heat, warm the olive oil. Add the onion, garlic, and jalapeño and cook, stirring, for 2 minutes, or until they start to soften. Add the mushrooms and cook, stirring, for about 7 minutes, until the mushrooms release their juices. Stir in the reserved chile mixture and the wine, then add the tomato paste and season with salt. Stir to combine. Bring to a simmer, reduce the heat to medium-low, and cook, stirring occasionally, until the liquid reduces by about half, about 30 minutes.

Add the shrimp and crema to the pan and stir to combine. Continue to cook just until the liquid begins to bubble, 2 to 3 minutes. Remove from the heat and let cool for about 10 minutes. Stir in the chopped basil. Taste and season with salt if needed.

To fill and cook the tamales, follow the step-by-step instructions on page 31.

To serve, open the tamales, leaving them in the corn husks or removing the corn husks as you prefer. Top with salsa and garnish with the onion-cilantro mixture.

LAMB PICADILLO TETELAS
AND SALSA VERDE WITH PEAS AND MINT

Picadillo can be found across Latin America, with many local variations. The name comes from the word *picar*, which means "to chop," and the dish is always some version of ground or finely chopped meat, usually mixed with raisins, olives, onions, and some form of tomato. The unofficial history of Mexican picadillo recounts its appearance in a stuffed poblano pepper served to Agustín de Iturbide, the first constitutional emperor of Mexico, upon his coronation on July 21, 1822.

MAKES 6 TETELAS

To make the fresh masa for the tetelas, put the masa into a bowl, add the lamb fat and a pinch of salt, and mix well. Cover the bowl with a kitchen towel and let the masa rest at room temperature for 1 hour. (Otherwise, refrigerate it, then bring it to room temperature before working with it).

To make picadillo, in a saucepan, heat the oil over medium heat. Add the lamb and chorizo (removed from casing if necessary) and cook, breaking the meats up with a wooden spoon or spatula, for 5 to 6 minutes, or until cooked through. Using a slotted spoon, transfer the meat to a bowl, leaving some of the fat in the pan. Add the onion, garlic, and thyme to the pan and cook, stirring occasionally, for 3 to 4 minutes, or until they turn slightly golden brown and soften. Add the raisins, olives, tomato paste, and paprika, stir well, and cook, stirring often, for 2 minutes. Pour in the stock and reduce until the pan is almost dry. Return the cooked meats to the pan, mix well, and season with salt. Let cool completely before using. The picadillo can be made up to 2 days in advance and refrigerated in an airtight container.

To shape the tetelas, roll the masa into six 2-inch (5-cm) balls, each weighing about 2 ounces (55 g).

Follow the directions for pressing tortillas on page 25, place a ball on the press, press to make a tortilla, and then transfer the tortilla to a work surface. Repeat with the remaining balls.

To form each tetela, see the diagrams on page 57, starting with step 4. Add about ¼ cup (2 ounces/55 g) of the picadillo to the center of a tortilla. Fold the tortilla to form three corners, creating a triangle.

Preheat a large cast-iron pan, griddle, or comal over medium-high heat until very hot. Working in batches to avoid crowding, cook the tetelas, turning once, for about 1 minute on each side, or until nicely toasted. The tetelas are done when you can smell the toasted corn of the tortillas and the color of the masa has changed slightly. As each tetela is ready, transfer to a plate and keep warm until serving.

To serve, divide the tetelas among six plates. Top each tetela with 2 tablespoons of the salsa and garnish with cilantro, watercress, and avocado. Serve at once.

INGREDIENTS

12 ounces (340 g) store-bought fresh masa for tortillas (page 22) or Basic Masa from Masa Harina (page 24)

⅓ cup (75 g) rendered lamb fat, lard, or butter

Kosher salt

1 tablespoon olive oil

1 pound (455 g) ground lamb

2 ounces (55 g) chorizo, homemade (page 213) or store-bought

1 cup (110 g) yellow onion, diced

2 cloves garlic, minced

2 tablespoons chopped fresh thyme

½ cup (75 g) raisins

¼ cup (40 g) green olives, pitted and chopped

2 tablespoons tomato paste

1 teaspoon smoked paprika

½ cup (120 ml) chicken stock

¾ cup (180 ml) Fresh Salsa Verde with Peas and Mint (page 266)

Fresh micro cilantro or cilantro leaves, for garnish

Watercress, for garnish

1 avocado, pitted, peeled, and thinly sliced, for garnish

WILD MUSHROOM TACOS
WITH AL PASTOR SAUCE

In his *Historia de la comida en México*, the first general history of Mexican gastronomy, Amando Farga described Mexican food as "the happy meeting between the indigenous clay pot and the Spanish copper cauldron. This 'fusion of two great peoples' [the Aztecs and the Spanish] had given rise to the 'lineage of today's Mexican cuisine.'" Tacos al pastor, "shepherd style," are filled with spit-grilled meat, usually pork, a cooking method based on traditional Lebanese lamb shawarma but with a flavor profile that is pure Mexico. Popular in Puebla, where there is a sizable Lebanese Mexican population, the meat is seasoned with a combination of Middle Eastern herbs and spices originally introduced by the Lebanese, including Mediterranean oregano (not to be confused with Mexican oregano; see page 274), cumin, and cinnamon, along with ingredients indigenous to central Mexico. It is served wrapped in pan árabe, a cross between a tortilla and pita. In this vegetarian take, the earthiness of a trio of wild mushrooms is the perfect foil for the smokiness of the chipotles in the salsa. If you can't find wild mushrooms, you can use 9 ounces (255 g) of cultivated mushrooms, such as cremini and shiitake.

MAKES 10 TACOS

Follow the instructions for making and cooking the tortillas. For this recipe, you want to undercook the tortillas; they should be done to the point that they don't stick to the comal, but they should not be cooked to the point that they color (fully cooked tortillas will be a little darker). As the tortillas are ready, set them aside wrapped in a clean kitchen towel. When parcooked this way, finishing the tortillas will take only about 30 seconds per side.

Clean all the mushrooms in warm water (see Note, page 54), then cut them into roughly 1-inch (2.5-cm) pieces, making sure the pieces are all about the same size. Line a sheet pan with a kitchen towel, lay the mushroom pieces on the towel in a single layer, and let dry for about 1 hour to rid them of excess water.

Heat a large sauté pan over medium heat. When the pan is hot, add the oil and tip the pan to spread the oil evenly over the bottom. Add the mushrooms and cook, stirring occasionally, until just lightly browned, 3 to 4 minutes. Add the garlic, season with salt, and cook, stirring, until fragrant, 1 to 2 minutes longer, making sure not to burn the garlic. If you do not have a large sauté pan, cook the mushrooms in two batches to avoid overcrowding, which will result in soggy mushrooms.

While the mushrooms are cooking, finish cooking the tortillas on a hot comal.

As you pull each tortilla from the comal, add a spoonful of the mushrooms hot from the pan. Top the mushrooms with 2 to 3 tablespoons of the salsa, then season with salt (remember, the cheese is also salty) and a squeeze of lime juice. Sprinkle about 2 tablespoons of the cheese over the top of each taco, then garnish with the onion-cilantro mixture. Serve at once with lime wedges on the side.

INGREDIENTS

10 homemade tortillas (page 25)

3 ounces (85 g) hen of the wood mushrooms

3 ounces (85 g) morels

3 ounces (85 g) king trumpet mushrooms

1 tablespoon olive oil

2 large cloves garlic, grated or minced

Kosher salt

1¼ to 1¾ cups (300 to 420 ml) Salsa Al Pastor (page 262)

Kosher salt

5 limes, cut into wedges, for serving

10 ounces (280 g) grated queso Cotija or Parmesan cheese

½ cup (65 g) minced Spanish white onion mixed with ½ cup (20 g) chopped fresh cilantro

BLUE CORN TOSTADAS
WITH YELLOWFIN TUNA, AVOCADO, AND CUCUMBER

I love serving yellowfin (ahi) tuna raw because of its buttery texture, beautiful red color, and mild flavor. Here, it is used with ingredients typical of aguachile (see page 171), Mexico's answer to ceviche, so it works beautifully on a crunchy, golden tostada. Be sure to purchase "sushi-grade" tuna for all raw preparations and use it within a day or two of purchase. You can swap out the blue corn tostadas for white or yellow tostadas.

INGREDIENTS

12 blue corn tostadas (page 28)

1 pound (455 g) sushi-grade yellowfin tuna, cut into ¼-inch (6-mm) dice

Grated zest and juice of 3 limes, plus more juice as needed

3 tablespoons lemon oil

1 serrano chile, minced

1 cucumber, cut into ¼-inch (6-mm) dice

Kosher salt

2 large avocados, pitted, peeled, and thinly sliced

MAKES 6 SERVINGS

Have the tostadas ready. These is no need to reheat them before serving.

In a large bowl, combine the tuna, lime zest and juice, lemon oil, chile, and cucumber, season with salt, and toss gently to mix. Taste the tuna to make sure it has enough acidity and salt and add more lime juice and salt, if needed.

Place 2 tostadas on each of six individual plates. Top the tostadas with the tuna mixture, dividing it evenly. Fan an equal number of avocado slices over each tuna portion and season the avocado with salt and a squeeze of lime juice. Serve at once.

HUARACHES WITH CHORIZO
AND QUESO PANELA

If you look up the word *huarache* online, the first thing you'll see are photos of handmade sandals, which is how this antojito, with its sandal-like shape, got its name. Huaraches may first be filled with refried beans (see page 26) and then topped with almost anything you like. Or, for a quicker preparation, you can skip the filling as I have here. I like mine topped with a layer of refried beans, chorizo, queso panela, and salsa and finished with finely chopped cilantro and onion.

MAKES 8 TO 12 SERVINGS

If you are using chorizo in casings, remove and discard the casings. Place a skillet over medium-high heat and add the chorizo, breaking it up with a wooden spoon or spatula. Cook, stirring often, until cooked through, 20 to 25 minutes. Using a slotted spoon, transfer to paper towels to drain. Keep warm.

When ready to serve, generously coat the bottom of a cast-iron skillet with oil and heat over medium-high heat until the oil shimmers. Working in batches to avoid crowding, crisp the huaraches, turning once, until warmed through, about 3 minutes. As each batch is ready, transfer to a large plate lined with paper towels and keep warm.

When all the huaraches are ready, spread a layer of refried beans evenly over the entire huarache. Sprinkle the reserved chorizo on top of the beans, dividing it evenly. Drizzle each serving with an equal amount of the salsa and then top with the cheese, dividing it evenly. Garnish with the onion-cilantro mixture and serve.

INGREDIENTS

1 pound (455 g) Mexican chorizo, homemade (page 213) or store-bought

Vegetable or canola oil, for cooking

8 to 12 unstuffed huaraches, cooked (page 26)

½ to 1 cup (120 to 240 g) Refritos (Refried Beans), page 260

1½ cups (360 ml) Salsa Verde con Chiles de Àrbol (page 265)

1 cup (150 g) crumbled queso panela

½ cup (65 g) minced Spanish white onion mixed with ½ cup (20 g) chopped fresh cilantro

HUARACHES WITH SHRIMP
AND SALSA A LA DIABLA

Camarones a la Diabla are one of the most common—if not *the* most common—Mexican seafood dishes in both the US and Mexico. Using these "deviled shrimp" to top huaraches and adding fennel curtido are my own special twists.

INGREDIENTS

For the shrimp:

Juice of 2 limes

1 tablespoon chopped fresh cilantro

1 serrano chile, seeded and finely chopped

1 teaspoon garlic powder

1 teaspoon onion powder

½ teaspoon sweet paprika

½ teaspoon smoked paprika

½ teaspoon kosher salt

1½ pounds (680 g) medium shrimp, shelled, deveined, and halved lengthwise

Olive oil, for cooking

4 to 6 huaraches, cooked (page 26)

1 cup (220 g) Fennel Curtido (page 259)

½ cup (120 ml) Salsa a la Diabla (page 262)

Leaves from ½ bunch fresh cilantro

MAKES 4 TO 6 SERVINGS

To marinate the shrimp, in a bowl, stir together the lime juice, cilantro, serrano chile, garlic powder, onion powder, both paprikas, and the salt and mix well. Add the shrimp and toss to coat evenly. Cover and refrigerate for 30 minutes.

Drain the shrimp, discarding the marinade. In a large skillet, warm 3 tablespoons oil over medium heat. Add the shrimp and cook, stirring occasionally, until they take on color, about 5 minutes.

While the shrimp are cooking, heat a comal until very hot. Working in batches to avoid crowding, crisp the huaraches, turning once, until warmed through, about 3 minutes. As each huarache is ready, transfer to a large plate lined with a paper towel and keep warm.

To serve, divide the huaraches evenly among four to six individual plates. Divide the curtido evenly among the huaraches, covering the entire surface of each one. Top each huarache with the shrimp, dividing evenly. Drizzle the shrimp with the salsa, dividing it evenly, and garnish with the cilantro leaves. Serve at once.

WINE PAIRING Perfectly pairs with Ceja Vineyards' Vino de Casa Red Blend, an irreverent, playful, and adventurous blend of pinot noir, Syrah, and merlot that successfully mingles these distinct varieties for a delicious romp. Crushed violets and black pepper meet black plum and dark fruit aromas and flavors.

SOPES WITH SONOMA ARTICHOKES THREE WAYS
AND VERDOLAGAS SALSA VERDE

In this inspired antojito, sopes, lightly fried masa bases, are topped with locally grown artichokes and a pleasantly tart salsa verde made with purslane and tomatillos. Many farmers and home gardeners consider the fast-spreading purslane—verdolaga in Spanish—an invasive weed. But its small, fleshy, mildly acidic leaves are actually quite tasty. If you cannot find purslane, watercress makes a good substitute. You can prep and cook the artichoke hearts a couple of days in advance and refrigerate them, but wait until just before serving to fry them.

MAKES 6 SERVINGS

To prep the baby artichokes, working with 1 artichoke at a time, snap off and discard the tough outer layer of leaves, then cut off the fibrous end—roughly the bottom ¼ to ½ inch (6 to 12 mm) of the stem. (1) Rub the exposed stem end with the cut side of a lemon half.

Snap or pull off five to six layers (or more) of external leaves (set them aside if you'd like to steam and eat them) until you reach an inner layer of fresh-looking, pale yellow leaves that are white at the base. Use a paring knife to trim away any tough, dark green parts that may remain on the base of the artichoke, leaving only tender, light flesh. (2)

Using a sharp chef's knife, slice off the remaining crown of leaves, cutting across the entire choke to divide the darker part from the whitish bottom. (3)

A grapefruit spoon works best for removing the furry, inedible center, or choke. (4) Be sure to scrape off all the inedible fuzzy bits. Rub all the exposed areas with the cut side of a lemon half. (5) The artichoke heart is now ready to cook.

To braise the artichoke hearts, in a large stockpot, combine the oil, stock, vinegar, lemon juice, bay leaf, garlic, and salt and bring to a simmer. Add the 24 prepared baby artichoke hearts and cook for 10 to 20 minutes, or until fork-tender. Remove from the heat with a slotted spoon or spider and set aside to cool.

Cut 12 of the artichoke hearts into quarters and set aside until ready to plate. Cut the other 12 artichoke hearts in half and reserve for frying. The artichoke hearts can be made up to 2 days in advance and refrigerated in an airtight container before proceeding.

CONTINUED...

INGREDIENTS

For prepping the baby artichokes:

30 medium baby artichokes (each about 2 to 3 ounces/55 to 80 g)

1 lemon, cut in half, plus 1 lemon slice for cooking

For braised artichoke hearts:

3 cups (720 ml) olive oil

2 cups (480 ml) vegetable stock or water

¾ cup (180 ml) champagne vinegar

1 tablespoon fresh lemon juice

1 bay leaf

2 cloves garlic

2 teaspoons kosher salt

24 baby artichoke hearts, prepped and halved

 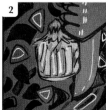 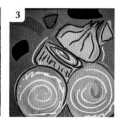 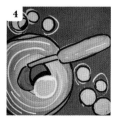 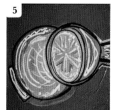

For fried baby artichoke hearts:

Canola oil, for deep-frying

2 cups (480 ml) buttermilk

3 tablespoons kosher salt

2 cups (320 g) rice flour

2 cups (260 g) cornstarch

12 braised baby artichokes,
from above

For the shaved artichokes:

6 cups (1.4 L) of water

1 lemon

6 baby artichoke hearts, prepped

To assemble:

12 sopes (page 27)

1 cup (245 g) black bean paste
(page 261)

12 braised baby artichoke hearts,
quartered

12 fried baby artichoke heart halves

6 raw baby artichoke hearts, shaved
on a mandoline or very thinly sliced

2 cups (480 ml) Verdolagas Salsa
Verde (page 266)

Verdolaga leaves, for garnish

½ pound (225 g) queso fresco,
crumbled for garnish

To make the fried artichoke hearts, pour the oil to a depth of 2 inches (5 cm) into a deep fryer or deep pot and heat to 325°F (165°C). Line a large plate or sheet pan with paper towels and set it near the stove.

In a shallow bowl, combine the buttermilk and 1 tablespoon of the salt and mix well. In a second shallow bowl, whisk together the rice flour, cornstarch, and the remaining 2 tablespoons salt.

One at a time, dip each artichoke heart half into the buttermilk, letting any excess drip off, and then dip into the flour mixture, coating evenly and tapping off the excess. Set aside on a large plate or sheet pan.

When the oil is ready, working in batches if necessary to avoid crowding, carefully add the coated artichoke to the hot oil and cook, turning once or twice, for about 2 minutes, or until golden brown. Using a skimmer, transfer the artichokes to the paper towels to drain.

For the shaved artichokes, place the water in a bowl and squeeze the lemon into it. Add the prepped artichoke hearts to the water to prevent oxidation and set aside until needed. When ready to assemble, thinly slice each heart with a mandoline, you will be using about ½ of an artichoke heart per sope.

To assemble, arrange 2 warm sopes on each of six individual plates. Spread 1 to 2 tablespoons of the black bean paste into the bottom of each sope. It should come about halfway up the sides of the sope. For each sope, arrange the quarters of 1 braised baby artichoke heart over the top of the black bean paste, then top each sope with 2 fried baby artichoke heart halves, placing them in a neat fashion. Finish with a good amount of shaved artichoke hearts over the top of each sope. Drizzle each with a spoonful of the Verdolaga Salsa Verde, then garnish with the verdolaga leaves and queso fresco.

TLAYUDAS
WITH MUSHROOMS, AVOCADO, AND QUELITES PESTO

Tlayuda, an iconic Oaxacan antojito, is Mexico's answer to pizza. The thin, crisp masa disk can be loaded with any number of toppings. Here, I have used a mix of five different mushrooms and a pesto made from quelites, or lamb's-quarters, a wild green with a mild, spinach-like flavor. A favorite of foragers, it is also occasionally sold at farm stands. If you can't get lamb's-quarters, spinach can be substituted.

MAKES 6 TO 8 TLAYUDAS

To make the tlayuda dough, in a stand mixer fitted with the paddle attachment, combine the masa harina, all-purpose flour, bacon fat, and salt and mix on low speed until the bacon fat is evenly mixed into the flours. With the mixer still on low speed, slowly drizzle in the warm water, starting with a little less than the full 2 cups (475 ml) and continuing to mix until a dough forms that is soft and smooth but not sticky. If it seems too dry, add more water, 2 tablespoons at a time, until you achieve the correct consistency.

Divide the dough into balls, each weighing 1¾ ounces (50 g); keep the balls covered with a damp kitchen towel so they don't dry out. You can shape the tlayudas with a pasta machine with a 6- to 8-inch (15- to 20-cm) roller or with a rolling pin. If using a pasta machine, pass each dough ball through the rollers until you reach the #2 thickness on the dial. Your tlayudas will have corners rather than be round. You can leave them as they are or trim the edges so they are round. As the tlayudas are shaped, set them aside and cover with a kitchen towel to prevent drying. Alternatively, on a work surface, roll out each ball into a round 6 to 8 inches (15 to 20 cm) in diameter. You may need to lightly dust the work surface with flour to prevent sticking. Cover with a kitchen towel to prevent drying.

To cook the tlayudas, heat a plancha (griddle) over low heat. When the plancha is hot, working in batches to prevent crowding, add the tlayudas and cook, turning once, for 5 to 6 minutes on each side, or until toasted on both sides and crispy. As they are ready, transfer to a wire rack.

To make the mushrooms, in a large sauté pan, heat the oil over medium heat. Add all the mushrooms and sauté until tender and lightly browned, 8 to 10 minutes. Add the shallot and cook, stirring occasionally, for about 6 minutes. Reduce the heat to medium-low and add the garlic. Cook, stirring frequently, for another 6 to 8 minutes, until the shallot is golden brown. Remove from the heat, season with salt, and let cool. If you do not have a large sauté pan, cook the mushrooms in two batches to avoid overcrowding, which will result in soggy mushrooms.

CONTINUED...

INGREDIENTS

For the tlayuda dough:

2⅓ cups (275 g) masa harina, preferably Masienda brand

1½ cups (190 g) all-purpose flour

3 tablespoons bacon fat, at room temperature, or olive oil

1½ teaspoons kosher salt

2 cups (480 ml) warm tap water

For the mushrooms:

3 tablespoons olive oil

1 cup (70 g) roughly chopped lobster mushrooms

1 cup (60 g) each thinly sliced black trumpet, king trumpet, shiitake, and cremini mushrooms

1 small shallot, minced

3 cloves garlic, minced

Kosher salt

For the pesto:

1 bunch fresh cilantro, roughly chopped

1 cup (30 g) roughly chopped lamb's-quarters

½ cup (70 g) pine nuts

1 clove garlic, minced

1 teaspoon cumin seeds, toasted and ground (see page 271)

1 tablespoon honey

2 teaspoons red wine vinegar

Juice of 1 lime

¼ cup (60 ml) olive oil

Kosher salt

2 cups (520 g) refried beans (page 260), warmed

2 avocados, pitted, peeled, and cut into ¼-inch (6-mm) dice

Pickled Red Onions and Jalapeños (page 259), for garnish

To make the pesto, in a blender, combine the cilantro, lamb's-quarters, nuts, garlic, cumin, honey, vinegar, and lime juice. Turn on the blender to low speed and blend slowly while gradually adding the oil in a thin stream. The finished pesto should have a chunky consistency. Season with salt. You should have about 1½ cups (360 ml). The pesto can be made up to 5 days in advance and refrigerated in an airtight container.

To assemble, spread a thin layer of the refried beans over the top of each tlayuda. Add the mushrooms, followed by the avocado. Drizzle with the pesto. Garnish with the pickled onions and jalapeños and serve at once.

NOTE Before trimming and slicing or chopping mushrooms, I rinse them in warm water to remove all the dirt. I find that using a large bowl of warm water works best, as the dirt falls to the bottom and the mushrooms rise to the top. Line a sheet pan with a kitchen towel, then remove the mushrooms from the water and spread them on the towel to dry for about 1 hour before cutting them. This will ensure they develop a nice sear when you cook them.

BLACK BEAN AND CORN TETELAS
WITH SQUASH BLOSSOMS

Tetelas are triangle-shaped filled masa "pockets." They typically conceal beans and cheese, and here I have used black bean paste and queso Oaxaca, which is similar to string cheese (a type of mozzarella) in that it pulls apart into "strings" or strands—or rajas in Spanish. The addition of a squash blossom embedded in the masa makes for a particularly eye-catching presentation. Craving these tetelas but squash blossoms are not in season? Any edible flower or even a sprig of cilantro works too.

MAKES 6 TETELAS

To make the fresh masa for the tetelas, put the masa into a bowl, add the lard and a pinch of salt, and mix well. Cover the bowl with a kitchen towel and let the masa rest at room temperature for 1 hour. (Otherwise, refrigerate it for up to 1 day, then bring it to room temperature before working with it.)

To shape the tetelas, roll the masa into six 2-inch (5-cm) balls, each weighing about 2 ounces (55 g).

Open each squash blossom and gently remove the stamen or pistil with your fingers or culinary tweezers. (1) Following the directions for pressing tortillas on page 25, place a ball on the press and do a first, very gentle press to form a thickish tortilla (more or less double the thickness of a typical tortilla). (2) Now place a squash blossom in the middle of the thick tortilla. (3) Do a second press, again lightly, with the tortilla press. (4) The result should be a tortilla of regular thickness. Now, using your dominant hand, and starting from one side of the tortilla, gently release the tortilla from the plastic onto a work surface, flipping it as you do so the squash blossom side is face down.

In a bowl, stir together the bean paste and corn kernels and then season with salt. Add one-sixth of the bean paste mixture to the center of the tortilla and top with one-sixth of the cheese "strings." (5) Fold the tortilla to form three corners, creating a triangle. Repeat with the remaining masa balls, bean paste, and cheese to form five more tetelas.

Preheat a large cast-iron pan, griddle, or comal over medium-high heat until very hot. Working in batches to avoid crowding, cook the tetelas, turning once, for about 1 minute on each side, or until nicely toasted. The tetelas are done when you can smell the toasted corn of the tortillas and the color of the masa has changed slightly. As each tetela is ready, transfer to a plate and keep warm until serving.

Serve the tetelas flower side up, with the salsa spooned on top. (6)

INGREDIENTS

12 ounces (340 g) store-bought fresh masa for tortillas (page 22) or Basic Masa from Masa Harina (page 24)

1½ teaspoons lard, unsalted butter, or olive oil

Kosher salt

6 squash blossoms

1 cup (245 g) black bean paste (page 261)

Kernels from 2 ears yellow corn (see page 271)

1 cup (110 g) "pulled" queso Oaxaca

¾ cup (180 ml) Salsa Irma (page 264)

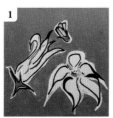    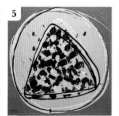 

FEATURED MENU:
RECALENTADO

In Mexico, there's always a get-together the next afternoon after a big party, as parties typically last until the wee hours. This is when the guests return for recalentado (reheated leftovers) and to chismear (gossip) about the previous night's adventures. New Year's Day usually starts this way: everyone returns to where they spent New Year's Eve (if they left, that is!), the great feast is reheated, and all pitch in to get the house back in order. As afternoon gives way to evening, it's time to eat again. The menu is festive but lighter.

RECALENTADO MENU

Atole de Avena with Ponche Fruit Syrup 155

Blood Orange Margaritas with Chile-Salt Rim 160

Huevos Motuleños with Smoked Duck and Mushrooms a la Cazuelita 243

Enmoladas with Roasted Black Sesame Mole 60

Cinnamon–Red Wine Coricos 63

Café De Olla 261

ENMOLADAS
WITH ROASTED BLACK SESAME MOLE

A cousin of the better-known enchilada (which was originally simply a corn tortilla fried and dipped in salsa but is more typically now served with a protein filling), the enmolada is dipped in mole instead of the usual salsa. Enmoladas are a great way to stretch your leftovers for the recalentado. If you use leftover mole from the Roasted Black Sesame Mole Rib Eyes recipe (page 237), it makes for a super-easy process.

INGREDIENTS

24 large corn tortillas (page 25)

1 cup (240 ml) olive oil

3 cups (720 ml) roasted black sesame mole (page 237)

1 pound (455 g) queso fresco, crumbled

2 to 3 avocados, pitted, peeled, and sliced

1 Spanish white onion, minced, mixed with 1 bunch fresh cilantro, chopped

MAKES 24 ENMOLADAS; 8 TO 12 SERVINGS

Warm your tortillas on a comal and place them near the stove. Set up two skillets and two pairs of rubber-tipped tongs (one for each skillet) and have dinner plates in a pile to the side of the stove.

Pour the oil into one skillet and heat over medium-high heat. Pour the mole into the second skillet and heat over low heat. Using tongs, grab a tortilla and quickly dip it into the hot oil, turning to coat on both sides. If you prefer your enmoladas with less mole, as in the photo (right), stop here and follow the instructions for plating below. For smothered enmolodas, using the second pair of tongs, dip the same tortilla into the mole, again turning to coat both sides. This time, however, leave it in the mole for about 3 seconds on each side, or until softened (it will soften more the longer it sits).

Transfer the tortilla to a dinner plate, roll it up, and repeat with the remaining tortillas (always roll them right away as they are harder to roll if left to sit). Serve 2 to 3 enmoladas per person. Smother with more mole once all the tortillas are dipped and rolled, then top with the cheese, avocado, and onion-cilantro mixture. Serve at once.

ENFRIJOLADAS No leftover mole? No worries! Substitute the same amount of extra runny Refritos (Refried Beans, page 260) for the mole to make enfrijoladas, a variation on enmoladas but in a savory bean sauce.

CINNAMON–RED WINE CORICOS

One of Mexico's sixty-eight distinct Indigenous peoples, the Rarámuri of La Sierra Madre and Copper Canyon in Chihuahua, make a version of coricos using pinole, grinding and toasting their own corn. In communities and rural settlements in Baja California, Sonora, and Sinaloa, you'll find homemade coricos made with masa harina. Home cooks bake batches of these ring-shaped cookies year-round, but especially for Catholic Holy Week and Easter. In larger cities, commercial versions are sold in supermarkets. For my wine country version, I've added cabernet. If you prefer a cookie with no alcohol, substitute ½ cup (120 ml) whole milk for the wine. Serve these with your favorite Mexican hot chocolate or the Brentwood Corn Champurrado (page 34).

MAKES 40 COOKIES

In a stand mixer fitted with the paddle attachment, combine the butter and granulated sugar. Starting on medium speed, beat together the butter and sugar, gradually increasing the speed to medium-high until white and fluffy. Add the eggs one at the time, beating after each addition until incorporated. Add the wine and vanilla and beat until well mixed.

In a bowl, stir together the masa harina, all-purpose flour, brown sugar, baking powder, cinnamon, and salt. On low speed, add the masa harina mixture to the butter mixture and beat until a soft, moist cookie dough forms. You should be able to squeeze the dough easily but it should not stick to your fingers.

Transfer the dough to a clean countertop and shape into a thick roll. Wrap in plastic wrap and refrigerate for 30 minutes. While the dough rests, preheat the oven to 350°F (175°C). Line a large sheet pan with parchment paper.

Remove the dough from the refrigerator and divide it into forty 1-ounce (28-g) portions. Each will be about the size of an apricot. Working with one portion at a time, roll it into a ball and then into a rope 6 to 8 inches (15 to 20 cm) long. Gently press the ends of the rope together to make a ring and place it on the prepared sheet pan. Repeat with the remaining dough portions, making sure the cookies don't touch one another on the pan. If the dough gets too soft, refrigerate the shaped cookies for 15 minutes before baking.

Bake the cookies for about 20 minutes, or until they are golden brown. Let cool completely on the pan on a wire rack. They will develop some crunch once they have cooled. Store in an airtight container at room temperature for up to 5 days or freeze for up to 2 months.

INGREDIENTS

1 pound (455 g) unsalted butter, at room temperature

1 cup (200 g) granulated sugar

3 large eggs

½ cup (120 ml) cabernet sauvignon or other dry, full-bodied red wine

1 teaspoon pure vanilla extract

3½ cups (420 g) masa harina, preferably Masienda brand

1 cup (125 g) all-purpose flour

½ cup (110 g) packed light brown sugar

2 teaspoons baking powder

1 tablespoon ground cinnamon

1 teaspoon kosher salt

WHEAT-BASED RECIPES

The History of Baking in Mexico

Starting with the arrival of the Spanish conquistadors, baking gained a foothold in Mexico and eventually flourished. Wheat was needed by the Catholic Church for the Holy Communion wafer, and bread played an important cultural role as a marker of elite social status.

Baking in Mexico experienced a further boost a few centuries later during the French Intervention, the occupation of Mexico by Napoleon III in the 1860s. Although brief, the culinary contributions of that period are significant, resulting in what is called la comida afrancesado (a fusion of Mexican ingredients and French techniques), with baked goods arguably the most impactful development. For example, pan de muerto, an integral part of Día de los Muertos celebrations and altars, would not exist without the influence of the country's Basque bakeries, as the basic ingredients—butter, cane sugar, and wheat flour—were not known in Mesoamerica prior to conquest.

Ancient and Modern Food Politics in Mexico

According to the Mayan creation myth, the gods formed the first humans from corn dough, while wheat was not introduced to what we now call Mexico until the Spanish invaded. What ensued was a kind of "battle of the grains" and an early example of food politics in which the Spanish looked to convert and Europeanize Mexico by replacing corn with wheat.

In fact, the "Indians" of Mexico, as the Spanish called them, were viewed by the colonizers as backward and unproductive—an obstacle to progress in New Spain. The transformation of Indigenous food habits, perceived as a root cause of what the Spaniards called "Indian deprivation," became an important social program. But despite public cooking classes during the colonial era, the focus of which was to wean the Mexican lower class off both chiles and corn, the local foodways continued to flourish. In fact, the native population "rejected [wheat] bread as being 'like famine food . . . like dried maize stalks.'" In *The Conquests of Wheat: Culinary Encounters in the Colonial Period,* John Pilcher relates that Indigenous women, catering to the colonial Spanish, sold wheat bread in the market squares of Mexico City as early as 1550, a "first step toward acculturation. . . . But Indians typically entered the baking trade only by force . . . [via] labor drafts [that] included bakeries. Moreover, criminals commonly served eight-to-ten-year sentences kneading dough."

Si Maíz No Hay País

Today, a different kind of battle is underway. In 2007, a movement was born to protect corn varieties native to Mexico and to raise awareness around the challenges facing small farmers. Made up of an informal network of organizations across the county, its rallying cry is "sin maíz no hay país" (without corn there is no country). A December 2020 decree by President Andrés Manuel López Obrador put in place a ban on genetically modified (GM) corn for human consumption by 2024. And in October 2021, Mexico, for the first time in its history, refused to permit the import of GM corn. In the ensuing case brought by Bayer, the parent company of the Monsanto, an international powerhouse of genetically engineered crops, the ruling was upheld, an important victory for Mexico's anti-GMO movement.

SAN FRANCISCO SOURDOUGH FLOUR TORTILLAS

What could be more representative of Mexican cooking in the San Francisco Bay Area than a sourdough tortilla? Surprise your friends and family with this twist on the traditional recipe. These tortillas are so good you will want to eat them spread with butter straight off the comal. If you do not have your own sourdough starter, it is widely available online.

MAKES TWELVE 7- TO 8-INCH (17- TO 20-CM) TORTILLAS

In a small bowl, sprinkle the yeast over the lukewarm water, stir to dissolve, and let stand for about 10 minutes, or until it blooms, or looks bubbly. Stir in the oil.

In a bowl, combine the flour and salt. Add the sourdough starter and yeast mixture and stir with a wooden spoon until a shaggy dough forms. Turn the dough out onto a lightly floured surface and knead for about 10 minutes, or until the dough looks smooth on the outside without roughness. Cover the dough with a kitchen towel and let rest for about 2 hours.

Divide the dough into 12 equal pieces, each about 2 ounces (55 g). Shape each piece into a ball. Let the balls sit on the work surface, covered with a kitchen towel, for 1 hour.

On a lightly floured work surface, working with 1 ball at a time and using a rolling pin, roll out each dough ball into a paper-thin round 7 to 8 inches (17 to 20 cm) in diameter.

To cook the tortillas, heat a dry cast-iron skillet or comal over medium heat. Place a tortilla on the hot surface and cook for about 30 seconds on each side, or until dark speckles appear As the tortillas are ready, stack and then wrap them in a clean cloth. Serve warm.

INGREDIENTS

1 teaspoon active dry yeast

1 cup (240 ml) lukewarm water (105° to 115°F/41° to 46°C)

1½ tablespoons olive oil or lard

2½ cups (320 g) all-purpose flour

1 tablespoon kosher salt

½ cup (125 g) sourdough starter

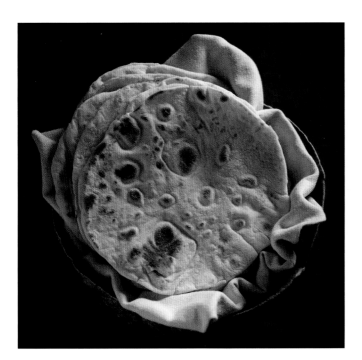

BRAIDED HONEY-GLAZED PAN DE MIEL

For this honey-glazed loaf bread, I like to use white Sonora flour from Frog Hollow Farms, based in nearby Brentwood, a place long known as an agricultural center. Frog Hollow first planted the heirloom white wheat, which was introduced to the American Southwest and Mexico by the Spanish in the early seventeenth century, in 2018 and began milling it in 2020. The flour imparts a mild, sweet flavor to this popular bread.

INGREDIENTS

1½ cups (360 ml) whole milk

⅓ cup (65 g) sugar

3 tablespoons honey

1 tablespoon active dry yeast

4½ cups (565 g) all-purpose flour

2 teaspoons kosher salt

7 tablespoons (100 g) unsalted butter, softened

Canola or vegetable oil, for greasing

Clarified butter (page 269), melted, for brushing

MAKES 2 LOAVES

In a saucepan over medium heat, combine the milk, sugar, and 1 tablespoon of the honey. Gently warm to 105° to 115°F (41° to 46°C). Remove from the heat, sprinkle the yeast on top, and stir to dissolve. Set aside until it looks bubbly, 5 to 10 minutes.

In a large bowl, stir together the flour and salt. Add the yeast mixture and butter and stir with a wooden spoon until a rough, shaggy mass forms. Turn the dough out onto a lightly floured work surface and knead for 5 to 7 minutes, or until smooth and elastic. Form the dough into a ball.

Grease a large bowl with oil, transfer the dough to the bowl, and cover the bowl with plastic wrap. Let the dough rise in a warm, draft-free area for about 1 hour, or until doubled in size. Uncover the bowl, punch down the dough, re-cover the bowl, and let the dough rise again for about 45 minutes, or until doubled in size.

Lightly brush 2 baking sheets with oil. After the second proof, turn the dough out onto a lightly floured work surface and using lightly floured hands, divide it into 2 equal pieces. To form the braided loaves, divide one piece of dough into 3 equal pieces. Roll each piece on the work surface into a rope that is about 16 inches (40 cm) long and about 1 inch (2.5 cm) thick; you will have 3 ropes. Arrange the 3 ropes on the prepared baking sheet. Pinch the ropes together at one end, then braid them together by crossing the outside ropes over the center rope; first cross the right and then the left rope over the center, alternating. When you reach the end, pinch the ropes together, tucking the ends of the ropes neatly underneath. Repeat to braid the other piece of dough and place on the second baking sheet. Let the bread rise until bouncy to the touch, about 2 hours.

About 15 minutes before the breads finish proofing, position two oven racks evenly in the oven and preheat to 375°F (190°C) or to 350°F (175°C) on the convection setting.

Bake the loaves, rotating them between the racks halfway through baking, until golden brown and they bounce back when gently pushed, 20 to 30 minutes. Brush the loaves with the clarified butter once or twice while baking, about every 10 minutes. As soon as the loaves are ready, immediately brush them generously with the remaining 2 tablespoons honey. Serve warm.

SESAME BREAD Immediately after brushing with the honey, sprinkle with a light dusting of roasted black sesame seeds, preferably Kuki brand.

SOURDOUGH TELERAS

These traditional Mexican bread rolls are not made with sourdough starter in Mexico, of course. That's my special San Francisco twist! Teleras are oval, about 6 inches (15 cm) long, flatter than a typical bread roll, and have distinctive indentations on top. They are de rigueur for tortas, traditional Mexican sandwiches. Use this recipe for the California Pambazos with Farmers' Market Vegetables and Queso Panela (page 72). If you do not have your own sourdough starter, it is widely available online.

MAKES 12 TELERAS

In a bowl, combine the water and sugar then sprinkle the yeast on top and stir to dissolve. Let stand for about 10 minutes, or until it blooms, or looks bubbly. Add the oil and stir to mix.

In a stand mixer fitted with the dough hook, stir together the flour and salt. Add the starter and the yeast mixture and mix on medium-high speed for about 10 minutes, or until a wet dough forms. A wet dough means soft, tender buns, so resist the urge to add more flour.

Turn the dough out onto a sheet pan, lightly spray it with nonstick cooking spray to prevent sticking, and cover with a kitchen towel. Alternatively, transfer the dough to a large bowl and cover the bowl with a kitchen towel. Let the dough rise until it doubles in size, about 1 hour.

Once the dough has proofed, line a large sheet pan with parchment paper. Turn the dough out onto a lightly floured work surface. As noted above, add as little flour as possible to the work surface and your hands to ensure the finished rolls will be soft and tender. Divide the dough into 12 equal portions; each should weigh about 4½ ounces (130 g). Loosely shape each portion into a football shape, tapering the ends. The rolls should be 5½ inches (14 cm) long and 2 inches (5 cm) wide at the center.

Transfer the teleras to the prepared pan, spacing them 1 to 2 inches (2.5 to 5 cm) apart on the pan. Loosely cover the pan with greased plastic wrap and let sit in a warm, draft-free area for about 30 minutes, or until the teleras have doubled in size. About 15 minutes before the teleras have finished proofing, preheat the oven to 400°F (205°C).

Once the oven is preheated, place a 9 x 13-inch (23 x 33-cm) baking dish half filled with water on the bottom rack of the oven to create steam. Using a sharp knife, score the center of each roll from end to end. Brush the tops of the rolls with water. Bake the rolls for 7 to 10 minutes. Rotate the pan 180 degrees and continue to bake until golden brown, the top is crispy, and a toothpick inserted into the center of a roll comes out clean, 7 to 15 minutes longer. Transfer to a wire rack and let cool completely. The teleras will keep in an airtight container at room temperature for up to 2 days.

INGREDIENTS

2¼ cups (540 ml) lukewarm water (105° to 115°F/41° to 46°C)

3 tablespoons sugar

2 tablespoons active dry yeast

¼ cup (60 ml) tablespoons extra-virgin olive oil

4½ cups (610 g) bread flour

2 teaspoons kosher salt

½ cup (50 g) sourdough starter

Nonstick cooking spray, for spraying on dough

HERBED SOURDOUGH TELERAS Add ½ cup (50 g) grated Parmesan cheese, 1 teaspoon garlic powder, 1 teaspoon onion powder, 1 tablespoon very finely minced fresh Mexican oregano, and 1 tablespoon very finely minced fresh basil to the mixer bowl with the starter and yeast mixture. I like to use Burlap & Barrel–brand Porcelain or Purple Stripe garlic powder and toasted onion powder.

LEEK AND QUESO PANELA EMPANADAS WITH MOJO VERDE

Empanadas were introduced to Mexico by the Spanish, and today, regional specialties are found throughout the country, with seafood fillings along the coasts, pork in Chiapas, and chicken in yellow mole in Oaxaca. In this version, I have paired leeks with queso panela, a white, fresh, mild cow's milk cheese available in Mexican markets and well-stocked supermarkets. Empanadas are served both fried and baked in Mexico, and both cooking methods are included here. The mojo verde is not a typical "green sauce"— the addition of the avocado gives it a rich creaminess.

MAKES 24 EMPANADAS

To make the empanada dough, in a large bowl, combine the water, melted butter, vinegar, salt, and sugar and mix well. Slowly add the flour to the butter mixture while stirring constantly with a wooden spoon until a shaggy dough comes together. Turn the dough out onto a lightly floured work surface and knead for about 5 minutes, or until a smooth and slightly shiny dough forms. Wrap the dough in plastic wrap and let rest in the refrigerator for at least 10 minutes or up to 2 days before using. (The longer it rests the easier it will be to stretch the dough; it will keep for up to 2 days as long as it is covered.) Remove the dough from the refrigerator 10 minutes before you are ready to roll it out. A very cold dough or a warm dough is hard to roll and shape.

To make the filling, preheat the oven to 350°F (175°C). Rinse the leeks well in cold water, making sure to dislodge any dirt hidden in the leaves, then pat dry. Pile the leeks on a large sheet pan, drizzle with the olive oil, season lightly with salt, and toss to coat evenly. Spread the leeks in a single layer. Place in the oven and roast for 30 minutes, or until tender. Let cool, roughly chop, and transfer to a bowl. Add the cheese and toss to mix evenly. Set aside.

Portion the empanada dough into 3-ounce (85-g) balls. On a lightly floured work surface, roll out each ball into a thin round about 5 inches (12 cm) in diameter. Place about 3 tablespoons of the filling in the center of each round. Brush the edge of one half of the round with egg wash to help bind the two edges. Now, fold the round in half to create a half-moon, making sure the filling stays in the center. Using fork tines, press down along the edges to seal securely closed.

To pan-fry the empanadas, pour enough oil into a large sauté pan to cover the bottom (about ¼ cup/60 ml) and heat over medium heat. When the oil is hot, working in batches to avoid crowding, add the empanadas and fry, turning once, for 2 to 3 minutes on each side, or until golden brown and cooked through, making sure to spoon over some hot oil to cook the edges of the dough. Transfer to a platter and keep warm. Add more oil to the pan as needed to cook the remaining batches.

To bake the empanadas, preheat the oven to 350°F (175°C). Line a large sheet pan with parchment paper. Arrange the empanadas on the sheet pan, spacing them about 1 inch (2.5 cm) apart. Brush the top of the empanadas with the egg wash. Bake until golden brown and cooked through, about 20 minutes.

Serve the empanadas warm, with the mojo verde.

INGREDIENTS

For the empanada dough:

2 cups (480 ml) lukewarm water (105° to 115°F/41° to 46°C)

½ cup (115 g) unsalted butter, melted

1 tablespoon apple cider vinegar

2 tablespoons kosher salt

2 tablespoons sugar

6 cups (750 g) all-purpose flour, sifted, plus more for dusting

For the filling:

2 pounds (910 g) trimmed leeks or spring onions, white parts only, rinsed and dried

2 tablespoons olive oil

Kosher salt

1 pound (455 g) queso panela, shredded on the large holes of a box grater-shredder

Canola or vegetable oil, if frying

1 large egg, lightly beaten, for egg wash, if baking

Mojo Verde (page 267), for serving

CALIFORNIA PAMBAZOS
WITH FARMERS' MARKET VEGETABLES AND QUESO PANELA

Pambazos are a popular street food in Guadalajara, where you can't walk more than a few blocks without finding a puesto (food stand) selling this "wet" sandwich. The word *pambazo* is derived from the term *pan basso* (literally, "low bread"), which was historically used for peasant bread made with the poorest-quality and oldest flour. The people who could afford only pan basso soaked it in salsa guajillo to soften it, thus making the bread edible. In this California version of the pambazo, I've stuffed the sandwich with farm-fresh vegetables and soaked it in an árbol chile salsa. For a non-vegetarian version, add chorizo patties (page 213) and use half the quantity of vegetables.

INGREDIENTS

For the vegetables:

3 tablespoons olive oil, plus more if needed

2 yellow onions, thinly sliced

3 cloves garlic, minced

1 small head green cabbage, thinly sliced

4 red bell peppers, halved and cut lengthwise into strips ¼ inch (6 mm) wide

1 bunch broccolini, cut crosswise into 1-inch (2.5-cm) pieces

1 bunch dinosaur (Tuscan) kale, stems and ribs removed and leaves cut crosswise into 1-inch (2.5-cm) strips

Kosher salt

Grated zest and juice of 2 lemons

1 tablespoon Salsa Macha "Chilango" (page 265)

1 cup (140 g) raw peanuts, toasted and roughly chopped

12 Sourdough Teleras (page 69)

3 cups (780 g) refried beans (page 260), warmed

2 pounds (910 g) queso panela, cut into slices ⅛ inch (3 mm) thick, plus more crumbled for garnish

6 cups (1.4 L) Salsa Verde con Chiles de Árbol (page 265)

Coarsely chopped fresh cilantro, for garnish

MAKES 12 SERVINGS

Preheat the oven to 325°F (165°C).

To prepare the vegetables, in a large, shallow, ovenproof pot, heat the oil over medium-high heat. Add onions and garlic and cook, stirring often, for about 5 minutes, or until translucent. If the onions and garlic soak up all the oil, add a little more to the pan.

Add the cabbage and bell peppers and cook, stirring often, until the cabbage begins to wilt, about 5 minutes. Add the broccolini and continue to cook, stirring, until the florets are tender enough to be pierced with a fork, about 5 minutes. Add the kale, season with salt, and continue to cook, stirring often, until the kale is wilted and vegetables are tender, about 2 minutes more. Make sure not to overcook the vegetables. Transfer the pan to the oven and roast the vegetables for about 20 minutes, or until they release their natural flavors.

Remove the vegetables from the oven, season them with the lemon zest and juice, and then stir in the Salsa Macha and peanuts, mixing gently. Taste and adjust the seasoning with salt if needed.

To make each pambazo, split a telera horizontally, stopping just short of cutting all the way through. Open the telera and, using a rubber spatula, lightly spread the cut sides with beans. Add a couple slices of the queso panela and then a generous portion of the vegetables. Close the sandwich. Repeat until all the sandwiches are filled.

Pour half of the salsa verde into a shallow bowl. Preheat a large skillet over medium-low heat. Add a sandwich to the bowl with the salsa, coating the first side, then flip the sandwich and coat the second side. Add the sandwich to the hot skillet. Repeat with more sandwiches, being careful not to crowd the pan. Toast the pambazos, turning once, for 2 to 3 minutes on each side, or until both sides are a toasty golden brown. Repeat to toast the remaining sandwiches.

To serve each pambazo, spoon 2 tablespoons of the salsa verde onto an individual plate, top with the sandwich, and spoon 2 tablespoons of the salsa verde over the top. Garnish with the crumbled cheese and the cilantro and serve at once.

"EL MOJADO" MOLTEN MEXICAN CHOCOLATE CAKE

I love this molten chocolate cake, which I playfully call el mojado, or "the wet one," because the cake is gooey on the inside. The recipe is easy and almost foolproof. As with any recipe using chocolate, the quality of the chocolate is paramount. Here, I've blended two quality chocolates from our friends at Dandelion Chocolate and Rancho Gordo to create a Mexican version of this popular dessert. Add the recommended spices from Burlap & Barrel for a special flavor twist.

MAKES 8 TO 10 SERVINGS

Fill a saucepan about one-third full with water, place over medium heat, and bring to a gentle simmer. Meanwhile, in a heatproof bowl that will rest snugly in the rim of the pan without touching the water, combine 5 ounces (140 g) of the dark chocolate, the Mexican chocolate, butter, piloncillo, granulated sugar, and salt. Set the bowl in the rim of the pan and heat the mixture, stirring occasionally. Just before the mixture is completely melted, remove from the heat. Add the chile powder and the cocoa powder, cinnamon, and wild mesquite, if using, and stir until well mixed and smooth.

Add the eggs to the chocolate mixture and mix well. Then add the flour and baking powder and mix well. Spoon the cake mix into a piping bag fitted with a ½-inch- (12.7-mm-) diameter plain tip. Set aside.

To make the ganache, put the remaining 5 ounces (140 g) dark chocolate in a bowl. In a small saucepan, bring the cream to a simmer over medium-low heat. Pour the cream over the chocolate and let sit for 5 minutes, then stir until smooth. Let cool to room temperature.

Preheat the oven to 450°F (230°C). Have ready eight to ten 4- to 6-ounce (120- to 180-ml) ramekins.

Pipe a thin layer (about ½ inch/12 mm thick) of the cake mix onto the bottom of each ramekin. Using a ½-ounce (15-ml) ice-cream or cookie scoop, add a scoop of ganache to the center of each ramekin, using your fingers to push the ganache down into the cake mix layer. Pipe the remaining cake mix to fill the ramekins. Arrange the ramekins on a large sheet pan and place in the oven. Bake the cakes until the sides have puffed and set but the centers are still jiggly when gently shaken, 4 to 5 minutes.

Serve warm, topped with whipped cream, if desired.

WINE PAIRING Hoopes Merlot from Howell Mountain is an incredible accompaniment alongside chocolate with chili.

INGREDIENTS

10 ounces (280 g) 70 percent cacao dark chocolate, preferably Dandelion brand, coarsely chopped

5 ounces (140 g) Mexican chocolate, preferably Rancho Gordo brand (2 tablets), coarsely chopped

½ cup (115) unsalted butter

¼ cup (55 g) grated piloncillo (see page 274) or packed dark brown sugar

¼ cup (50 g) granulated sugar

¼ teaspoon kosher salt

1 tablespoon ancho chile powder

2 tablespoons cocoa powder, preferably Burlap & Barrel Morogoro cacao powder (optional)

1 teaspoon ground cinnamon, preferably Burlap & Barrel royal cinnamon (optional)

½ teaspoon Burlap & Barrel wild mesquite powder (optional)

6 large eggs, at room temperature, lightly beaten

½ cup (65 g) all-purpose flour

2 teaspoons baking powder

6 tablespoons (90 ml) heavy cream

Whipped cream or ice cream, for serving (optional)

CHESTNUT CINCO LECHES CAKE WITH CHOCOLATE DUST

Mexico's well-known tres leches cake was either inspired by the English trifle, a layered dessert of soaked cake layers and custard, or by a milk-soaked sponge cake dessert from Nicaragua, where it was promoted by canned milk products, like Nestlé and Borden, with recipes provided on the can labels. I've taken the classic and increased the number to cinco leches (five milks).

INGREDIENTS

For the soaking milk:

1¼ cups (300 ml) organic sweetened condensed milk

1 cup (240 ml) organic evaporated milk

½ cup (120 ml) whole milk

½ cup (120 ml) chestnut liqueur

½ cup (120 ml) heavy cream

For the cake:

Cooking spray or butter, for greasing the pans

10 large eggs, separated

2 cups (400 g) sugar

⅔ cup (165 ml) whole milk

1½ teaspoons pure vanilla extract

2¼ cups (280 g) all-purpose flour

1 tablespoon baking powder

½ teaspoon kosher salt

1 cup (240 ml) dulce de leche or cajeta (goat milk caramel spread)

Whipped cream, ground chocolate (page 273), and seasonal berries, for garnish

MAKES 8 TO 10 SERVINGS

To make the soaking milk, in a bowl, combine the condensed milk, evaporated milk, whole milk, liqueur, and cream and mix well. You should have 3¾ cups (900 ml). Divide the mixture in half and reserve.

To make the cake, preheat the oven to 350°F (175°C). Lightly grease two 9-inch (23-cm) spring forms or cake pans. Line the pan bottoms and sides with parchment paper.

Put the egg whites into a large bowl. Using an immersion blender fitted with the whisk attachment or a handheld mixer, beat the whites on high speed while slowly adding 1 cup (200 g) of the sugar, beating until stiff peaks form.

In a second large bowl, beat together the egg yolks and the remaining 1 cup (200 g) sugar on medium-high speed until the mixture is pale yellow and reaches the ribbon stage. To check, lift some of the mixture with the beater; it should fall back on itself like a ribbon and then slowly dissolve into the surface. Add the milk and vanilla and beat on medium-high speed for 1 more minute.

In a small bowl, stir together the flour, baking powder, and kosher salt. Whisk the flour mixture into the yolk mixture, making sure there are no lumps. The mixture will be quite thick, but it will lighten up once the egg whites are mixed in.

Pile one-third of the beaten egg whites on top of the yolk mixture and then fold them in with a rubber spatula just until no white streaks remain. Repeat with the remaining egg whites in two batches, folding after each addition just until well blended.

Divide the batter evenly between the two prepared pans. Bake the cakes for 35 to 45 minutes, or until a toothpick inserted into the center of each cake comes out clean. Let cool in the pans on wire racks for 30 minutes.

Invert the cakes onto the racks, lift off the pans, and gently peel off the parchment. Return the cakes to the pans. Pour half of the soaking milk over each cake. Place the pans on a sheet pan and refrigerate for 1 hour.

To assemble, pull the cakes out of the refrigerator. Invert each cake onto a cake stand or a serving plate. If not making a layered cake, spread the dulce de leche over the top of the cakes. If you are an experienced baker, you can create a layered cake: Invert one cake onto a cake stand or serving plate and drizzle it with ½ cup (120 ml) of the dulce de leche. Turn out the second cake on top of the first and finish it with the remaining ½ cup (120 ml) of the dulce de leche. Garnish with whipped cream, dust with chocolate dust, and finish with berries.

WINE PAIRING Bouchaine 2019 Bouche d'Or Late Harvest Chardonnay, a golden dessert wine with the aroma of stone fruit, is balanced with acidity and crispness.

MILPA

MILPA

MILPA

THREE SISTERS: A HEALTHY BALANCE FOR LAND AND LIFE

The word *milpa* comes from the Nahuatl word phrase *mil-pa*, meaning "cultivated field." It refers to both an actual field and a farming practice: a traditional intercropping system that has played a central role in the protection of Mexican biodiversity. Corn, squash, and climbing beans, known as the "three sisters," are the main crops grown in the milpa cycle. The planting system allows these species not only to coexist but also to thrive as they share resources, including water, light, and nutrients from the soil. The genius of the system lies in its natural symbiosis. The corn stalks offer the climbing bean vines support as they reach for sunlight, while the beans pump beneficial nitrogen back into the soil, fertilizing the corn and squashes. The squashes, in turn, act as a natural weed suppressant, and their spiny, broad leaves protect the bean plants from predatory animals and provide ground cover. This trio of crops works together, leaving healthy and sustainable soil season after season. Ancient wisdom being its own kind of magic, the three sisters also form the basis of a healthy diet, followed by Mexicans since pre-Columbian times.

In November 2022, the Food and Agriculture Organization (FAO) of the United Nations formally recognized the Mayan milpa system of the Yucatán Peninsula for its complexity as a production model. It merits its designation as a Globally Important World Agricultural Heritage System (GIAHS) because it dates back millennia and because of its resilience to climate change and its contributions to the conservation of both culture and biodiversity.

PATATAS BRAVAS MEXICANAS
WITH CREMA AND CILANTRO

Although wild potato species are native to Mexico, the Spanish are credited with introducing the first cultivated varieties in the sixteenth century. It would take another three hundred years before these Andean imports were widely planted in the country. Today, potatoes turn up in myriad ways on Mexican plates, from stirred into chorizo and served with tortillas, pickled with carrots and onions, or mixed with onion and cheese to make croquettes. Here is my modern Mexican riff on a favorite Spanish tapa.

MAKES 12 SERVINGS

In a large saucepan, combine the milk, garlic, shallot, thyme, a pinch of salt, and the potatoes. Add water to cover the potatoes by about 1 inch (2.5 cm) and place the pan over medium-low heat. Bring to a gentle simmer and cook the potatoes for 10 to 12 minutes, or until fork-tender. Drain, discard the shallot, garlic, and thyme, and let the potatoes cool.

Slightly smash the potatoes, leaving them chunky enough so they have a surface area for browning. Pour the oil into a large skillet or sauté pan, adding enough to coat the bottom well, and heat over medium-low heat. When the oil is hot, add the potatoes and fry, turning as needed to color evenly, for 10 to 15 minutes, or until the potatoes are golden and crispy on all sides. (If you do not have a large pan, fry the potatoes in two pans.)

Transfer the potatoes to a serving plate, season with salt and lemon zest, and toss and turn gently. Top with 2 to 3 tablespoons of the salsa and then drizzle the crema over the top. Garnish with the cilantro and serve at once.

Note: If you cannot find small Yukon Gold potatoes, other all-purpose potatoes, such as Kennebec or Katahdin, can be used. Or you can cut larger Yukon Golds into 1½-inch (4-cm) pieces.

INGREDIENTS

2 quarts (2 L) whole milk

1 clove garlic

1 shallot, halved

1 fresh thyme sprig

Kosher salt

3 pounds (1.4 kg) Yukon Gold potatoes, 1½ inches (4 cm) in diameter (see Note)

3 to 4 tablespoons (45 to 60 ml) olive oil

Grated lemon zest, for seasoning

2 cups (480 ml) Salsa de Ancho Chile Brava (page 263)

2 cups (480 ml) crema or crème fraîche

Leaves from 1 bunch fresh cilantro, coarsely chopped

WINE PAIRING Ceja Pinot Noir, Los Carneros, Napa Valley is floral and lively with a beautiful exploration of lavender, red cherry, and cinnamon. Soft and juicy, it has a full-bodied figure of ripeness with polished tannins and structured spiciness, which pairs nicely with Salsa de Ancho Chile Brava.

BROCCOLINI AND SPINACH TORTITAS
WITH FRESH SALSA VERDE WITH PEAS AND MINT

These vegetarian tortitas, or "patties," are a delicious way to make sure you are getting a big share of the vegetables you need in your daily diet. They are also a great way to make sure your kids eat their vegetables!

INGREDIENTS

For the tortitas:

Kosher salt

6 ounces (170 g) spinach leaves

2 bunches broccolini, cut into large chunks

1 cup (115 g) grated Monterey cheese

1 yellow onion, finely diced

3 cloves garlic, minced

2 large eggs, lightly beaten

1 cup (125 g) all-purpose flour mixed with 2 teaspoons kosher salt, plus ⅓ cup (40 g) flour for dusting

⅓ cup (40 g) all-purpose flour

Olive oil, for frying

2 cups (480 ml) Fresh Salsa Verde with Peas and Mint (page 266), or your favorite salsa

MAKES 12 TORTITAS; 6 SERVINGS

To make the tortitas, fill a large bowl with water and ice and set it near the stove. Bring a large pot of water to a boil. Add 2 tablespoons salt, then add the spinach and broccolini and blanch for about 3 minutes. Drain the vegetables well and then plunge them into the ice bath to cool completely.

When the spinach and broccolini are cool, drain well, pressing out any excess moisture. Finely chop the spinach and broccolini by hand with a knife or pulse in a food processor (be sure not to purée). If the vegetables feel wet after chopping, wrap them in a kitchen towel and wring out the excess moisture. A dry mixture is key to success.

Transfer the spinach and broccolini to a bowl, add the cheese, onion, garlic, eggs, and a pinch of salt and stir to mix. While continuing to stir, slowly add ½ cup (65 g) of the seasoned flour. Then slowly stir in more seasoned flour until the mixture holds together well; you may not need all the flour.

Divide the vegetable mixture into 12 equal portions. Each should weigh about 3 ounces (85 g). Form each portion into a patty about ½ inch (12 mm) thick. Put the ⅓ cup (40 g) flour into a shallow bowl. Have ready a sheet pan. One at a time, coat the patties on both sides in the flour, tapping off the excess, and set aside on the sheet pan.

Pour the oil to a depth of ¼ inch (6 mm) into a large skillet and heat to 325° to 350°F (165° to 175°C). Line a large plate with paper towels and set it near the stove. When the oil is ready, working in batches to avoid crowding, add the patties and fry, turning once, for about 2 minutes on each side, or until golden brown on both sides and cooked through. Transfer the patties to the paper towels to drain and keep warm. Repeat with the remaining patties.

Serve the tortitas warm with 2 to 3 tablespoons of salsa per person on the side.

SEARED CAULIFLOWER
WITH PEANUTS AND SALSA MACHA "CHILANGO"

Marinating the cauliflower first, just as you would a protein, transforms it and adds a depth of flavor to the dish that holds up beautifully when paired with spicy, nutty Salsa Macha "Chilango" (page 265). Serve with my Agridulce Chicken Wings with Verde Goddess Dressing (page 224) or Baby Back Rib Carnitas (page 230).

MAKES 6 TO 8 SERVINGS

To make the marinade, in a large bowl, combine all the ingredients and mix well.

Using your fingers, break the cauliflower heads into thumb-size florets. When you are close to the top of each head, use a small knife to cut up the larger pieces so they are the same size as the smaller florets. Add the florets to the marinade, turn to coat well, cover, and refrigerate for 1 hour.

Remove the florets from the marinade and discard the marinade. Using a large skillet or sauté pan, heat the oil over medium-high heat. When the oil is hot, add the cauliflower and sauté for 3 to 4 minutes, or until it just begins to brown. Reduce the heat to medium-low, season with salt, and continue cooking, stirring often, for 6 to 8 minutes, or until fork-tender.

Add the spinach and cook, stirring often, for 2 to 3 minutes, or until wilted. Season with a squeeze or two of lemon juice, then taste and adjust with more salt if needed. Fold in the peanuts and cilantro and remove from the heat.

Transfer to a serving dish, drizzle with the salsa, and serve at once.

INGREDIENTS

For the marinade:

1 cup (240 ml rice vinegar

1 cup(240 ml) fresh lime juice

1 cup (240 ml) fresh orange juice

½ cup (120 ml) white soy sauce

¼ cup (60 ml) regular soy sauce

1 teaspoon Asian fish sauce, preferably Red Boat brand

2 to 3 cloves garlic, grated

1½ teaspoons peeled, chopped fresh ginger

2 heads cauliflower

⅓ cup (75 ml) olive oil

Kosher salt

4 cups (80 g) spinach leaves

½ lemon

1 cup (150 g) raw peanuts, toasted

1 bunch fresh cilantro, roughly chopped

¾ cup (180 ml) Salsa Macha "Chilango" (page 265)

CAULIFLOWER AND CUCUMBER CEVICHE
WITH COCONUT AND AVOCADO

A lighter alternative to traditional seafood ceviche, this antojito is perfect for vegetarian and vegan dinner guests (and easy on the host's pocketbook). If you like your food spicy, increase the amount of jalapeño chiles or substitute serrano chiles.

INGREDIENTS

½ cup (120 ml) fresh lime juice

½ cup (120 ml) coconut milk

2 tablespoons white soy sauce

1 tablespoon agave nectar

¼ cup (10 g) chopped fresh cilantro leaves

1 tomatillo, husked, peeled, and coarsely chopped

1 jalapeño chile, stem removed and then seeded if desired (for less spice)

Kosher salt

1 head cauliflower, 1½ to 2 pounds (680 to 910 g) in weight

1 avocado, pitted, peeled, and thinly sliced

1 cucumber, thinly sliced into coins

1 cup (85 g) cancha (toasted corn nuts), chopped (page 272; optional)

¼ cup (25 g) furikake (Japanese condiment)

MAKES 4 SERVINGS

In a blender, combine the lime juice, coconut milk, soy sauce, agave nectar, cilantro, tomatillo, and jalapeño and blend on medium-high speed until puréed, about 30 seconds. Season with salt to taste.

With a small knife, separate the larger florets from the head and set aside. You should have about 8 florets, each the size of a small lime. (Save the smaller florets and stem for another recipe or see Note, below.)

Using a mandoline, thinly slice the reserved large florets. As you slice the cauliflower some parts will crumble and some will look like Parmesan shavings in the shape of a little tree. Save these pretty shavings and reserve the crumbled cauliflower alongside the small florets and stems separated earlier. You will end up with about 8 ounces (225 g) of shavings for the dish.

To assemble, fan the avocado slices in the center of a serving plate. Alternate the cucumber coins and reserved cauliflower slices, shingling them over the top of the avocado to cover. Pour the lime-coconut mixture to the side of the cauliflower. Let sit for about 3 minutes to marinate.

Sprinkle the cancha over the top, if using, and finish with the furikake. Serve at once.

NOTE For a beautiful contrast in texture and appearance, blanch the smaller cauliflower florets in boiling water, then sear them slightly using a kitchen torch. If you do not have a chef's torch, follow the third step in Seared Cauliflower with Peanuts and Salsa Macha "Chilango" on page 91 to sear the cauliflower.

WINE PAIRING Ceja Chardonnay, Los Carneros, Napa Valley bursts with aromas of pineapple, Granny Smith apple, and apricot. Subtle hints of vanilla, pear, and Meyer lemon add to the incredibly complex aromas.

FEATURED MENU:
DÍA DE LOS MUERTOS

One testament to the success the Catholic Church had in converting Mexico's Indigenous people is that few, if any, of their rites have survived intact except in some of the smaller pueblos. Of these, the only national festival period that is a true carryover from pre-Hispanic times is Día de los Muertos (Day of the Dead), which draws upon the Aztec custom of holding festivals celebrating death. The festivities marry the ancient rituals of the Aztecs with Catholic customs and symbols in a joyful celebration fueled with food and drink.

Día de los Muertos actually lasts three days, from October 31 through November 2, during which family and friends come together to remember loved ones who have died. While sweets, skeletons, and spirits are associated with both Día de los Muertos and Halloween, and the dates overlap, that is where the similarities end. Dressing in costumes and asking for candy are recently "imported" practices that occur in only a handful of regions of Mexico. Rather than evoking fear, Día de los Muertos is an occasion for celebration, complete with gaily dressed catrinas (skeletons) and beautiful altars (ofrendas) replete with photos of the departed along with candles, flowers, memorabilia, and some of their favorite things, from foods to tequila.

Although now highly commercialized, Día de los Muertos remains very family focused. During the holiday, Mexicans believe the living reunite with the spirits of the deceased, who are shown the path "home" by colorful marigolds. On October 31, the gates of heaven are said to open so the spirits of deceased children can return to their families for one day, November 1. All Saints' Day, which honors Mexico's myriad saints, is also celebrated on November 1. The principal celebration takes place on November 2, or All Souls' Day, when the spirits of adults who have passed enjoy a brief reunion with their friends and families.

Modern Day of the Dead Rituals

Late in October, Mexican families begin preparing for the upcoming celebration. Streets are lined with market stalls selling sweets, the most famous of which are the intricately decorated sugar skulls (alfeñiques) and Day of the Dead bread (pan de muertos). Most people go to the cemetery (pantheon) and some even picnic at the gravesite, spending the entire night visiting with the spirits of their loved ones. Family members clean and dress up the graves, attracting vendors selling flowers and decorations. Musicians, hoping to earn a few pesos, come to entertain the deceased and their families.

A Guide to Elements of the Modern Altar

Decorating Día de los Muertos altars with personal objects of the deceased, along with food and offerings, most likely grew out of the Aztec belief that when people die, they travel through the region of Mictlan (the underworld) on their way to Tlalocan (Aztec heaven). On that long journey, the deceased needed food, water, and even candles to light their way. Historians believe these traditions may have become conflated with altars found in Catholic churches.

Altars typically have three levels. On the first are photographs of the deceased, four veladoras (blessed candles) to guide the departed souls on their journey, their lights symbolic of eternal love, and seven additional candles representing the seven deadly sins. This first level is also where marigolds (cempasúchitl) are placed, the traditional flowers of Día de los Muertos. Their vivid orange-yellow color represents the brightness of the sun and provides a colorful path that guides the spirits of the dead, while their pungent scent attracts the departed to the altars prepared in their honor.

Oranges and other fruits are placed on the second level along with the intricate hand-cut paper banners known as papel picado (literally "cut paper"). These colorful banners also line streets all across Mexico and Mexican neighborhoods in the United States, where they wave in the wind in celebration of the freedom that death brings. Every color has a meaning: purple signifies Christian mourning, orange is reserved for Aztec mourning, white for purity, and pink for celebration.

The third level of the altar is reserved for recuerdos, favorite belongings or even favorite foods of the deceased. It also holds items such as a hand towel and maybe even a mirror so the deceased can "wash up" before "eating." It is not expected that the dead will actually consume the food, but rather that their spirits will be nourished by absorbing the aromas and energy of the dishes and beverages offered. These often include mole, tamales, atole, and sometimes cigarettes and tequila. Typically, family and close friends partake of the food and drink and may even wear a favorite article of the deceased's

clothing while they do so. Pan de muertos and alfeñiques are also found on this last level, as well as an ash cross and incense (copal), both meant to ward off evil spirits.

DÍA DE LOS MUERTOS MENU

Red Beet Sangria 97

Carrot-Piloncillo Soup with Cilantro-Lime Crema 98

Brined Chicken with Pumpkin Mole 101

Marigold–White Sweet Potato Tortitas with Tomatillo Applesauce 103

Mexican Rice a la Robles 104

Calabaza en Tacha Flan with Candied Honeynut Squash Seeds 107

Dark Chocolate Pan de Muertos 109

RED BEET SANGRIA

As beautiful as it is delicious, this beet juice and red wine sangria is almost bloodred, making it the perfect beverage for your Day of the Dead—or Halloween—celebration.

MAKES 6 TO 8 SERVINGS

In a large pitcher, combine the apple and orange pieces and piloncillo and muddle with a wooden spoon for 45 seconds. Add the beet juice, apple juice, orange juice, lime juice, brandy, and Aperol and muddle for another 45 seconds.

Pour in the wine and add the cinnamon sticks. Taste and adjust the flavor to your liking: If you like your sangria more on the sweet side, stir in more piloncillo. If you prefer a stronger sangria, add more brandy. Cover and refrigerate until well chilled.

To serve, fill each glass about ⅔ full of ice cubes, then top the ice with the strawberries and blueberries, dividing them evenly. Give the sangria a good stir, pour over the ice and fruit, and serve at once.

INGREDIENTS

1 apple, halved, cored, and cut into eighths

1 orange, cut into eighths

½ cup plus 2 tablespoons (140 g total) grated piloncillo (see page 274) or packed dark brown sugar, plus more if needed

1 cup (240 ml) red beet juice, homemade in a juicer (from 4 large beets) or store-bought

¼ cup (60 ml) apple juice

¼ cup (60 ml) fresh orange juice

¼ cup (60 ml) fresh lime juice

¼ cup (60 ml) brandy, or more if needed

2 tablespoons Aperol

1 bottle (750 ml) dry red wine, preferably Ceja Vineyards Vino de Casa Red Blend

2 cinnamon sticks (3 inches/7.5 cm), preferably Mexican cinnamon

Ice cubes

6 to 8 strawberries, hulled and cut into quarters, for garnish

2 cups (290 g) blueberries, for garnish

CARROT-PILONCILLO SOUP
WITH CILANTRO-LIME CREMA

The earthy smokiness of piloncillo, the "brown sugar of Mexico," perfectly complements the woody, sweet flavor of the carrots in this colorful autumn soup. The carrots are tossed with the piloncillo and first cooked in the oven, which imparts both color and savor, and then finished on the stovetop. The agria (sourness) of the crema Mexicana adds a savory, tangy flavor and creaminess, which tempers the sweetness of the soup.

INGREDIENTS

1 large yellow onion, julienned

1 fresh sage sprig

1 cup (225 g) unsalted butter

5 large carrots (1¼ pounds/570 g), peeled and cut into rounds about ½ inch (12 mm) thick

2 tablespoons grated piloncillo (see page 274)

Kosher salt and freshly ground black pepper

½ cup (120 ml) crema

2 tablespoons roughly chopped fresh cilantro

Grated zest and juice of 1 lime

MAKES 8 SERVINGS

In a large pot, combine the onion, sage, butter, and ½ cup (120 ml) water, place over low heat, and sweat, stirring occasionally, for about 30 minutes, or until the onion is translucent. Do not allow the onions to color. Remove from the heat and set aside.

Preheat the oven to 400°F (205°C). In a baking dish, toss the carrots with the piloncillo, coating evenly. Add water to the dish to reach halfway up the sides of the carrots. Transfer the dish to the oven and bake for 20 to 25 minutes, or until the carrots are tender. Adding water to the baking dish allows the carrots to steam at the bottom while getting some color on top.

Add the contents of the baking dish to the pot holding the onion, then add 4 cups (960 ml) water to the pot and stir well. Place over medium heat, bring to a simmer, and simmer gently, stirring occasionally, for 10 minutes to blend the flavors. Remove from the heat, season with salt and pepper, and let cool for a few minutes.

There should be enough liquid to blend the mixture until smooth without adding more water. You are looking for a thickish consistency, similar to a tomato sauce. Transfer the soup to a blender and blend until smooth. (You may need to do this in batches, depending on the size of your blender.) Transfer the puréed soup to a clean saucepan and heat over low heat, stirring often, until piping hot.

Meanwhile, in a small bowl, combine the crema, cilantro, and lime zest and juice and stir well.

When the soup is hot, divide it evenly among eight individual bowls. Garnish with the crema mixture and serve at once.

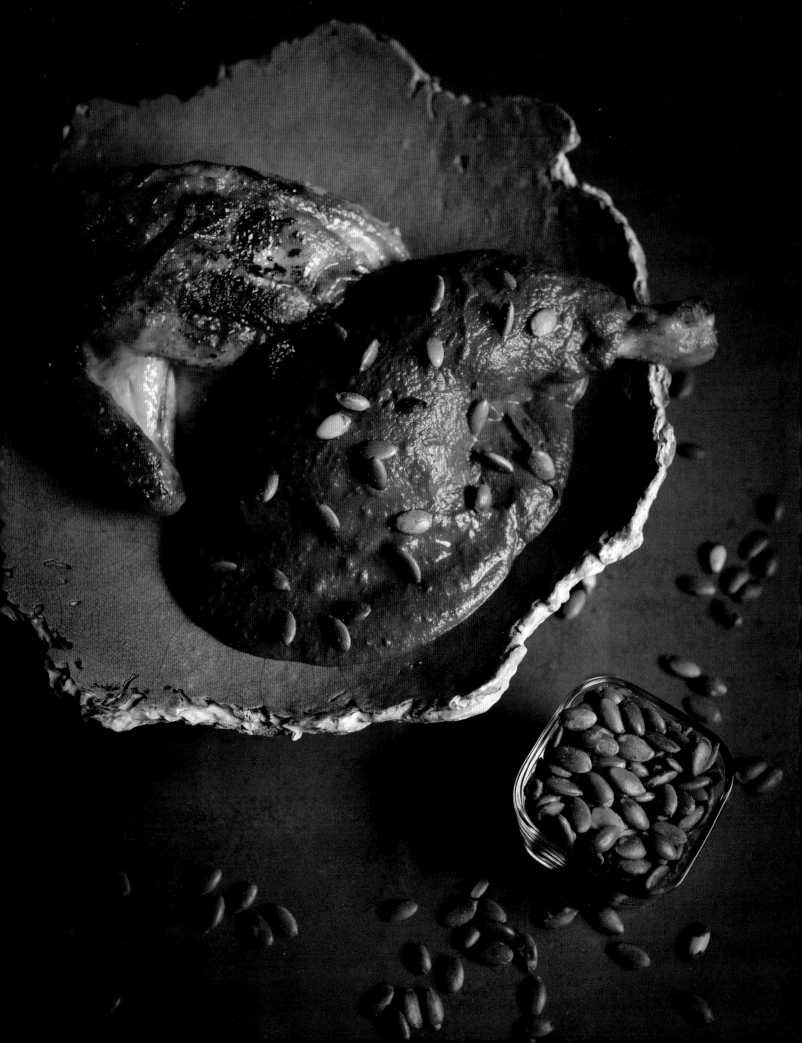

BRINED CHICKEN
WITH PUMPKIN MOLE

Mole de calabaza, or "pumpkin mole," is typically served during Día de los Muertos celebrations. Here, it is paired with chicken that is first brined to ensure moister, more tender meat and then roasted. The mole recipe makes more than you will need for the chicken, but the leftovers will keep in an airtight container in the refrigerator for up to 1 week and in the freezer for up to 3 months. If you do not want to store the mole, you can cut the recipe in half. In Mexico, it is common to eat mole with a side of beans (page 260), a pile of tortillas, and no protein.

MAKES 8 SERVINGS

To prepare the chicken, make the brine as directed. Once cool, add the chicken quarters, making sure they are submerged in the liquid. Cover and refrigerate overnight.

The next day, make the mole. In a large pot, combine the butter and onion over medium-low heat and cook for 1 to 2 minutes, or until the butter melts and begins to sweat the onion. Add the pumpkin and continue to cook, stirring occasionally, for 3 to 5 minutes, or until the pumpkin just begins to brown. Add 4 cups (960 ml) of the stock and the sage, increase the heat to medium, bring to a gentle simmer, and cook for 15 to 20 minutes, or until the pumpkin is tender. Carefully transfer the pumpkin and its liquid to a blender and blend until smooth. Leave the pumpkin purée in the blender for now.

Line a large plate or sheet pan with paper towels and set it near the stove. Select a large cast-iron skillet (this will allow space for the nuts and seeds to spread out in a single layer and toast more or less evenly) and place over medium-low heat. Pour the oil into the pan and heat the oil until it is hot. When the oil is ready, add the peanuts and toast them, turning them as needed, until they begin to color, then scoop them out onto the paper towels to drain. Repeat with the pepitas and drain on the paper towels.

Next, add the plantain to the same oil and toast, turning as needed, until nicely colored, then transfer to the paper towels. Continue using the same oil to toast the pasilla chiles, garlic cloves, and white onions and to bloom the clove, juniper berries, star anise, and cinnamon, always adding just one ingredient to the pan at a time to ensure evenly coloring and draining them on the paper towels. Once all the ingredients are toasted or bloomed, turn off the heat and reserve the oil.

You may need to blend the mole in two batches, depending on the size of your blender. Add all the toasted and bloomed ingredients, the raisins, chocolate, piloncillo, and sesame seeds to the blender with the pumpkin and blend well, starting on low speed and gradually increasing the speed to high. You want a perfectly smooth mole.

The mole should have the consistency of a thick pudding. If the mole is too thin, use tongs to hold the tortilla directly over a lit gas burner on your stovetop until it burns around the edges and has a few burnt spots in the center, then tear it into pieces, add to the blender, and blend until smooth. (If you don't have a gas stove, use a comal or dry cast-iron pan and overcook your tortillas until they start to burn around the edges.) If your mole is too thick, add more stock and blend again.

CONTINUED...

For the chicken:

12-Hour Poultry Brine (page 270)

2 whole chickens, cut into quarters

For the pumpkin mole:

1 cup (225 g) unsalted butter

1 small yellow onion, thinly sliced

One 2-pound (910-g) piece Cinderella pumpkin or 2-pound (910-g) butternut squash, seeded, peeled, and cut into medium-size chunks

4 to 6 cups (960 ml to 1.4 L) chicken stock (or vegetable stock for a vegetarian mole)

2 fresh sage sprigs

1 cup (240 ml) olive oil

¼ cup (40 g) raw peanuts

⅓ cup (45 g) pepitas

1 sweet plantain, peeled and sliced

4 pasilla chiles, stems and seeds removed

3 cloves garlic

2 Spanish white onions, cut into rounds ¼ inch (6 mm) thick

1 whole clove

2 juniper berries

1 star anise

1 cinnamon stick (3 inches/7.5 cm)

¼ cup (35 g) raisins

3 ounces (85 g) Mexican chocolate, chopped

2 tablespoons grated piloncillo (see page 274)

¼ cup (40 g) toasted white sesame seeds (see page 271), plus more for garnish

1 corn tortilla, if needed

To cook the mole, add the reserved oil to a large cazuela or other wide, shallow pot and heat over medium-high until the oil ripples or smokes very slightly. Keep a splatter screen nearby and add the mole to the hot oil. If needed, rinse the blender with some leftover stock to get every last bit and add it to the cazuela. Lower the heat to a simmer and cook for 15 to 20 minutes. As the mole cooks, use a large wooden spoon to stir it occasionally, being sure to scrape the sides and bottom of the pot and to stir in any oil that collects around edges as you do. The mole will darken slightly as it cooks, and it is ready when it coats the back of the spoon—the classic test for the correct mole thickness. If the mole is too thin, continue cooking until you have achieved the desired consistency. You should have about 3 quarts (2.8 L) mole. You will need only half of it for this recipe. Let the remainder cool and then store as suggested.

While the mole cooks, roast the chicken. Preheat the oven to 400°F (205°C). Line a large sheet pan or two smaller sheet pans with parchment paper. Remove the chicken from the brine and pat dry. Place the pieces, skin side down, on the prepared pan(s) and roast for about 15 minutes. Flip the chicken pieces and roast for 5 to 10 minutes longer, or until the skin is golden brown and an instant-read thermometer inserted into the thickest parts away from bone registers 165°F (74°C). Remove from the oven.

To serve, divide the chicken quarters among eight individual plates, smother the chicken in the piping-hot mole, and garnish with sesame seeds. Serve at once.

THE MANY MOLES OF MEXICO Mole poblano, with its iconic chocolate-chile flavor profile, is no doubt the best known of Mexico's hundreds of mole recipes. The word *poblano* means "from the state of Puebla," which is widely considered "the cradle of mole" and gives weight to a culinary myth that credits the kitchen skills of the sisters of Puebla's Convento de Santa Clara with creating this quintessential Mexican fiesta dish. In fact, mole clearly has pre-Columbian roots: the word *molli* or *mulli* appears repeatedly in the *Florentine Codex*, the sixteenth-century ethnography that is widely considered a primary source for the culinary history of Mexico.

Moles are thick sauces typically made from nuts, seeds, and any number of different chiles along with a multitude of other ingredients, depending on the variation (red, green, yellow, black, pink, white, and more); the region (Puebla and Oaxaca are the biggest players); and the particular family recipe. In addition to nuts, seeds, and chiles, mole recipes can include bread or tortillas as a thickener, raisins, plantains, chocolate, cloves, cinnamon, sweet and/or black pepper, and cumin.

There are over three hundred moles prepared in the various towns in the state of Puebla alone, each with its special variation. These complex, bold-flavored sauces are often the star at weddings, quinceañeras, and baptisms in central and southern Mexico. Recipes are passed down through the generations and are closely held family secrets. Abuelitas (grandmothers) have even been known to hide their recipes from the younger women in their families, especially their daughters-in-law.

MARIGOLD–WHITE SWEET POTATO TORTITAS
WITH TOMATILLO APPLESAUCE

In Mexico, marigolds begin to bloom in abundance at the end of the rainy season, just in time for Day of the Dead celebrations. The brightly colored blossoms are used not only to decorate the graves and altars of the departed but also in the kitchen. Here, I add their vibrant orange petals to crisp tortitas made with white sweet potatoes. Whip up an extra batch of the applesauce, as this apple-tomatillo version is addictive!

MAKES 4 TO 6 SERVINGS

In a large saucepan, combine the sweet potatoes with water to cover and bring to a boil over medium-high heat. Cook for 20 to 25 minutes, or until fork-tender. Drain and let stand until cool enough to handle, then peel, transfer to a bowl, and mash with a potato masher.

Add the raisins, marigold petals, cheese, egg, and ½ teaspoon salt to the mashed sweet potatoes and mix well.

In a shallow bowl, whisk together the flour, the remaining 1 teaspoon salt, and the cinnamon.

Have ready a sheet pan. Divide the sweet potato mixture into 10 equal portions. Each portion should weigh about 3 ounces (85 g). One at a time, loosely shape each portion into a ball about the size of a lime and place the ball in the bowl with the flour mixture. Use the flour to help prevent the potato mixture from sticking to your hands as you shape the ball into a patty about 3 inches (7.5 cm) in diameter and ½ inch (12 mm) thick. Tap off the excess flour and set aside on the sheet pan. Repeat until all the patties are shaped.

Pour the oil to a depth of ½ inch (12 mm) into a large skillet and heat to 300°F (150°C). Line a large plate with paper towels and set it near the stove. When the oil is ready, working in batches to avoid crowding, add the patties and fry, turning once, for about 2 minutes on each side, or until golden brown on both sides and cooked through. Transfer to the paper towels to drain and keep warm. Repeat with the remaining patties.

Serve the tortitas warm with the applesauce on the side.

INGREDIENTS

3 white sweet potatoes (about 1 pound/455 g)

½ cup (75 g) raisins

Petals from 4 organic marigold flowers, finely chopped

¼ cup (30 g) shredded queso Oaxaca

1 large egg

1½ teaspoons kosher salt

1 cup (125 g) all-purpose flour

½ teaspoon ground cinnamon

Light olive oil, for frying

1 cup (240 ml) Tomatillo Applesauce (page 267)

MEXICAN RICE A LA ROBLES

In an article published in August 2019, research fellow Raúl Matta wrote the following: "Cocineras tradicionales—traditional female cooks—are women of Mexican Indigenous descent who embody the status of food tradition bearers . . . [seen as both] esteemed social figures and . . . a driving force" behind the preservation of Mexico's culinary traditions. I am so fortunate that my mother, Irma Robles, is one of these cocineras tradicionales and passed not only her knowledge but also her passion for cooking on to me. The is one of the dishes we would have on special occasions. I always knew when my mother was making her famous rice because of the amazing smells that filled the house: first, the smell of the rice as she toasted it and then of the steam from the rice as she lifted the lid to check its doneness. The stuffed chiles placed over the top were like regalitos (little presents). Every family member would race to grab a pepper, as my mom, I suspect deliberately, never made quite enough for everyone.

INGREDIENTS

For the stuffed jalapeños:

1 pound (455 g) queso panela

10 jalapeño chiles, stems on

For the rice:

2 cups (480 ml) chicken stock

5 Roma tomatoes, cut into eighths

3 tablespoons olive oil

2 cups (400 g) Calrose rice or other medium-grain white rice such as Carolina rice

1 yellow onion, finely diced

1 clove garlic, minced

1 tablespoon tomato paste

1 bay leaf

1 teaspoon kosher salt

MAKES 10 SERVINGS

To make the stuffed jalapeños, cut the cheese into 10 pieces the thickness of your pinkie finger and just a little shorter than a chile.

Dry roast the jalapeños on a comal as directed on page 271. Let cool.

The seeds and veins are the spiciest parts of a chile. For a spicy stuffed jalapeño, use a small, sharp knife to remove the "cap" where the stem is. Slip a piece of the cheese into the chile, put the cap back in place, and secure it with a toothpick. For a less spicy stuffed jalapeño, using a small, sharp knife, make an incision from just below the stem to the tip of the chile, taking care not to pierce the opposite side. Scrape out the seeds and veins or even just the seeds with the knife or a small spoon. Slip a piece of the cheese into the chile and secure the incision closed with a toothpick.

To make the rice, in a blender, combine the stock and tomatoes and blend until the tomatoes have liquefied. Set the "tomato water" aside.

In a large, deep sauté pan with a lid, heat the oil over medium-high heat. Add the rice and toast, stirring frequently, for 3 to 4 minutes. The rice will first turn translucent and then start to turn light brown. Add the onion and garlic and cook, stirring frequently to prevent sticking or scorching, for 2 to 4 minutes, or until they release their aroma. Add the tomato paste and stir until well-blended, cooking for just another 30 seconds to 1 minute.

Add the "tomato water" to the rice, stir well, and bring to a simmer. Add the bay leaf and salt, stir one last time, taste the liquid, and adjust with salt if needed. Insert the stuffed jalapeños, stuffed side up, evenly over the top of the rice. Cover the pan, adjust the heat to medium, and cook for 30 to 45 minutes, or until the liquid is absorbed and the rice is tender.

Serve the rice warm. Remove the toothpicks from the jalapeños before serving, and make sure each diner receives a jalapeño.

CALABAZA EN TACHA FLAN
WITH CANDIED HONEYNUT SQUASH SEEDS

This dish takes its name from the copper cauldrons, known as tachos or tachas, used in sugar mills in colonial Mexico for boiling down sugarcane juice to a thick syrup, which was then crystallized into sugar. Authentic tachas are almost exclusively produced in Santa Clara de Cobre in the Mexican state of Michoacán, where the indigenous Purépecha have been crafting them since pre-Hispanic times and are widely recognized as master coppersmiths. With the addition of spices to the syrup, sweet preparations, like calabaza en tacha, or candied pumpkin, were introduced. Nowadays, the syrup-doused pumpkin is a popular dessert or snack, especially for Día de los Muertos. Here, I've transformed this classic sweet into a base for a rich, creamy flan.

MAKES 8 TO 10 SERVINGS

Cut each squash in half and scoop out the seeds. Cut the squash into large chunks and set aside.

To make the candied seeds, thoroughly rinse the seeds with water, removing as much pulp as possible. Cover a work surface with paper towels and spread the seeds on the towels in a single layer. Air-dry the seeds for 15 to 20 minutes. While the seeds are drying, preheat the oven to 300°F (150°C). Line a small sheet pan with parchment paper.

Measure out ¼ cup (28 g) of the squash seeds and add them to a small bowl. (Save the remaining seeds for another use.) Add the melted butter, piloncillo, cinnamon, and vanilla and toss until the seeds are well coated. Using a slotted spoon, transfer the seeds to the prepared pan, spreading them in a single layer.

Roast the seeds for 20 to 25 minutes, or until lightly browned and crispy. Let cool completely before using to garnish the flan.

To prepare the squash, adjust the oven temperature to 400°F (205°C).

Place the squash pieces in a baking pan just large enough to hold them comfortably. Top with the unsalted butter, 1 cup (220 g) of the brown sugar, and 1 cup (240 ml) water and cover the pan with aluminum foil.

Bake the squash for about 45 minutes, or until fork-tender and the liquids have reduced slightly. (You can reserve the cooking liquid from the squash, reduce it to a syrup consistency in a small saucepan over low heat, and then use it as a dessert sauce or for sweetening a caffe latte.)

While the squash bakes, make the caramel. Have ready a 9-inch (22-cm) cake pan or eight to ten 6- to 8-ounce (180- to 240-ml) ramekins. In a small heavy saucepan, combine the granulated sugar and ½ cup (120 ml) water and stir until the sugar is evenly moistened. Place over medium-low heat and bring to a simmer, stirring just until the sugar dissolves. Once the sugar has dissolved, immediately stop stirring

CONTINUED...

INGREDIENTS

2 Honeynut squashes
(see page 108)

For the candied seeds:

Seeds from Honeynut squashes

¼ cup (55 g) salted butter, melted

2 tablespoons grated piloncillo
(see page 274)

2 teaspoons ground cinnamon

2 teaspoons pure vanilla extract

For the squash:

¼ cup (55 g) unsalted butter,
at room temperature

1 cup (220 g) plus 2 tablespoons
packed dark brown sugar

2 tablespoons honey

½ teaspoon kosher salt

½ teaspoon ground ginger

½ teaspoon ground cinnamon

For the caramel:

½ cup (100 g) granulated sugar

For the custard:

3 large eggs

3 large egg yolks

1 cup (240 ml) whole milk

1 cup (240 ml) heavy cream

(if you continue, the sugar will crystallize) and continue to cook until the mixture turns a dark amber. Remove from the heat and quickly pour the caramel into the single large cake pan or divide evenly among the small ramekins. Tilt the mold or molds to coat the bottom evenly. Set aside to cool and harden.

When the squash is ready, remove from the oven and let cool slightly. Using a slotted spoon, transfer the squash to a blender. Add the remaining 2 tablespoons brown sugar, the honey, salt, ginger, and cinnamon. Blend until smooth.

Adjust the oven temperature to 350°F (175°C).

To make the custard, add the eggs, egg yolks, milk, and cream to the blender with the blended squash and continue blending until a batter is formed.

Place the mold or molds into a large baking pan. Pour the flan mixture into the mold or molds. Pour hot water into the baking pan to come halfway up the sides of the mold(s). Cover the pan with aluminum foil.

Bake for 40 to 60 minutes for a cake pan or 25 to 30 minutes for ramekins. The flan is ready if it jiggles slightly when the mold is gently shaken. Remove the pan from the oven, uncover the pan, and allow the flan to cool down to room temperature. Cover and refrigerate for at least 3 hours or up to overnight.

To serve, have ready a wide, shallow bowl filled with hot water. Gently run a sharp knife around the inside edge of the large mold. Now briefly dip the base of the mold into the hot water to help loosen the caramel, then invert a round, deep serving platter over the mold, quickly and decisively invert them together, and lift off the mold. Pour any caramel remaining in the mold over the flan. Unmold the small molds the same way. Decorate the top of the mold(s) with the candied squash seeds. Cut the large mold into slices to serve.

HONEYNUT SQUASH You've probably never heard of the Honeynut squash, which is still not widely available commercially but is starting to pop up in farmers' markets across the country. They are cute—they look like tiny Butternut squashes—and they cook up sweet and are richly flavored. Their skin is thin and edible, and it takes on a caramelly flavor when the squashes are roasted. The flesh is smooth and tender and has none of the stringiness you get from larger squashes.

Honeynuts are a winter squash, so they're the perfect side dish for your Day of the Dead dinner or even for Thanksgiving. They were created by the produce dream team of chef Dan Barber and vegetable breeder Michael Mazourek, who, along with seed farmer Matthew Goldfarb, founded the seed company Row 7. "Part of the goal of the company is not only to increase the flavor of vegetables: it's to look at how we, as chefs, can change the culture of eating," explains Barber.

DARK CHOCOLATE PAN DE MUERTOS

Traditional Mexican pan dulces, or "sweet breads," take on special shapes in late October as the Day of the Dead approaches. Pan de muertos (bread of the dead) traces its roots to the conquest years, when the Spaniards first arrived in Mesoamerica and were horrified to discover that Aztecs were making a type of bread from ground amaranth seeds, honey, and human blood, which they regarded as a sacred food. In an attempt to eliminate what they perceived as a barbaric practice, the Spaniards created a heart-shaped bread coated with red sugar simulating blood. The acceptance of this stand-in for the human heart was the first time the Aztecs gave bread divine attributes and marked the beginning of their slow transition to Catholicism. Today, folk Catholicism, in which Catholic traditions and expressions commingle with aspects of vernacular religion, is practiced by an estimated 50 percent of Mexico's Catholics (about 78 percent of Mexicans identify as Catholic). The Day of the Dead is an excellent example of this embrace of two belief systems. Pan de muertos is made in countless shapes, from simple rounds and crescent moons to animals, human figures, and angels.

MAKES 4 SERVINGS

In a small saucepan, combine the ¼ cup milk and the ½ cup sugar. Place over medium-low heat, and heat, stirring to dissolve the sugar, to 105° to 115°F (41° to 46°C). Remove from the heat and pour into the bowl of a stand mixer. Sprinkle the yeast on top, stir to dissolve, and let stand for 15 minutes, or until it blooms (looks bubbly).

Add the flour, salt, butter, chocolate, and orange zest to the yeast mixture. Fit the mixer with the dough hook and mix on medium-low speed until combined. With the mixer running, add 4 of the whole eggs, one at a time, mixing until the dough is soft. Then continue to knead on medium-low speed for about 10 minutes, or until the dough is smooth and elastic. Remove the bowl from the mixer stand, cover the bowl with plastic wrap, and let the dough rise in a warm, draft-free area for 1 to 2 hours, or until it doubles in size

Preheat the oven to 350°F (175°C). Line a baking sheet with parchment paper.

Punch down the dough and divide it into four 4-ounce (115-g) pieces for the 4 breads and one 6-ounce (170-g) piece for making the "bones" and the knobs for the breads.

Shape the four 4-ounce (115-g) dough pieces into balls and set aside on the prepared baking sheet. Using the 6-ounce (170-g) piece of dough, make the "bones" and knobs. For each "bone," shape ½ ounce (14 g) of the dough between your fingers into a log and then press slightly at the center to create a bone shape. To make each knob, roll ½ ounce (14 g) of the dough into a ball. Each bread will need 2 bones for the sides and a knob for the top.

CONTINUED...

INGREDIENTS

¼ cup (60 ml) plus 1 tablespoon whole milk

½ cup (100 g) sugar, plus more as needed for decorating

2 tablespoons active dry yeast

4 cups (500 g) all-purpose flour

1 teaspoon kosher salt

¾ cup (170 g) unsalted butter, at room temperature

3 tablespoons finely chopped 70 percent dark chocolate, preferably Dandelion-brand Camino Verde

Grated zest of 2 oranges

5 large eggs

1 large egg yolk

½ cup (115 g) salted butter, melted

In a bowl, whisk together the remaining 1 whole egg and the egg yolk with the remaining 1 tablespoon milk to make an egg wash. Using a pastry brush, lightly brush each dough ball with the egg wash. Stick the "bones" to the top of each egg-washed bun. Brush the "bones" with egg wash and position the knob on top, pressing it into the dough to stay in place. Brush the knob with egg wash.

Set aside until the bread is puffed and jiggles slightly when the baking sheet is gently shaken, about 30 minutes. (Placing the baking sheet over the preheating oven will help accelerate the process).

Gently brush the tops of the buns again with egg wash. Bake until golden brown, 15 to 20 minutes.

Transfer the buns to a platter and let cool. Brush the cooled buns with melted butter then sprinkle with sugar to coat. Serve.

BEET AND MANGO AGUACHILE
WITH PEANUTS

Beets have an earthiness and an almost "meaty" texture, making them a good vegetarian alternative in aguachile, or "chile water," which is traditionally prepared with seafood.

MAKES 6 SERVINGS

To prepare the beets, preheat the oven to 375°F (190°C). In a baking pan large enough to hold the beets in a single layer, combine 2 cups (480 ml) water, the vinegar, and kosher salt and stir to mix well. Add the beets and bake for 45 minutes to 1 hour, or until fork-tender. The timing will depend on the size of the beets.

Remove from the oven, transfer the beets to a plate, and let cool.

To make the aguachile, in a blender, combine the beet juice, lime juice, orange juice, white soy sauce, cilantro, jalapeño chile, and shallot and blend until well mixed. Pour the mixture through a fine-mesh sieve set over a bowl, pressing against the solids to extract all the liquid. Season with kosher salt and set aside.

Once the beets are cool enough to handle, wearing gloves, remove the skins. Cut the cooked beets in half and divide them evenly among six shallow bowls, with two halves of each color in each bowl.

Divide the mangoes, radishes, and cucumber evenly among the bowls. Pour a generous portion of the aguachile over the top of each serving, then garnish with the avocados. It should look watery. Sprinkle the slices of serrano chile and the peanuts (if using) over the beets as a garnish. Finish with the sea salt and serve.

INGREDIENTS

For the beets:

2 cups (480 ml) water

2 tablespoons red wine vinegar

1 tablespoon kosher salt

12 small mixed golden and red beets (about 1½ pounds/680 g), trimmed and peeled

For the aguachile:

1 cup (240 ml) store-bought beet juice

½ cup (120 ml) fresh lime juice

½ cup (120 ml) fresh orange juice

⅓ cup (75 ml) white soy sauce

¼ cup (10 g) fresh cilantro

1 jalapeño chile, stem removed, roughly chopped

½-inch (12-mm) piece shallot

Kosher salt

3 mangoes, peeled, pitted, and cut into large cubes

6 breakfast radishes, cut into quarters

1 English cucumber, cut into slices ¼ inch (6 mm) thick

3 avocados, pitted, peeled, and cut into large cubes

1 serrano chile, stem removed, thinly sliced

1 cup (150 g) roasted, unsalted peanuts for garnish (optional)

Coarse sea salt, for finishing

ROASTED BEETS IN MOLE ROSADA WITH BEET CHIPS

You will need to source ruby chocolate, a product of celebrated chocolate-maker Callebaut, for my mole rosada (pink mole). Made from ruby cocoa beans harvested from trees grown in and influenced by the unique terroir in Ecuador, Brazil, and West Africa, the chocolate has a natural rose color and distinctive berry-like taste. Mole is traditionally served with beans and tortillas, and I love the idea of serving a pot of Rancho Gordo's King City pink beans (see Clay Pot Beans, page 260, for cooking method) and a stack of warm red corn tortillas—the perfect color and flavor companions to complement this unusual mole.

INGREDIENTS

For the beet chips:

2 large red beets or 1 large red and 1 large golden (10 ounces/280 g each)

1 tablespoon olive oil

⅛ teaspoon kosher salt

For the oven-roasted beets:

6 medium red beets (about 1½ pounds/680 g), trimmed

6 medium golden beets (about 1½ pounds/680 g), trimmed

12 cloves garlic

6 fresh rosemary sprigs, cut in half

¼ cup (60 ml) olive oil

¼ cup (60 ml) sherry vinegar

Kosher salt

MAKES 6 SERVINGS

To make the beet chips, trim off the root end and top from each beet but leave the peel on. Using a mandoline or sharp chef's knife, slice the beets paper-thin. Transfer the slices to a large bowl, keeping the golden beets (if using) separate from the red beets. Drizzle with the oil, and sprinkle with the salt. Let sit for 15 to 20 minutes.

Meanwhile, preheat the oven to 300°F (150°C). Line two or three sheet pans with parchment paper.

Drain the beets and discard any liquid that was released as they sat. Arrange the slices in a single layer on the prepared pans, taking care the slices do not overlap. Bake for 45 to 60 minutes, or until the slices are crisp. Do not allow them to brown. Let cool completely and set aside until needed. The chips can be made up to 2 days in advance and stored in an airtight container at room temperature.

To make the oven-roasted beets, adjust the oven temperature to 400°F (205°C). Cut twelve aluminum foil squares each large enough to wrap a single beet. Put a beet, a garlic clove, and ½ rosemary sprig on each foil square and drizzle the beet with a little of the oil. Wrap the beets in the foil and place the foil packets on a sheet pan.

Bake the beets for 50 to 60 minutes, or until fork-tender. Remove the pan from the oven, unwrap the beets, and let cool just until they can be handled. Slip the skins off the beets and put the red beets in one bowl and the golden beets in a second bowl. Season each bowl with 2 tablespoons of the vinegar and a few pinches of salt. Toss to coat well and set aside until needed.

To make the mole, place a comal (preferred) or griddle over high heat. Have ready a bowl of water. When the comal or griddle is very hot, dry roast the chipotle chiles on the first side until charred. Watch closely to make sure they do not burn. (Use a bacon press or metal spatula to make sure the entire chile is touching the hot surface.) Flip and char on the second side. The chiles will start to puff up. Transfer the chiles to the bowl of water, making sure they are submerged. Let the chiles sit in the water for about 20 minutes, or until softened. When the chiles have rehydrated, stem them and add them to a blender.

CONTINUED...

For the mole:

4 chipotle meco chiles or, for a milder sauce, chipotle morita chiles

¾ cup (105 g) raw almonds

¾ cup (105 g) pine nuts

⅔ cup (100 g) white sesame seeds

½ white Spanish onion, cut into slices ¼ inch (6 mm) thick

6 cloves garlic

¼ cup (60 ml) canola oil

1 cinnamon stick (3 inches/7.5 cm)

1 star anise

½ sweet plantain, peeled and sliced

1 cup (240 ml) coconut milk

2 to 3 tablespoons cabernet sauvignon, preferably Napa Valley

½ pound (225 g) ruby chocolate discs, preferably Callebaut

⅔ cup (95 g) red (flame) raisins or dried currants

¼ cup (40 g) beet root powder (see Note)

2 to 3 cups (480 to 720 ml) beef, chicken, or vegetable stock

1 corn tortilla, if needed

¼ cup (60 ml) olive oil

Kosher salt

Pickled red onions (page 259), for garnish

Chopped fresh chives, for garnish

While the chiles soak, one ingredient at a time, dry roast the almonds, pine nuts, sesame seeds, onion slices, and garlic cloves on the hot comal, until each ingredient is fragrant. As each ingredient is ready, transfer it to a blender.

Add 2 tablespoons of the canola oil to a skillet and preheat over medium heat. Add the cinnamon stick and star anise and bloom for about 30 seconds, or until aromatic. Transfer the bloomed spices to the blender with the dry-roasted ingredients.

Add the remaining 2 tablespoons canola oil to the skillet over medium heat, add the plantain slices, and cook, turning as needed, for 1 to 2 minutes per side, or until evenly golden brown. Do not allow them to burn or the oil will have a burned taste. Transfer the slices to the blender. Reserve the oil in the pan.

Add the coconut milk, wine, chocolate, raisins, beet powder, and 1 cup (240 ml) of the stock and blend until a smooth, velvety paste forms. You may need to blend the mole in two batches, depending on the size of your blender. Adjust the consistency by slowly adding more stock to achieve a rich, sauce-like mixture.

The mole should have the consistency of a thickish pancake mix and coat the back of a wooden spoon. Making mole is part art and part science. If your mole is too thin, use tongs to hold the tortilla directly over a lit gas burner on your stovetop until it burns around the edges and has a few burnt spots in the center, then tear it into pieces, add to the blender, and blend until smooth. (If you don't have a gas stove, use a comal or dry cast-iron pan and overcook your tortilla until it starts to burn around the edges.) If your mole is too thick, add more stock and blend again.

To cook the mole, add the reserved oil from cooking the plantain and spices along with the olive oil to a cazuela or other wide, heavy, shallow pot and heat over medium-high until the oil ripples or smokes very slightly. Keep a splatter screen nearby and add the mole to the hot oil. If needed, rinse the blender with some leftover stock to get every last bit and add it to the cazuela. Lower the heat to a simmer and cook for 15 to 20 minutes. As the mole cooks, use a large wooden spoon to stir occasionally, being sure to scrape the sides and bottom of the pot and to stir in any oil that collects around the edges as you do. The mole will darken slightly as it cooks, and it is ready when it coats the back of a spoon—the classic test for the correct mole thickness. If the mole is too thin, continue cooking until you have achieved the desired consistency. Season with salt. You should have about 4 cups (960 ml) mole. It can be made in advance and stored in an airtight container in the refrigerator for up to 1 week or in the freezer for up to 3 months.

To assemble, if the mole has cooled, reheat to piping hot. Divide the beets evenly among six plates, putting one of each color on each plate. Smother the beets in about ½ cup (120 ml) of mole. Add more as needed until the beets are well coated in the sauce and to your liking. Top each serving with a handful of beet chips, some pickled onions, and a sprinkling of chives.

Note: Beetroot powder is available in natural foods stores and online. If you cannot source it, omit it or roast an additional red beet and add as much as needed to the mole so it more closely resembles the color of the ruby chocolate.

WINE PAIRING Ceja Oxomo is a stellar blend of cabernet sauvignon and merlot. Broad and rich with a deep core of wild berry, blueberry, and spice, this wine hits the palate with pure, textured fruit and offers up a full body and a long, sexy finish.

THREE SISTERS' SUCCOTASH
WITH NOPALES

In the States, cooks in the Northeast and South claim succotash as their own, with corn and beans being the two constants. In my version of modern Mexican succotash, the three sisters—corn beans, and squash—are the stars, with nopales, tender paddles of the prickly pear (nopal) cactus, playing an important supporting role. In Mexico, the cactus is both an important food source—the fruits can be eaten raw or made into juice or preserves, and the paddles turn up in everything from salads to tacos to soups and stews—and an important symbol: the Mexican flag displays an eagle perched atop a string of nopales. According to the Mayo Clinic, the prickly pear cactus may also be good for you, with some research suggesting that it can decrease blood sugar levels in people with type 2 diabetes and may even counter the effects of a hangover.

MAKES 6 TO 8 SERVINGS

To prepare the cranberry beans, pick them over, discarding any grit or other debris. Put the beans in a bowl, cover with water, and let soak for 4 to 6 hours

In a large saucepan over medium heat, warm 2 tablespoons olive oil. Add the shallot, 1 clove garlic, and the thyme and cook, stirring, until fragrant. Drain the beans then add them to the saucepan along with enough water to cover by at least 2 inches (5 cm). Bring to a boil, stirring occasionally, then reduce the heat to low and simmer until the beans are tender, 1 to 3 hours (see method for Frijoles de Olla, page 260). Once the beans start to soften, add 1 tablespoon salt.

To prepare the nopales, in a saucepan, combine the nopales with water to cover and the remaining 1 tablespoon salt and bring to a simmer over medium heat. Reduce the heat to medium-low, being sure to maintain a simmer, cover, and cook for 15 to 20 minutes, or until tender. Drain into a colander and rinse under cold running water to remove any slimy residue. Drain well and set aside.

Finely mince the remaining 2 garlic cloves. In a large skillet, heat the remaining 3 tablespoons olive oil over medium-high heat. When the oil is hot, add the onion and garlic and cook, stirring often, for 2 to 3 minutes, or until translucent. Add the corn, zucchini, and bell peppers and cook, stirring often, for 5 to 6 minutes, or until all the vegetables are tender but still have "tooth." (If you don't have a large skillet, cook the vegetables in batches to prevent crowding.)

Add the butter and season with salt, then reduce the heat to medium-low and stir in the nopales, basil, parsley, and paprika.

Once the cranberry beans are tender, strain and combine with the vegetables. Finish the dish with the lemon juice and zest and stir once more to combine.

INGREDIENTS

1 cup (210 g) dried cranberry beans, preferably Rancho Gordo brand

5 tablespoons olive oil

1 small shallot

3 cloves garlic

1 fresh thyme sprig

2 tablespoons kosher salt

2 nopales (cactus paddles), cleaned and rinsed (see page 274), then cut into ¼-inch (6-mm) dice

1 yellow onion, diced

Kernels from 2 ears yellow corn (see page 271)

2 zucchini, cut into ¼-inch (6-mm) dice

2 red bell peppers, roasted, peeled, and seeded (see page 271), then cut into ¼-inch (6-mm) dice

2 tablespoons unsalted butter

2 tablespoons fresh basil chiffonade

2 tablespoons fresh flat-leaf parsley chiffonade

1 teaspoon smoked paprika

Grated zest and juice of 1 lemon

CALDO DE CODORNIZ
WITH SUMMER CORN, ZUCCHINI, AND KOSHIHIKARI RICE

Quail are upland game birds (so not poultry) and weigh 5 to 8 ounces (140 to 225 g) each. They have all dark meat, which is lean, has a delicate texture, and a mild "wild" flavor, and they are delicious roasted or grilled to medium-rare. Squab, also upland game birds, weigh about 1 pound (455 g) each. Their meat is dark, tender, and lean, with a flavor similar to duck, and, like quail, they are excellent roasted or grilled. In this recipe, I make a caldo (broth) that is richly flavored with quail and then use it for a summertime soup. You can make the broth with squab or even Cornish game hen, simply adjust the number of birds, using 1½ to 2 pounds (680 to 910 g) total weight.

MAKES 8 SERVINGS

To make the caldo, in a large stockpot, combine 4 quarts (3.8 L) water, the quail, onions, garlic, jalapeño chile, bay leaf, and salt and bring to a simmer over medium heat, skimming off any foam that forms on the surface. Simmer, uncovered, for 20 minutes, skimming as needed. Reduce the heat to medium-low and continue to cook, skimming off any foam or excess fat from the surface, for 40 to 50 minutes, or until a rich broth has formed.

Remove from the heat and strain through a fine-mesh sieve into a clean large pot. (If you like, pick out the quail halves and set aside to add the meat to the soup later.)

To make the soup, return the caldo to medium heat and bring to a gentle boil. Add the potatoes, corn, and carrots and cook for 10 minutes. Lower the heat and allow the caldo to simmer before adding the zucchini, oregano, and rice, stir well, and continue to simmer the soup.

While the soup cooks, scoop out 1 cup (240 ml) of the caldo, add it to a blender along with the tomatillos, and blend just until the mixture is the consistency of a chunky salsa. Pour the tomatillo mixture into the soup, season with salt and lime juice, and continue cooking for about 20 minutes, or until the rice is tender. If you like, shred the meat from the quail halves and stir it into the soup.

To serve, ladle the soup into eight bowls, dividing it evenly, and garnish with the petite zucchini and baby corn (if using), and the cilantro. If desired, shred some of the quail meat or serve the quarters of quail, bone and all, and add it into the caldo. Serve at once.

NOTE Koshihikari is a short-grain white rice cultivar that originated in Japan and is now grown in Japan and California. Tamanishiki is a hybrid short-grain variety that combines two rice strains, Koshihikari and Yumegokochi. If neither rice can be found, any high-quality short-grain Japanese rice variety can be substituted.

INGREDIENTS

For the caldo:

4 quail, cut in half lengthwise

2 yellow onions, cut into quarters

1 head garlic, cut in half lengthwise

1 jalapeño chile, stems and seeds removed and cut into quarters

1 bay leaf

2 tablespoons kosher salt

For the soup:

½ pound (225 g) Yukon Gold potatoes, 1½ inches (4 cm) in diameter (see Note, page 87)

4 ears yellow corn, each cut into 4 equal lengths

3 carrots, peeled and each cut into 6 equal lengths

2 medium zucchini, each cut into 6 equal lengths

½ teaspoon dried Mexican oregano

2 cups (410 g) Koshihikari or Tamanishiki rice (see Note)

6 tomatillos, husks removed, rinsed, and halved

Kosher salt

Fresh lime juice, for seasoning

For garnish:

1 pound (455 g) petite zucchini (optional)

1 pound (455 g) baby corn, blanched and cooled (optional)

1 cup (40 g) chopped fresh cilantro

STREET FOOD–STYLE CORN ON THE COB WITH MEXICAN AIOLI

In Mexico, corn on the cob is known as elote, from the ancient Nahuatl word *elotitutl*, or "tender cob." Today, it is the name of a popular street food: the corn is boiled or grilled, bathed in a creamy sauce, rolled in queso Cotija, and served with a wooden stick pushed well into the stem end of the cob as a handle.

MAKES 6 SERVINGS

To make the aioli, crack the eggs into a molcajete (mortar) and add the lime juice, jalapeño, and garlic. Work the ingredients together with a tejolote (pestle) until smooth. While stirring constantly with the tejolote, slowly add the butter in a thin, steady stream until the mixture is emulsified. It should be thick, creamy, and smooth. Alternatively, in a blender, combine the eggs, lime juice, jalapeño, and garlic and blend just until well combined. With the blender running, slowly add the butter in a thin, steady stream until mixture emulsifies and is thick, creamy, and smooth. Transfer to a bowl, stir in the cilantro, and season with the salt. Set aside.

Prepare a charcoal or gas grill for direct cooking over medium-high heat.

Working with 1 corn ear at a time, pull back the husk and silk, discarding the silk and leaving the husk attached at the stem end. Tie the husk together with kitchen string or a narrow strip of husk to create a "handle" for maneuvering the ear on the grill.

When the grill is ready, place the ears directly over the fire and grill, using the husk "handles" to turn the ears as needed, until evenly browned on all sides. The timing will depend on the heat of your fire, but they should be ready in 15 to 20 minutes. Allow to cool enough to handle before proceeding with the next step.

Spread the cheese on a large, flat plate. Spread the cilantro on a separate plate. Evenly spread the aioli on each warm corn ear, coating it completely. Then roll the corn in the cheese, coating lightly on all sides. Sprinkle each ear on all sides with the chile-lime salt, then roll in the cilantro to coat evenly. Serve at once.

WINE PAIRING 2022 Brown Estate Chaos Theory began as a one-off (and back then, irreverent) blend of cabernet sauvignon and zinfandel that David Brown created for the winery's first participation in the annual Premiere Napa Valley trade auction over fifteen years ago. It has become a shape-shifter, each vintage its own unique blend. This full-body vintage has a juicy, creamy mouthfeel and supple tannins with notes of maraschino cherry, effervescent citrus, rose, warm spice, and leather.

INGREDIENTS

For the aioli:

2 large eggs, at room temperature

1 tablespoon fresh lime juice

1 jalapeño chile, dry roasted (see page 271) and stem removed

1 clove garlic, grated

1 cup (115 g) clarified butter (page 269), melted and cooled

½ teaspoon kosher salt

6 ears very fresh yellow corn in husks

3 cups (300 g) grated queso Cotija or Parmesan cheese

Leaves from 1 bunch fresh cilantro, roughly chopped

2 to 3 teaspoons chile-lime salt, preferably Burlap & Barrel brand, or chili powder

FEATURED MENU:
DACA DINNER

My coauthor, Andréa Lawson Gray, and I met when she organized a fundraising dinner to support DACA (Deferred Action for Childhood Arrivals) recipients in 2018. The night stands out for me because it was the first time I knew I was really able to help my immigrant community.

At the time, I was the chef at the Commissary, chef Traci Des Jardins's restaurant in San Francisco's Presidio, and I am grateful to have been able to arrange for the event to be held at her landmark restaurant, Jardinière. Andrea and I, along with two other chefs, cooked courses for the event, the goal of which was to raise money to help DACA applicants cover the $495 application fee, which was out of reach for many of them. We raised $10,000 that night, and the event was widely covered by both local and national media, shining a light on the plight of these "Dreamers," who were facing a quickly approaching application deadline. The featured menu includes a contribution from Traci Des Jardins.

DACA DINNER MENU

Braided Honey-Glazed Pan de Miel 66

Grilled Stone Fruit Salad with Mezcal Vinaigrette 124

Beef Cheek Tacos with Árbol Salsa 212

Pistachio-Crusted Duck Breasts with Black Cherry Mole and Pistachio Tortillas 127

Thumbelina Carrots Al Pastor 130

Café de Olla Ahogado with Hazelnut-Horchata Ice Cream 132

GRILLED STONE FRUIT SALAD
WITH MEZCAL VINAIGRETTE

Grilling stone fruits brings out their flavor and caramelizes their sugars while also adding a pleasant hint of smoke. In this recipe, they are paired with crisp cucumber, fennel, and peppery arugula along with a colorful array of toppings. Always use locally grown, just-picked fruits if you can. My go-to source for this recipe is Frog Hollow Farm (see page 276), which grows a wide assortment of stone fruits.

INGREDIENTS

½ cup (50 g) thinly sliced red onion

¼ cup (60 ml) olive oil

Pinch of sugar

Kosher salt

2 ripe but firm peaches, pitted and cut into eighths

2 ripe but firm plums, pitted and cut into quarters

6 cups (120 g) arugula

1 fennel bulb, trimmed and thinly shaved lengthwise

1 large English cucumber, peeled and cut into coins ½ inch (12 mm) thick

Freshly ground black pepper

½ cup (120 ml) Mezcal Vinaigrette (page 268)

12 cherry tomatoes, cut in half

½ cup (75 g) pitted Niçoise olives

¼ cup (30 g) slivered almonds

½ cup (50 g) grated queso Cotija or Parmesan cheese

MAKES 4 SERVINGS

Preheat the oven to 425°F (220°C). In a large bowl, toss the onions with 2 tablespoons of the oil, the sugar, and a pinch of salt. Spread the onions into an even layer on a rimmed baking sheet. Roast, stirring once or twice, until soft and browned, about 20 minutes.

Prepare a charcoal or gas grill for direct cooking over medium-high heat, or heat a cast-iron griddle over medium-high heat.

Brush the stone fruit pieces lightly on both sides with the remaining 2 tablespoons oil. Place the fruit pieces on the grill rack directly over the fire or on the griddle and cook, turning once, for about 1 minute on each side, or until lightly etched with grill marks. The timing will depend on the ripeness and size of each piece. As the pieces are ready, transfer them to a sheet pan and set aside.

In a large bowl, combine the arugula, fennel, cucumber, and red onion. Sprinkle with salt and pepper and toss lightly to season the cucumber and fennel. Add the vinaigrette and toss to coat.

Divide the arugula mixture evenly among four large salad bowls. Arrange the cherry tomato halves over the top. Place the peaches and plums around the edge of each plate, with the salad in the middle, then finish with the olives, almonds, and cheese. Serve.

WINE PAIRING 2022 Scalon Sauvignon Blanc has a grassy, sensory impression and a zesty and vibrant nose with mineral notes.

PISTACHIO-CRUSTED DUCK BREASTS WITH BLACK CHERRY MOLE AND PISTACHIO TORTILLAS

In this modern Mexican riff on the traditional pairing of duck and cherries, the duck breasts are coated with a pistachio crust that is echoed in the pistachios in the cherry mole. Developing this recipe was special to me, and I had many versions to choose from. I decided to add the pistachio crust as it is a classic, and my coauthor, Andréa Lawson Gray, has been making this black cherry mole for years. It made perfect sense for us to collaborate on this recipe. As mole is time-consuming to prepare; I always make a big batch. This recipe yields more than you will need for the duck breasts, but the leftover mole keeps well, and you can reheat it as many times as you like, as it only gets better. The mole will also work well with chicken or steak. In Mexico, it is common to serve mole without an animal protein, with a generous side of beans, and, of course, fresh tortillas.

MAKES 4 SERVINGS

Place the duck breasts, skin side up, on a small sheet pan or large plate and refrigerate uncovered for 48 hours. This step dries out the skin, which helps it become crispier when cooked.

To make the mole, place a comal (preferred) or griddle over high heat. Have ready a large bowl of water. When the comal or griddle is very hot, toast the chipotle chiles on the first side until charred (do not allow to burn). (Use a bacon press or metal spatula to make sure the entire chile is touching the hot surface.) Flip and char on the second side. The chiles will start to puff up. Transfer the chiles to the bowl of water, making sure they are submerged. Repeat with the ancho chiles and the pasilla chiles. Let the chiles sit in the water for about 20 minutes, or until softened.

While the chiles soak, add the star anise to the comal and toast until fragrant, then transfer to a blender. Next, toast the sesame seeds. Watch them closely, and as soon as they start to jump, transfer them to the blender.

Continue working with the hot comal, first charring the onion slices on both sides and then the garlic. Add them to the blender.

Finally, char the tomatillos on all sides. They will turn from bright to paler green when done. Transfer them to the blender.

Select a large cast-iron skillet (this will allow space for the nuts and seeds to spread out in a single layer and toast more or less evenly) and place over medium-high heat. Pour in enough oil to coat the bottom of the pan—about ¼ cup (60 ml)—and heat the oil until it is hot. When the oil is ready, add the almonds and toast them, turning them as needed, until they begin to color, then scoop them out and add to the blender. Toast the pepitas, pecans, and pistachios the same way, adding them to the blender as they are ready. Be sure to remove all residual bits of seeds or nuts before adding the next

CONTINUED...

INGREDIENTS

4 duck breast halves, preferably Liberty Ducks brand

For the mole:

4 chipotle meco chiles

4 ancho chiles

4 pasilla chiles

1 star anise

6 tablespoons (55 g) unhulled white sesame seeds

2 slices Spanish white onion, each ¼ inch (6 mm) thick

4 cloves garlic

6 to 8 tomatillos, husks discarded and rinsed

4 to 6 tablespoons (60 to 90 ml) olive oil, for toasting the nuts and seeds, plus ¼ to ½ cup (60 to 120 ml) for cooking the mole

¼ cup (25 g) sliced almonds

¼ cup (35 g) pepitas

¼ cup (30 g) pecan pieces

2 tablespoons pistachios

4 to 5 cups (960 ml to 1.2 L) chicken or duck stock (see Note)

4 cups (620 g) pitted fresh or thawed frozen black cherries

¼ cup (45 g) coarsely ground 70 percent cacao dark chocolate, preferably Dandelion Camino Verde Chef's Chocolate (see page 273)

About ¼ cup (55 g) grated piloncillo (see page 274)

1½ teaspoons kosher salt

1 corn tortilla, if needed

For the tortillas:

½ cup (65 g) pistachios, toasted

12 ounces (340 g) store-bought fresh masa for tortillas (page 22) or Basic Masa from Masa Harina (page 24)

2 tablespoons rendered duck fat, bacon fat, or olive oil

½ teaspoon kosher salt

For the pistachio crust:

Canola oil, for deep-frying

3 dinosaur (Tuscan) kale leaves, stems and ribs removed

½ cup (65 g) pistachios, toasted and finely chopped

Grated zest of 4 lemons

Kosher salt

½ cup (120 ml) honey

Kosher salt

batch, as the burned bits will make the oil taste burned. If needed, add a little more oil between batches, as some of the oil will end up in the blender as you scoop out the nuts and seeds. Add any the residual oil, which now is full of flavor, to the blender jar.

Next, scoop the chiles out of the water (they should be soft and pliable) and remove and discard the stems. Then, remove the seeds from the chiles and reserve the seeds and the chile water (it's fine if there are seeds in the chile water). Add the chiles to the blender.

You may need to blend the mole in two batches, depending on the size of your blender. Add 4 cups (960 ml) of the stock, the cherries, chocolate, piloncillo, and salt to the blender and blend well, starting on low speed and gradually increasing the speed to high. You want a perfectly smooth mole. Taste for salt, sweetness, and spice and balance as needed with more salt, more piloncillo (the amount you will need will depend on the sweetness of the cherries), and the chile seeds and water for additional spice. Continue tasting and blending until you achieve the desired result.

The mole should have the consistency of a thickish pancake batter. Making mole is part art and part science. If your mole is too thin, use tongs to hold the tortilla directly over a lit gas burner on your stovetop until it burns around the edges and has a few burnt spots in the center, then tear it into pieces, add to the blender, and blend until smooth. (If you don't have a gas stove, use a comal or dry cast-iron pan and overcook your tortilla until it starts to burn around the edges.) If your mole is too thick, add more stock and blend again.

To cook the mole, pour ¼ inch (6 mm) of oil into a cazuela or other wide, shallow pot and heat over medium-high heat until the oil ripples or smokes very slightly. Keep a splatter screen nearby and add the mole to the hot oil. If needed, rinse the blender with some leftover stock to get every last bit and add it to the cazuela. Lower the heat to a simmer and cook for 15 to 20 minutes. As the mole cooks, use a large wooden spoon to stir it occasionally, being sure to scrape the sides and bottom of the pot and to stir in any oil that collects around edges as you do. The mole will darken slightly as it cooks, and it is ready when it coats the back of the spoon—the classic test for the correct mole thickness. If the mole is too thin, continue cooking until you have achieved the desired consistency. Remove from the heat and set aside until needed. You should have about 2 quarts (2 L). You will need only about 2 cups (480 ml) for the duck breasts. The remainder will keep in an airtight container in the refrigerator for up to 2 weeks or in the freezer for up to 3 months.

To make the tortillas, chop all but a few of the pistachios to a sand-like consistency. I like to chop the remaining nuts more coarsely so they are visible in the tortillas, which gives the tortillas an appealing look. In a bowl, combine the masa, pistachios, duck fat, and salt and knead everything together for about 10 minutes, or until you have a smooth dough. Cover the bowl with a damp kitchen towel and let the masa mixture sit at room temperature for 1 hour. Uncover and knead the masa mixture for 2 minutes longer. It should be malleable and not sticky.

Divide the masa into 1-ounce (28-g) portions, or about 2 tablespoons each, and shape into balls. They should be about the size of a golf ball. Cover the balls with a sheet of parchment paper to prevent them from drying out as you shape and cook them.

Follow the instructions for shaping and cooking tortillas on page 25, undercooking them slightly so you can finish them to order, which takes only about 30 seconds per side.

To make the pistachio crust, pour the oil to a depth of 2 inches (5 cm) into a deep skillet or sauté pan (no more than half full) and heat to 350°F (175°C). Line a plate with paper towels and set it near the stove. Dry the kale leaves well to avoid splatters. When the oil is ready, one at a time, add the kale leaves to the hot oil and fry, making sure they are submerged in the oil and moving then around gently so they emerge evenly crisp, for about 1 minute, or until they darken slightly. Transfer the leaves to the paper towels to drain and let cool completely.

Finely chop the cooled kale leaves and transfer them to a small bowl. Add the pistachios and lemon zest, season with salt, and mix well. Pour the mixture onto a flat plate or small sheet pan, shaking the plate or pan to create a thin, even layer. Set aside.

To cook the duck breasts, first score the skin in a crisscross pattern, being careful not to cut into the flesh. Season the breasts with salt. Put the breasts, skin side down, in a large heavy skillet or sauté pan and place over medium-low heat. (If you don't have a pan large enough to hold all the breasts, use two pans.) Cook, pressing down on the breasts with a bacon press or metal spatula from time to time to create good contact between the breasts and the pan, for 20 to 25 minutes, or until the fat renders, allowing the skin to become golden brown and crispy. Flip the duck breasts and cook on the meaty side for 1 to 2 minutes, or until browned, taking care not to overcook. The breasts should be medium-rare.

Transfer the breasts to a plate and let rest for 10 minutes before proceeding with the crust.

While the duck breasts are resting, finish cooking the tortillas and wrap them in a cloth for serving. Reheat about 2 cups (480 ml) of the mole until piping hot.

Once the duck breasts have rested, using a pastry brush, brush the skin side of each breast with the honey. One at a time, turn each breast skin side down onto the crust mixture, press gently to adhere, and then turn the breast right side up on a cutting board.

Cut each duck breast in half, plate the duck breasts on four individual plates, and either smother in the mole or offer the mole on the side. Serve at once with the tortillas.

Note: To make the mole vegetarian, substitute vegetable stock or corn stock (page 269) for the chicken or duck stock.

WINE PAIRING Scalon Cellars 2019 Merlot, Barking Dog Select has notes of ripe plum, cedar, and oak spice aromas, which are lifted and lingering. This wine is velvety lush on the palate, bolstered by fleshy, chewy tannins and a tick of caffè mocha.

THUMBELINA CARROTS AL PASTOR

Thumbelina carrots are mini carrots. They are often spherical, about the size of a golf ball, and their flavor is reminiscent of a mild beet with a slightly sweet finish and mild herbaceous undertones. The pineapple in the salsa highlights the carrots' natural sweetness while the mild chiles provide a nice counterpoint. Here, the carrots are served as a side dish, but they can also be spooned into tortillas and topped with the pineapple and cilantro for a vegetarian taco.

INGREDIENTS

¼ cup (60 ml) olive oil

1 pound (455 g) Thumbelina carrots, peeled

Kosher salt

1 cup (240 ml) Salsa al Pastor (page 262)

1 cup (165 g) diced pineapple, in ¼-inch (6-mm) dice, for garnish

Fresh cilantro leaves, for garnish

MAKES 4 SERVINGS

In a large skillet, heat the oil over medium-high heat. Add the carrots, season with salt, and sauté for 4 minutes, covered. Uncover and cook, stirring, for 3 to 4 minutes, or until tender, making sure they are evenly caramelized.

Add the salsa to the carrots and stir to coat the carrots evenly, then cook, stirring, just until the salsa is heated through.

Divide the carrots among four small bowls. Garnish each serving with one-fourth of the pineapple and a scattering of cilantro leaves and serve at once.

EARLY MESOAMERICAN FARMERS As with the practice of nixtamalization (see page 21), the sound nutritional science behind the foodways that flourished in Mesoamerica is nothing short of remarkable. Ingeniously, the "three sisters" at the heart of Mexican cuisine, corn, climbing beans, and squash, form the basis of a nutritionally complete diet, with the corn providing carbohydrates, the beans delivering much-needed protein, and squash contributing a wide range of minerals and vitamins.

The Mayans, who date from approximately 2000 BCE, gradually evolved from a hunter-gatherer society to an agricultural one. They abandoned their nomadic lifestyle to farm crops that had once been growing together in the wild near Oaxaca, Mexico: beans, squash, and teosinte (the ancestor to corn). Of these three, squash was domesticated first. A multitasker, squash was initially grown for its hard rind—useful for bowls and utensils—later for its nutritious seeds, and eventually for its flesh, as Mexico's Indigenous people learned to breed the naturally bitter flavor out of the vegetable and develop a crop with a more palatable flavor and texture.

CAFÉ DE OLLA AHOGADO
WITH HAZELNUT-HORCHATA ICE CREAM

This is a twist on affogato al caffè, an Italian dessert in which a scoop of vanilla gelato is affogato (drowned in) a shot of hot espresso. Here, ice cream made with a horchata (sweet rice drink) base infused with hazelnut is ahogado (drowned in) café de olla, Mexico's traditional sweetened and spiced coffee.

INGREDIENTS

For the horchata:

1 tablespoon olive oil

1 cup (135 g) hazelnuts, roughly chopped

1½ cups (285 g) jasmine rice

2 cinnamon sticks (3 inches/7.5 cm each)

2 cups (480 ml) whole milk

2 cups (480 ml) heavy cream

½ cup (110 g) grated piloncillo (see page 274)

For the ice cream:

4 large egg yolks

1 cup (220 g) grated piloncillo (see page 274)

Seeds from 1 vanilla bean

1 teaspoon kosher salt

Horchata (above)

3 cups (720 ml) Café de Olla (page 261)

MAKES 8 TO 10 SERVINGS

To make the horchata, in a saucepan, heat the oil over medium-high heat. Add the hazelnuts, rice, and cinnamon sticks and toast, stirring often, for 5 to 7 minutes, or until the ingredients are aromatic. Remove from the heat, add the milk, cream, and piloncillo, and stir until the piloncillo dissolves. Let steep at room temperature for 2 hours or cover and refrigerate for up to overnight.

Strain the steeped mixture through a fine-mesh sieve into a heavy saucepan, pressing against the solids to extract as much liquid as possible. This is the horchata for the ice cream base.

To make the ice cream, fill a large bowl with water and ice, nest a medium heatproof bowl in the ice bath, and set the ice bath near the stove. In a second heatproof bowl, whisk together the egg yolks, piloncillo, vanilla, and salt, blending well. Place the saucepan holding the horchata over low heat and heat, stirring occasionally, until the horchata is hot. Remove from the heat. While whisking constantly, slowly stream the hot horchata into the yolk mixture to form a custard. Return the custard to the saucepan, place over medium-low heat, and bring to a simmer, stirring constantly. Cook, stirring, for about 5 minutes, or until the custard thickens enough to coat the back of a spoon (about 180°F/82°C). To test if it is ready, draw your finger along the back of the spoon; it should leave a path in the custard. Remove from the heat and strain through a fine-mesh sieve into the bowl nested in the ice bath. Let cool, stirring occasionally, then remove the custard bowl, cover, and refrigerate until well chilled or up to overnight.

Transfer the chilled custard to an ice-cream maker and freeze according to the manufacturer's instructions. Transfer the ice cream to an airtight container and place it in the freezer until serving. You should have about 1 pint (480 ml). It will keep for up to 2 months.

To serve, make the café. Put a scoop of ice cream into eight to ten small glass bowls or mugs and pour an equal amount of the café over each scoop. Serve at once.

LAVENDER-HORCHATA ICE CREAM To make lavender-horchata ice cream, omit the hazelnuts. Add 2 or 3 fresh sprigs or 1 teaspoon dried culinary lavender to the milk-cream mixture. Steep for at least an hour and up to 4 hours in the refrigerator to infuse the lavender. Proceed as directed.

TORTITAS DE PAPA
WITH TOMATILLO APPLESAUCE

Who doesn't love potato pancakes with applesauce? Here is a Mexican take on that iconic pairing. The cotija cheese adds a tangy flavor, the perfect foil for the spicy applesauce.

MAKES 10 TO 12 TORTITAS; 4 SERVINGS

To make the spicy applesauce, dry roast the jalapeño or serrano on a comal (see page 271). Make the Tomatillo Applesauce, adding the roasted chile to the blender along with the tomatillos and poached apples (see page 267).

In a large pot, combine the potatoes and 1 teaspoon of the salt with water to cover generously. Place over high heat and bring to a boil, then reduce the heat to medium and cook at a rapid simmer for 20 to 30 minutes, or until fork-tender. Drain the potatoes well and let sit just until cool enough to handle. Then, one at a time, hold the potatoes with a towel with your nondominant hand and carefully peel them. As each potato is peeled, drop it into a large bowl.

When all the potatoes are in the bowl, mash them with a potato masher. Then add 1 cup (125 g) of the flour, the eggs, and the cheese and mix until evenly incorporated. Do not season with salt, as the cheese is salty.

Divide the potato mixture into 10 to 12 equal portions, each weighing about 3 ounces (85 g). Form each portion into a patty about ½ inch (12 mm) thick.

In a shallow bowl, whisk together the remaining 1 cup (125 g) of the flour and 2 teaspoons of the salt. Have ready a sheet pan. One at a time, coat the patties on both sides with the seasoned flour, tapping off the excess, and set aside on the sheet pan.

Pour the oil to a depth of ¼ inch (6 mm) into a large skillet and heat to 325° to 350°F (165° to 175°C). Line a large plate with paper towels and set it near the stove. When the oil is ready, and working in batches to avoid crowding, add the patties and fry, turning once, for about 2 minutes on each side, or until golden brown on both sides and cooked through. Transfer to the paper towels to drain and keep warm until serving.

Serve the warm tortitas with the salsa on the side.

INGREDIENTS

For the applesauce:

1 jalapeño or serrano chile, stem and seeds removed

½ cup (120 ml) Tomatillo Applesauce (page 267)

For the tortitas:

6 Yukon Gold potatoes (about 1¼ pounds/570 g), not peeled (see Note, page 87)

3 teaspoons salt

2 cups (250 g) all-purpose flour

3 large eggs, lightly beaten

1 cup (100 g) grated queso Cotija or a mixture of ½ cup (50 g) grated Parmesan and ½ cup (75 g) crumbled feta cheese

Olive oil, for frying

GUACAMOLE DE REINA

I call this the "Queen's Guacamole" because of the unusual presentation: the guacamole goes back into the avocado halves after the fruit has been removed, and then each stuffed avocado half is presented on a glittering mountain of crushed ice, fit to serve royalty!

INGREDIENTS

4 ripe avocados

1 jalapeño or serrano chile

1 bunch fresh cilantro, finely chopped

Juice of 2 limes

Kosher salt

Crushed ice, for serving

Tortilla chips, for serving

MAKES 8 SERVINGS

Halve and pit the avocados. Score an avocado half with a knife to create cubes, being careful not to pierce the skin. Ease a spoon between the skin and the flesh and gently scoop out the flesh into a bowl. Preserve the avocado skin to use for serving. Repeat with the remaining avocado halves.

Stem the chile (use the jalapeño for a milder guacamole or the serrano for a spicier one), then remove the seeds if you prefer less heat. Finely chop the chile and add to the avocado with the cilantro, lime juice, and a pinch of salt. Mash everything until somewhat smooth, then taste and adjust with salt if needed. If time permits, cover tightly and refrigerate for 1 hour before serving.

To serve, line a platter with crushed ice. Scoop the guacamole into the reserved avocado skins, nestle the filled skins in the ice, and serve. Accompany with tortilla chips.

SQUASH BLOSSOM AND MAITAKE RICE PILAF
WITH POBLANO CHILE AND KALE

This unusual pilaf is made with flavorful maitake mushrooms, best described as woodsy, or earthy and peppery, with a distinctive aroma and succulent texture. They can be difficult to source and are pricey, but they are worth the time and money. Maitakes work beautifully with the kale, which is also earthy and peppery and contrasts nicely with the mild spice of poblanos for a perfectly balanced dish. The squash blossoms add a beautiful finishing touch.

MAKES 4 TO 6 SERVINGS

Heat a large skillet with a lid over medium-high heat. When the pan is hot, melt the butter with the oil. Add the rice, reduce the heat to medium, and toast, stirring occasionally, for 5 minutes. The rice will first turn translucent and then start to turn light brown. Add the onion, kale, maitake, poblano, and garlic and cook, stirring often, for 3 minutes. Add the zucchini and paprika and cook, stirring, for 1 minute. Pour in the stock, bring to a simmer, and stir in the salt. Reduce the heat to medium-low, cover, and cook for 10 to 12 minutes, or until the liquid has been absorbed and the rice is tender. Remove from the heat and let sit, covered, for another 10 minutes.

While the rice sits, remove the stamens and pistils from the squash blossoms and rinse them (see page 57).

Uncover the skillet, taste the pilaf, and adjust the seasoning with salt if needed. Fold in the whole squash blossoms and cheese and serve at once.

INGREDIENTS

2 tablespoons unsalted butter

3 tablespoons olive oil

1 cup (190 g) jasmine rice

1 yellow onion, finely diced

2 cups (130 g) stemmed and roughly chopped dinosaur (Tuscan) kale

2 whole maitake mushrooms, roughly chopped (see Note, page 54)

1 poblano chile, charred, peeled, stemmed, and seeded (see page 271), then cut into ¼-inch (6-mm) dice

2 cloves garlic, minced

1 zucchini, cut into ¼-inch (6-mm) dice

1 teaspoon sweet smoked paprika

1½ cups (360 ml) chicken stock or water

2 teaspoons kosher salt

16 squash blossoms

1 cup (100 g) grated queso Cotija or Parmesan cheese

POBLANO VICHYSSOISE
HUITLACOCHE CRÈME FRAÎCHE AND TOASTED HAZELNUTS

In this Mexican-inspired version of a French classic, the addition of poblano chiles gives the soup a touch of heat. As with traditional vichyssoise, this creamy soup is delicious served hot or cold.

INGREDIENTS

For the vichyssoise:

3 tablespoons unsalted butter

1 yellow onion, thinly sliced

2 large leeks, white and tender green parts, thinly sliced

2 poblano chiles, charred, peeled, stemmed, and seeded (see page 271)

3 cloves garlic, thinly sliced

3 sprigs of fresh thyme

3 medium-large Yukon Gold potatoes (½ pound/225 g) peeled and cut into quarters (see Note, page 87)

3 quarts (2.8 L) chicken stock

½ cup (120 ml) heavy cream

Kosher salt

For the huitlacoche crème fraîche:

1 cup (240 ml) crème fraîche, preferably Bellwether Farms

¼ cup (40 g) canned huitlacoches, strained

Pinch of kosher salt

1 teaspoon of thinly sliced chives, optional

½ cup (55 g) hazelnuts, toasted and roughly chopped, for garnish

MAKES 6 TO 8 SERVINGS

To make the vichyssoise, in a large pot, combine the butter, onion, leeks, poblanos, garlic, and thyme sprigs over medium heat. Sweat the vegetables in the melted butter, stirring occasionally, for 20 minutes, or until the vegetables have softened. Watch closely to make sure the vegetables and butter do not turn brown.

Add the potatoes, stock, cream, and 1 cup (240 ml) water, stir well, and bring to a simmer. Reduce the heat to medium-low and cook for 45 minutes to 1 hour, or until the potatoes are fork-tender.

While the soup cooks, make the huitlacoche crème fraîche. In a bowl, blend the crème fraîche, huitlacoches, and salt until smooth. Add the chives, if desired, for a touch of freshness. The crème fraîche can be made up to 3 days in advance and stored in an airtight container in the refrigerator.

When the soup is ready, remove it from the heat and let cool for several minutes. Remove and discard the thyme sprigs. Transfer to a blender and blend on high speed until silky smooth. (You may need to do this in two batches, depending on the size of your blender.) Alternatively, purée directly in the pot with an immersion blender. Season the soup with salt to taste. If serving the soup hot, reheat over medium-low heat, stirring often, until piping hot. If serving the soup cold, let cool completely and refrigerate in a covered container until well chilled.

To serve, ladle the soup into individual bowls. Garnish each serving with a dollop of the crème fraîche and top with about 1 tablespoon of the hazelnuts.

CHILES Native to Mexico, evidence has been found of the use of chiles in the diet of Indigenous groups of Puebla's Tehuacán Valley as far back as 6500 BCE. The Europeans who arrived during the Second French Intervention of Mexico, an invasion launched at the behest of Napoleon III in the early 1860s with the intent of establishing a Mexican regime favorable to French interests, declared chiles dégueulasse, which roughly translates as "disgusting," and considered them a stimulant. The "love of chiles is a significant distinction between Mexicans and foreigners . . . thus form[ing] part of the national identity," notes Jeffrey Pilcher in his book, *¡Que vivan los tamales! Food and the Making of Mexican Identity.* This may explain a specific machismo around one's toleration for lo picoso (level of spiciness), which often manifests itself as a sort of competition at the dinner table, with diners trying to prove that they can tolerate a spicier chile than the person next to them!

Despite efforts by Europeans during the colonial era to change the way Mexicans cooked by replacing corn with wheat and eradicating chiles, the current-day popularity of corn tortillas and chile-laced salsa underscores what a miserable failure these attempts were.

GARNET YAM AND BLACK LENTIL QUESADILLAS
QUESO OAXACA AND SALSA BORRACHA

In Mexico, "That's more tangled than Oaxacan cheese" is sometimes used to described what in the States is called red tape. The saying comes from the long, twisted ropes of queso Oaxaca, a kneaded and stretched curd cheese made from cow's milk. In Mexico, the "ropes" are typically wound into balls, while in the States, the cheese is more often sold in large strips, or rajas. A good melting cheese, it is Mexico's answer to low-moisture mozzarella, which is an easily accessible substitute. Here it is tucked into quesadillas along with a mixture of sweet, earthy Garnet yams, cheese, and a paste of inky black lentils.

MAKES 4 TO 6 SERVINGS

Preheat the oven to 300°F (150°C). Place the yams on a small sheet pan. Using a fork, poke a few holes in each yam. Bake for 1½ hours, or until a small knife inserted into each yam goes through without any resistance.

While the yams bake, in a saucepan, combine the lentils, garlic, half of the onion, the cilantro sprig, salt, and 3 cups (720 ml) water. Bring to a boil over high heat, reduce the heat to low, and simmer for about 15 to 20 minutes, or until the lentils are tender but not mushy. Taste a couple of lentils to check if they are ready. Remove from the heat and drain into a sieve, capturing the liquid in a bowl. Add salt to taste.

Transfer the lentils and their vegetables to a blender, add just a small amount of the cooking liquid, and blend to a paste, adding more liquid as needed until the mixture is smooth. Taste and adjust with salt if needed. Set the lentil paste aside.

When the yams are ready, remove them from the oven, cut in half lengthwise, and let cool until they can be handled. Using a spoon, scoop the flesh of the yam halves into a bowl and discard the skins. Add the queso fresco and queso Cotija and mash together with the yams until well mixed.

To assemble the quesadillas, warm the tortillas. Spread a thin layer of the lentil purée over each tortilla. Top with a layer of the yam mixture. Lay 3 or 4 strips of queso Oaxaca on the yam layer, then fold each tortilla in half.

Place a comal or a large dry skillet (cast-iron works best) over medium-high heat. When the comal or skillet is hot, working in batches to avoid crowding, add the quesadillas and cook, turning once, for 30 to 60 seconds on each side, or until golden brown and the cheese has melted. Press down firmly on the quesadillas with a bacon press or metal spatula so they color evenly. As each batch is ready, transfer to a large plate and keep warm.

In a small bowl, mix together the remaining onion with an equal amount of the chopped cilantro. Just before serving, open each quesadilla and add a sprinkling of queso fresco and a little of the onion-cilantro mixture, then close back up. Serve at once with the salsa.

INGREDIENTS

2 Garnet yams (about 1 pound/455 g)

1 cup (200 g) black (Beluga) lentils, picked over and rinsed

2 cloves garlic

1 yellow onion, diced

¼ cup (10 g) roughly chopped fresh cilantro, plus 1 sprig

Kosher salt

8 ounces (225 g) queso fresco, crumbled, plus more for garnish

3 ounces (85 g) queso Cotija cheese, crumbled

8 to 12 corn tortillas (page 25; number depends on size)

8 ounces (225 g) queso Oaxaca, pulled into strips

¾ cup (180 ml) Salsa Borracha (page 263)

STUFFED CHILES
WITH FORBIDDEN RICE PILAF IN NOGADA

The most popular recipe for stuffed chiles in Mexico is chiles en nogada (walnut sauce), often called a "Mexican flag on a plate" because of its colors. This dish is so popular that there is even a Festival Internacional del Chile en Nogada in September as part of the Independence Day celebrations. Traditionally stuffed with a meat picadillo, I've opted for a vegetarian version with a nutrient-rich mix of forbidden rice (black rice) and vegetables.

MAKES 6 SERVINGS

To make the rice pilaf, in a saucepan, heat the oil over medium heat. Add the onion and garlic and cook, stirring occasionally, for 2 to 3 minutes, or until the onion begins to soften. Add the rice and toast, stirring often, for 4 to 5 minutes, or until a nutty aroma can be detected. Pour in the wine and cook, stirring frequently, until the liquid is reduced by half. Pour in 2 cups (480 ml) of the stock, reduce the heat to medium-low, and stir gently until almost all the liquid has been absorbed. Pour in the remaining 2 cups (480 ml) stock and stir gently until all the liquid is absorbed and the rice is tender. The total cooking time should be 35 to 40 minutes. Season the rice with the lemon zest and juice and salt, cover, and set aside off the heat.

Preheat the oven to 400°F (205°C).

Now that the rice is cooked and the oven is preheating, dry roast and peel the poblanos as directed on page 271. Make sure to leave the stems intact. Carefully remove the seeds by creating a lengthwise slit, making sure to keep the whole chile intact.

Preheat a medium skillet with a lid over medium-high heat. Add the butter and olive oil, and when the butter melts, add the onion, kale, red bell pepper, and garlic and cook, stirring occasionally, for 3 to 5 minutes, or until the vegetables begin to soften. Add the zucchini and corn, if using, season with the salt and paprika, and cook, stirring, for 1 to 2 minutes, or until all the ingredients are well incorporated. Remove the vegetables from the heat and fold them and the diced queso añejo into the rice. This is your forbidden rice pilaf.

Carefully fill the poblanos with the pilaf, stuffing them generously and taking care not to tear the chile walls. Arrange the chiles, stuffing side up, in a baking dish. Bake the chiles for 10 to 15 minutes, or until the top is slightly toasted and the stuffing is piping hot.

While the chiles are in the oven, prepare the nogada. Combine all of the ingredients in a blender and blend on medium speed until puréed. (The nogada can be made up to 3 days in advance and brought to room temperature before serving.)

Remove the chiles from the oven and top with the nogada. Garnish with a few pomegranate arils and leaves of parsley. Serve at once.

WINE PAIRING Bouchaine 2023 Vin Gris of Pinot Noir, Estate Selection has layers of guava, wild strawberry, and melon that sing on the refreshing and dry palate.

STUFFED CHILES WITH LAMB PICADILLO For a meat-based stuffing, use the picadillo from the Lamb Picadillo Tetelas (page 41) and make 1½ times the recipe.

INGREDIENTS

For the rice pilaf:

1 tablespoon olive oil
½ yellow onion, cut into small dice
2 cloves garlic, minced
1 cup (180 g) forbidden black rice
½ cup (120 ml) dry white wine
4 cups (960 ml) vegetable stock, warm
Grated zest and juice of 1 lemon
Kosher salt

For the chiles:

6 poblano chiles
2 tablespoons butter
2 tablespoons olive oil
1 yellow onion, cut into small dice
2 cups (130 g) stemmed and roughly chopped dinosaur (Tuscan) kale
1 red bell pepper, finely diced
2 cloves garlic, minced
1 zucchini, diced
1 cup (145 g) fresh corn kernels (see page 271)
2 teaspoons kosher salt
1 teaspoon sweet smoked paprika
1 cup (130 g) finely diced queso añejo

For the nogada:

1 cup (3 to 4 ounces/85 to 115 g) walnut pieces, blanched and inner skins removed
½ cup (50 g) crumbled queso fresco
¼ cup (60 ml) crema Mexicana
¼ teaspoon ground cinnamon
⅛ teaspoon freshly grated nutmeg

Fresh pomegranate arils and small parsley leaves, for garnish

CAMOTE EN LECHE
WITH CANDIED SPICED PECANS

Growing up, it was unusual for me and my siblings to have dessert, especially on a weeknight. But on Sunday, the smell of sweet potatoes cooking meant we were in for a treat, as my mother stood in front of the stove preparing camote en leche (sweet potato in milk), one of my favorites. I like to use Stokes purple sweet potatoes for this dish, as they have both purple skin and deep purple flesh, which results in an eye-catching dessert.

MAKES 8 TO 10 SERVINGS

To make the pecans, preheat the oven to 350°F (175°C). Line a baking sheet with aluminum foil, then spray the foil with cooking spray. Spread the pecans on the baking sheet and toast them in the oven until dark and fragrant, stirring a few times while baking, about 10 minutes.

In a bowl, whisk together the brown sugar, agave, butter, salt, cayenne, and cinnamon. Add the warm pecans to the mixture. Stir until the nuts are evenly coated, then return the coated nuts back to the baking sheet, spreading them into an even layer.

Bake for another 10 minutes, stirring after every 3 to 4 minutes, until browned. Set them aside on the baking sheet set on a wire rack to cool completely; the nuts will crisp up as they cool. Break the nuts apart or coarsely chop them. (The nuts can be stored in an airtight container at room temperature for up to 2 weeks in advance.)

To make the camote, using a vegetable peeler, remove the peels of both oranges, then juice the oranges. In a large, deep pot, combine 6 cups (1.4 L) water, the orange peel and juice, the piloncillo cones, cinnamon sticks, and salt, place over high heat, and bring to a boil, stirring occasionally, until the sugar dissolves. While the liquid heats, lay a small square of cheesecloth on a work surface. Place the star anise, cloves, allspice berries, and cardamom pods in the center, bring the corners together to form a pouch, and tie securely with kitchen twine. This pouch is known as a bolsita in the Mexican kitchen. Add the pouch to the pot.

Next, scrub the sweet potatoes clean, then cut them crosswise into slices ½ inch (12 mm) thick. When the liquid is at a boil, add the sweet potatoes, return the liquid to a boil, adjust the heat to a gentle simmer, and cook the sweet potatoes for 15 or 20 minutes, or until the fork-tender.

Meanwhile, preheat the oven to 250°F (120°C). Line a sheet pan with parchment paper. When the sweet potatoes are ready, remove the pot from the heat. Using a slotted spoon, transfer them to the prepared sheet pan. Cover the sheet pan with aluminum foil and place in the oven until needed.

Return the cooking liquid to medium-high heat and cook, uncovered, for 25 to 30 minutes, or until reduced to a syrup. Remove from the heat, strain through a fine-mesh sieve into a heatproof container, and set aside for about 5 minutes to cool slightly.

Divide the sweet potatoes evenly among eight to ten serving bowls. Spoon some of the cooking syrup over the top and finish with the milk, adding ¼ to ½ cup (60 to 120 ml) to each bowl. Dust with ground cinnamon and nutmeg, finish with the spiced candied pecans, and serve at once.

INGREDIENTS

For the spiced candied pecans:

Cooking spray

2 cups (200 g) pecan halves or pieces

3 tablespoons dark brown sugar

1½ tablespoons agave nectar

1 tablespoon unsalted butter, melted

1½ teaspoons kosher salt

¾ teaspoon cayenne pepper

½ teaspoon ground cinnamon

For the camote en leche:

2 oranges

6 whole piloncillo cones
(1¾ pounds/800 g total weight)
(see page 274)

4 cinnamon sticks (3 inches/7.5 cm)

Pinch of kosher salt

1 star anise

10 whole cloves

5 allspice berries

3 cardamom pods, crushed

3 pounds (1.4 kg) Stokes purple sweet potatoes, or any purple sweet potato available

4 cups (960 ml) whole milk or heavy cream

Ground cinnamon, for dusting

Freshly grated nutmeg, for dusting

"CONCHARONS"
WITH LAVENDER CREAM

A classic French confection, macarons are the perfect balance of almond flour, whipped egg whites, and sugar, paired with a decadent filling. For this recipe, I took a classic Mexican pastry, conchas, and used them to make French macarons with a twist. I dry and grind some of the sweet bread rolls and use fresh crumbs as part of the filling for an overall delicious taste and texture. Look for freshly made conchas at your favorite Mexican bakery; day-old ones work well here.

INGREDIENTS

For the concharon cookies:

½ cup (90 g) dried vanilla concha crumbs (see Note, page 146)

1 cup plus 2 teaspoons (120 g) almond flour

⅛ teaspoon kosher salt

1¼ cups (125 g) confectioners' sugar

5 fluid ounces (150 ml) pasteurized liquid egg whites

Lilac or purple food coloring (optional)

¾ cup plus 2½ tablespoons (180 g) granulated sugar

For the lavender buttercream:

¾ cup (170 g) unsalted butter, at room temperature

1 cup (180 g) dried vanilla concha crumbs (see Note, page 146)

2 cups (200 g) confectioners' sugar

1 tablespoon Lavender Syrup (page 261)

1 tablespoon whole milk or heavy cream

Pinch of kosher salt

MAKES 24 CONCHARONS

To make the cookies, in a large bowl, combine the concha crumbs, almond flour, salt, confectioners' sugar, and 2¼ fluid ounces (70 ml) of the pasteurized liquid egg whites. Stir until a paste forms. Color the paste with a few drops of food coloring, if desired. This is the cookie base. Set aside until needed.

Preheat the oven to 325°F (165°C). Line three baking sheets with parchment paper. Fit a piping bag with a ½-inch (12-mm) plain tip.

While the oven preheats, put the remaining 2¾ fluid ounces (80 ml) egg whites in a stand mixer fitted with the whisk attachment. In a small saucepan, combine the granulated sugar and ⅓ cup (75 ml) water and stir until the sugar is evenly moistened. Place over medium heat and bring to a simmer, stirring just until the sugar is dissolved. Once the sugar is dissolved, immediately stop stirring (if you continue, the sugar will crystallize) and continue to cook until the syrup registers 240°F (115°C) on a candy thermometer. Turn off the heat and leave the syrup in the pan until needed.

Right away, begin beating the egg whites on high speed until they begin to froth, 30 to 60 seconds. Reduce the speed to low and pour the hot sugar syrup down the side of the bowl in a slow, steady stream. Once the syrup has been added, increase the speed to medium-high and beat the egg whites for 2 to 3 minutes, or until the metal bowl is cool to the touch and the whites are firm. This is your meringue.

Pile one-third of the meringue on top of the reserved cookie base and then fold in with a rubber spatula just until no white streaks remain. Repeat with the remaining meringue in two batches, folding after each addition just until well blended.

Spoon the concharon batter into the prepared piping bag and pipe disks ¾ inch (2 cm) in diameter onto the prepared sheet pans, spacing them about 1 inch (2.5 cm) apart and making sure no little tip forms on the top. The disks should be as flat as possible (see photo). Tap the sheet pans firmly against the countertop two or three times to release any air bubbles.

Bake the cookies, rotating the pans back to front halfway through baking, for 12 to 15 minutes, or until the tops are dry and the batter has puffed up slightly. Let cool completely on the pans on wire racks.

CONTINUED...

To make the lavender buttercream, in the bowl of an electric mixer fitted with the paddle attachment, beat the butter until smooth and creamy, 2 to 3 minutes. With the mixer on low speed, add 1 cup (180 g) dried concha crumbs, the confectioners' sugar, lavender syrup, milk, and salt. Continue beating until light and fluffy. Transfer to a piping bag fitted with a ⅛-inch (3-mm) plain round tip.

To assemble, once the cookies are cool, carefully remove them from the pans. Turn half of the cookies bottom side up. Pipe each with a thin layer (about ¼ inch/6 mm) of the lavender buttercream, slightly smaller than the diameter of the cookie. Top with the remaining cookies, bottom side down, gently pressing the cookies together, making sure not to crack the top, until the filling starts showing on the edges. The concharons will keep refrigerated in an airtight container for up to 1 week.

NOTE: To make concha crumbs, cut 3 large plain vanilla conchas (each about 3 ounces/90 g) into ⅛-inch (3-mm) thick slices. Arrange in a single layer on a baking sheet and let sit uncovered overnight until dried out and stale. The next day, in a food processor, pulse the stale conchas to the consistency of almond flour. You should have about 1¼ cups crumbs (about 7⅔ oz/215 g). If the concha crumbs are still soft, dry them in a preheated 200°F (90°C) until they are dry like bread crumbs, making sure they do not darken too much. Let cool before using.

HORCHATA CONCHARONS Omit the lilac food coloring in the cookies. Omit the lavender syrup in the buttercream. To make horchata buttercream, after beating in the confectioners' sugar, add ½ cup (90 g) dried vanilla concha crumbs, the milk, ½ teaspoon ground cinnamon, and ½ teaspoon vanilla extract and beat to combine.

MEXICAN CHOCOLATE CONCHARONS Omit the lilac food coloring in the cookies. Omit the lavender syrup in the buttercream. To make Mexican chocolate buttercream, after beating in the confectioners' sugar, add ½ cup (90 g) dried vanilla concha crumbs, the milk, 1 tablespoon cocoa powder, 1 teaspoon ground cinnamon, and ½ teaspoon cayenne pepper and beat to combine.

PLUM-PILONCILLO MARMALADE AND BRIE EMPANADAS

These dessert empanadas are delicious on their own, but they are even better with a scoop of the hazelnut-horchata ice cream that I use in my Café de Olla Ahogado (page 132). You can swap out the plums for peaches, nectarines, or even apricots.

MAKES 24 EMPANADAS

To make the marmalade, roughly chop the plums or pulse them a few times in a food processor. Set aside. In a large saucepan, combine the granulated sugar, piloncillo, and ½ cup (120 ml) water and stir until the sugars are evenly moistened. Place over medium heat and bring to a simmer; do not stir. Continue to cook until the sugars have formed a thin, dark caramel syrup. Add the vinegar, orange zest and juice, and a squeeze of lime and deglaze the pan, stirring to scrape up any browned bits from the pan bottom. Add the plums and salt and cook, stirring often, for about 20 minutes, or until the mixture is the consistency of marmalade. Remove from the heat and let cool completely. Transfer to an airtight container and refrigerate until cold, about 1 hour. (The marmalade can be made up to 2 weeks in advance.)

Prepare the empanada dough as directed on page 71, using ⅓ cup (65 g) sugar instead of 2 tablespoons.

Portion out the dough into 3-ounce (85-g) balls, then roll out the balls as directed on page 71.

Place about 2 tablespoons of the cold plum marmalade and a piece of the cheese in the center of each round of dough. Brush the edge of one half of the round with egg wash to help bind the two edges. Now, fold the round in half to create a half-moon, making sure the filling stays in the center. Using fork tines, press down along the edges to seal securely closed.

Pan-fry, deep-fry, or bake the empanadas as directed on page 71. Serve warm.

INGREDIENTS

For the marmalade:

12 plums, pitted and cut into quarters

1 cup (200 g) granulated sugar

3 tablespoons grated piloncillo (see page 274)

½ cup (120 ml) red wine vinegar

Grated zest and juice of 1 orange

½ lime

Pinch of kosher salt

Empanada Dough (page 71), made with ⅓ cup (65 g) granulated sugar

2 wheels (10 ounces/280 g total) Brie cheese, preferably Laura Chenel brand, cut into 24 equal portions

1 large egg, lightly beaten, for egg wash

Canola or vegetable oil, if deep-frying or pan-frying

LAVENDER CUSTARD PIE
WITH MASA SUCRÉE CRUST

In the late 1990s, Charley Opper and Linda Barrett began cultivating lavender on a two-acre plot in Northern California's Capay Valley. Today, at their Cache Creek Lavender Farm, their harvest goes into everything from skin cream to bath salts to tea bags. I regularly use their high-quality, organic dried culinary lavender to make this rich, silky custard pie, as it adds just the right floral notes. This unusual custard pie has two distinctive components: a masa crust (a Mexican version of the traditional French pâte sucrée) and a lavender flan filling. The combination makes for a dessert that will surprise and delight—it's as pretty as it is flavorful.

MAKES ONE 9-INCH (23-CM) PIE; 8 TO 10 SERVINGS

A day before you want to make the pie, in a medium bowl, combine the milk, lavender, sweetened condensed milk, heavy cream, vanilla bean pod and seeds, egg yolks, whole eggs, and the granulated sugar and whisk until all ingredients are well combined. Cover the bowl and refrigerate overnight.

Preheat the oven to 325°F (165°C).

To make the dough, the bowl of a stand mixer fitted with paddle attachment, combine the flour, masa harina, brown sugar, and salt and mix for about 30 seconds, or until well combined. Add the butter and mix on medium speed until the mixture has a coarse sandy texture. Add 2 tablespoons of water, adding more water as needed 1 tablespoon at a time, just until the dough comes together when pressed.

Transfer the dough to a lightly floured work surface and press into a disk. Roll out the dough into a 10- to 11-inch (25- to 28-cm) round about ¼ inch (6 mm) thick. Gently ease the dough round into a 9-inch (23 cm) pie pan, pressing the dough snugly into the bottom and sides of the pan. Trim the edges so they extend about ½ inch (12 mm) beyond the pan. Tuck the dough over itself to create a rim, then crimp with your fingers or a fork.

Place the pie in the oven, then pour the lavender custard through a fine-mesh sieve into the crust-lined pie pan. Bake until the custard is set and it jiggles slightly in the center when gently shaken and the edges are light golden brown, about 1 hour.

Transfer the pie to a wire rack to cool completely, then transfer to the refrigerator to chill completely. Serve with whipped cream and dulce de leche.

INGREDIENTS

For the lavender-scented custard:

1½ cups (360 ml) whole milk

½ teaspoon dried lavender, or 1 fresh lavender sprig

½ cup (120 ml) canned sweetened condensed milk

1 cup (240 ml) heavy cream

1 vanilla bean, slit in half lengthwise and seeds scraped

4 egg yolks

2 whole eggs

¼ cup (50 g) granulated sugar

For the masa sucrée dough:

¾ cup (95 g) all-purpose flour

¾ cup (90 g) yellow or white masa harina, preferably Masienda brand

2 tablespoons dark brown sugar

⅛ teaspoon kosher salt

½ cup (115 g) very cold unsalted butter, thinly sliced or grated

3 to 4 tablespoons (45 to 60 ml) ice cold water

Whipped cream and dulce de leche, for serving

BUÑUELOS
WITH CHERRY ICE CREAM

Buñuelos are sweet fritters served year-round in Mexico, but they are especially popular during the Christmas holidays. One of the most delightful buñuelo traditions of the season takes place on El Noche de los Rábanos (Night of the Radishes), which is held each year in Oaxaca on December 23. On that evening, the city's central plaza is lined with stalls overseen by local artists displaying their elaborate sculptures of flowers, animals, saints, nativity scenes, and more, all carved from large red and purple radishes. Nearby, vendors are selling passersby buñuelos and small, rustic clay bowls filled with sweet syrup for dipping. Once celebrants have finished their buñuelos, they toss their bowl into the air and watch it shatter on the cobblestones, a simple ritual thought to ensure good fortune and prosperity in the new year.

MAKES 8 BUÑUELOS; 4 SERVINGS

To make the ice cream, in a bowl, combine the cherries, vanilla bean seeds, sugar, lime juice, and salt and stir and toss to mix well. Let sit at room temperature for 1 hour. Transfer the cherry mixture to a blender. Add the cream and milk and blend until smooth. Chill in the refrigerator for at least 4 hours or overnight.

Transfer the cherry mixture to an ice-cream maker and freeze according to the manufacturer's instructions. Transfer the ice cream to an airtight container and place in the freezer until serving. You should have 1 pint (480 ml). It will keep for up to 2 months.

To make the buñuelos, in a stand mixer fitted with the dough hook or paddle attachment, combine the flour, baking powder, sugar, and salt and mix on low speed until blended. Turn off the mixer and add the orange juice, melted butter, egg, and vanilla. Turn on the mixer to medium speed and mix until a smooth dough forms that comes away clean from the sides of the bowl. The dough will feel slightly moist to the touch but not really sticky. This is a sign of a good buñuelo dough, so resist the temptation to add more flour. Remove the bowl from the mixer stand, cover with a kitchen towel, and let rest at room temperature for 1 hour.

Pour the oil to a depth of 2 inches (5 cm) into a deep fryer or wide pot and heat to 350°F (175°C). Line a sheet pan with paper towels and set it near the stove.

While the oil heats, divide the rested dough into 8 equal portions of about 1¼ ounces (35 g) each (the size of an unshelled walnut). On a lightly floured work surface, roll out each portion into a thin round that is translucent and 8 to 10 inches (20 to 25 cm) in diameter.

When the oil is ready, add a dough round to the hot oil, pushing down on the center to make sure it remains flat. (If you fail to push down, the entire top will bubble up and cooking will be uneven.) Fry the buñuelo, turning once, for 1 to 2 minutes total, or until both sides are golden brown and covered with bubbles. Transfer to the paper towels to drain and dust on both sides with the cinnamon sugar. Keep warm.

Serve the buñuelos in a bowl with a scoop of the ice cream. To make an ice cream sandwich, split a buñuelo and stuff the center with ice cream.

INGREDIENTS

For the ice cream:

1 pound (455 g) Bing cherries, pitted

Seeds from 1 vanilla bean

½ cup (100 g) sugar

1 tablespoon fresh lime juice

1 teaspoon kosher salt

1½ cups (360 ml) heavy cream

½ cup (120 ml) milk

For the buñuelos:

1 cup (125 g) all-purpose flour

1½ teaspoons baking powder

1½ tablespoons sugar

½ teaspoon kosher salt

¼ cup (60 ml) fresh orange juice

3 tablespoons unsalted butter, melted

1 large egg

1 teaspoon pure vanilla extract, or seeds from ½ vanilla bean

Canola oil, for deep-frying

½ cup (100 g) sugar mixed with ¼ teaspoon ground cinnamon, preferably Mexican

PALETAS

It is most likely that Rafael Malfavón, a resident of the pueblo of Tocumbo, Michoacán, made the first paletas (ice pops) in the 1930s and sold them to residents of surrounding villages, transporting the paletas in wooden crates carried by donkeys. Other accounts credit two other Tocumbans, Agustín Andrade and Ignacio Alcázar, for the development of the informal "chain" of La Michoacana paleterías still known today for their state of origin. The two men, the story goes, moved to Mexico City in the 1940s, each opening competing shops all over the city. Today, many La Michoacana owners pride themselves on a direct family link to the original founders through a tío (uncle) or other relative from Michoacán. La Michoacana stores can be found throughout Mexico and in many places in the United States where there is a sizable Mexican immigrant community. Neither a brand nor a franchise, these retail sellers are independent businesses that take pride in linking their shops to the origin of the paleta.

MEXICAN CHOCOLATE PALETAS

INGREDIENTS

2 cups (480 ml) whole milk

2 cups (480 ml) heavy cream

⅓ cup (75 g) packed light brown sugar

½ teaspoon ground cinnamon

½ teaspoon pure vanilla extract

12 ounces (340 g) 70 percent dark chocolate, preferably Valrhona brand, coarsely chopped

2 tablespoons agave nectar

Pinch of kosher salt

MAKES 10 TO 12 PALETAS

In a small heavy saucepan, combine the milk, cream, sugar, cinnamon, and vanilla and bring to a simmer over medium heat, stirring occasionally to dissolve the sugar. Meanwhile, put the chocolate, agave nectar, and salt into a heatproof bowl. When the milk mixture reaches a simmer, remove it from the heat, pour the mixture over the chocolate, and stir until the chocolate melts and the mixture is smooth.

Pour the chocolate mixture into ice pop molds and freeze for at least 4 hours or up to overnight. To serve, run the molds under a bit of tap water until the ice pops slide out of the molds easily.

LIME PALETAS

INGREDIENTS

4 cups (960 ml) fresh lime juice

2 cups (400 g) sugar

3 tablespoons glucose syrup or agave syrup

Pinch of kosher salt

MAKES 12 TO 16 PALETAS

In a blender, combine the lime juice, sugar, glucose syrup, and salt and blend until the sugar dissolves.

Pour the lime juice mixture into ice pop molds and freeze for at least 4 hours or up to overnight. To serve, run the molds under a bit of tap water until the ice pops slide out of the molds easily.

COCONUT PALETAS

INGREDIENTS

1½ cups (360 ml) heavy cream

1 cup (240 ml) canned coconut milk

1 cup (240 ml) canned coconut cream

¼ cup (55 g) packed light brown sugar

½ teaspoon pure vanilla extract

1 cup (85 g) unsweetened shredded dried coconut

MAKES 8 TO 10 PALETAS

In a small heavy saucepan, combine the heavy cream, coconut milk, coconut cream, brown sugar, and vanilla over medium heat and heat, stirring, just until the sugar melts. Remove from the heat, let cool to room temperature, and fold in the shredded coconut.

Pour the coconut mixture into ice pop molds and freeze for at least 4 hours or up to overnight. To serve, run the molds under a bit of tap water until the ice pops slide out of the molds easily.

STRAWBERRY PALETAS WITH BASIL

INGREDIENTS

2½ pounds (1.2 kg) strawberries, hulled and cut into quarters, plus 10 strawberries, hulled and sliced into coins

1 cup (200 g) sugar

1 cup (240 ml) fresh orange juice

2 tablespoons fresh lime juice

2 tablespoons chopped fresh basil

MAKES 12 TO 16 PALETAS

In a blender, combine half each of the quartered berries, sugar, orange juice, lime juice, and 1 cup (240 ml) water and blend until the sugar dissolves and a smooth purée forms. Pour into a bowl. Repeat with the remaining quartered berries, sugar, orange juice, lime juice, and 1 cup (240 ml) water and add to the bowl. Let sit at room temperature for 30 minutes.

Stir the basil and the strawberry coins into the purée, then pour the purée into ice pop molds and freeze for at least 4 hours or up to overnight. To serve, run the molds under a bit of tap water until the ice pops slide out of the molds easily.

ORANGE PALETAS

INGREDIENTS

2 quarts (2 L) fresh orange juice

1 cup (240 ml) fresh lime juice

About 2 cups (400 g) sugar, depending on sweetness of oranges

3 tablespoons glucose syrup or agave syrup

Pinch of kosher salt

MAKES 12 TO 16 PALETAS

In a blender, combine half each of the orange juice, lime juice, sugar, and glucose syrup and blend until the sugar dissolves. Pour into a bowl. Repeat with the remaining orange juice, sugar, and glucose syrup and add to the bowl. Add the salt to the bowl and stir to mix.

Pour the orange juice mixture into ice pop molds and freeze for at least 4 hours or up to overnight. To serve, run the molds under a bit of tap water until the ice pops slide out of the molds easily.

ATOLE DE AVENA
WITH PONCHE FRUIT SYRUP

Ponche (punch) just isn't ponche without tejocotes. Tejocotes, the fruits of the Mexican hawthorn, resemble crab apples. Native to the mountainous regions of Mexico and Guatemala, the fruits have a sweet-sour flavor and are orange to golden yellow. If you live in an area with a large Mexican population, you may be able to locate fresh tejocotes during the Christmas holiday season. Otherwise, look for the fruits jarred or canned in Latin American markets. Here, the popular holiday punch is reduced so it's flavorful and syrupy and served over extra-thick atole de avena, a sweet, hot oatmeal drink.

MAKES 10 SERVINGS

To make the atole de avena, in a clay pot (preferably) or in a heavy saucepan, whisk together the oats, masa harina, milk, cream, piloncillo, cinnamon stick, vanilla, and salt, mixing well. Place over medium-low heat and bring to a gentle simmer while whisking constantly. Cook, whisking frequently to prevent scorching until the mixture is creamy and thick; note that you are looking for an atole that is thicker than the usual "drinking" version. The cooking time will depend upon the type of oats you use, follow the package directions. Remove from the heat and cover tightly to keep warm until serving.

To make the ponche reduction, if using fresh or frozen tejocotes (see below if using canned), combine the tejocotes with 2 quarts (2 L) water, the piloncillo cone, and cinnamon sticks in the clay pot or saucepan. Bring to a boil over medium-high heat. Reduce the heat to medium-low and cook until the fruit softens, 10 to 15 minutes; you will need to add time if you are working with frozen tejocotes. Strain the mixture through a fine-mesh sieve set over a bowl, reserving the cooking liquid, then transfer the cooking liquid back to the clay pot or saucepan. Transfer the tejocotes to a plate and let cool until they can be handled. Remove and discard the skin and seeds and set the fruits aside.

If using canned tejocotes, cut the fruits in half and set aside. Combine 2 quarts (2 L) water, the cinnamon sticks, and piloncillo in the clay pot or saucepan and bring to a boil over medium-high heat, stirring occasionally to dissolve the piloncillo.

Place the clay pot or saucepan filled with the piloncillo cooking liquid over medium heat. Add the tamarind, hibiscus, star anise, and cloves. Bring the ingredients to a boil and cook for 15 minutes.

Remove from the heat and strain through a fine-mesh sieve into a bowl. Discard the solids in the sieve. Return the strained liquid to the clay pot or saucepan and add the reserved tejocotes, guavas, apples, pears, prunes, and raisins. Place over medium heat, bring to a simmer, and cook, stirring often, for 30 to 35 minutes, or until all the fruits are soft and the liquid has reduced and is syrupy.

To serve, divide the atole de avena evenly among ten bowls and spoon the ponche fruit syrup over the top. Dust each serving with ground cinnamon and serve at once.

INGREDIENTS

For the atole de avena:

3 cups (270 g) rolled oats, instant or old fashioned (do not use steel-cut oats)

¾ cup (90 g) yellow masa harina, preferably Masienda brand

6 cups (1.4 L) whole milk

2 cups (480 ml) heavy cream

4 ounces (115 g) grated piloncillo (see page 274)

1 cinnamon stick (3 inches/7.5 cm)

1 teaspoon pure vanilla extract, or seeds scraped from 1 vanilla bean

Pinch of kosher salt

For the ponche:

8 tejocotes, fresh, frozen, or canned

1 large or 2 medium piloncillo cones (about 12 ounces/340 g) (see page 274), or 1½ cups (330 g) packed light brown sugar

3 cinnamon sticks

20 tamarind pods (3½ ounces/100 g), cracked open

1 cup (40 g) dried hibiscus flowers

1 star anise

2 whole cloves

4 to 6 guavas, cut into bite-size pieces

3 small yellow apples, cored and cut into bite-size pieces

2 small pears, cored and cut into bite-size pieces

1½ cups (195 g) pitted prunes

¾ cup (110 g) raisins

Ground cinnamon, for dusting

CHOCOFLAN
WITH STRAWBERRY-HIBISCUS SAUCE

Chocoflan is sometimes called "the impossible cake" because it goes into the oven with the chocolate cake batter on the bottom and the flan mixture on top, and it comes out of the oven with cooked flan on the bottom and baked chocolate cake on the top.

MAKES 10 TO 12 SERVINGS

To make the cake, sift together the flour, cocoa powder, baking powder, and baking soda into a bowl. In a large bowl, using an electric mixer on medium speed, beat together the butter and sugar until fluffy, stopping to scrape down the sides of the bowl. Add the egg and beat until incorporated. Add half each of the flour mixture and the buttermilk and, using a rubber spatula, gently fold into the eggs until well mixed. Add the remaining flour mixture and buttermilk and gently fold in until you have a fluffy chocolate cake base. Set aside.

To make the flan, in a blender, combine the whole milk, cream, condensed milk,,sugar, egg yolks, whole eggs, and vanilla and blend until smooth. Set aside.

To make the caramel, in a small saucepan, combine the sugar and ½ cup (120 ml) water and stir until the sugar is evenly moistened. Place over medium-low heat and bring to a simmer, stirring just until the sugar is dissolved. Once the sugar is dissolved, immediately stop stirring (if you continue, the sugar will crystallize) and continue to cook until the mixture turns a dark amber.

While the caramel cooks, preheat the oven to 325°F (165°C). Lightly spray a 10-inch (25-cm) Bundt cake pan with nonstick cooking spray. When the caramel is ready, immediately remove from the heat, carefully pour the hot caramel into the prepared pan, and swirl the pan to coat the bottom evenly. Set aside to cool and harden.

Once the caramel sets, add the cake batter to the pan. Slowly pour the flan mixture over the cake batter. The cake batter should float to the top. Place the Bundt pan in a large baking pan and pour hot water into the baking pan to come halfway up the sides of the Bundt pan. Cover the baking pan with aluminum foil. Bake for 1 hour 25 minutes to 1 hour 45 minutes, or until a knife inserted in the center comes out clean.

While the chocoflan bakes, make the strawberry-hibiscus sauce.

When the chocoflan is ready, let cool completely in the pan on a wire rack, then cover and refrigerate for 6 to 8 hours.

To serve, have ready a wide, shallow bowl filled with hot water. Gently run a sharp knife around the inside edge of the Bundt pan. Now briefly dip the base of the pan into the hot water to help loosen the caramel, then invert a round, deep serving platter over the mold; quickly and decisively invert them together and lift off the mold. Drizzle the chocoflan with the strawberry-hibiscus sauce and fill the center with the strawberries.

WINE PAIRING Brown Estate Duppy Conqueror NV Port is a balanced, ultradense, and plush port with a silky mouthfeel and long, luxurious finish. It has a dark berry nose and notes of brown sugar, eucalyptus, dried fig, and fruit leather.

INGREDIENTS

For the cake:

1¾ cups (220 g) all-purpose flour

⅓ cup (25 g) unsweetened cocoa powder

1 teaspoon baking powder

1 teaspoon baking soda

½ cup plus 2 tablespoons (145 g) unsalted butter, at room temperature

1 cup (200 g) sugar

1 large egg, at room temperature

1¼ cups (300 ml) buttermilk

For the flan:

1½ cups (360 ml) whole milk

1 cup (240 ml) heavy cream

½ cup (120 ml) sweetened condensed milk

¼ cup (50 g) sugar

4 large egg yolks

2 large eggs

Seeds from 1 vanilla bean, or 1 tablespoon pure vanilla extract

For the caramel:

1 cup (100 g) sugar

Strawberry-Hibiscus Sauce (page 261)

½ cup (75 g) strawberries, hulled and cut in half, for garnish

MEXICAN CHOCOLATE SANDWICH COOKIES
WITH HIBISCUS FILLING

Did you know that Oreos are the best-selling cookie in the world? More than 450 billion Oreo cookies have been sold around the globe since their introduction in 1912. I've put my own twist on this classic treat, reinterpreting the cookie with Mexican chocolate and the filling with hibiscus. Dunk these cookies in hazelnut-flavored horchata (page 132) or twist and open just as you might an Oreo.

INGREDIENTS

For the cookies:

1 pound (455 g) unsalted butter, at room temperature

2½ cups (315 g) confectioners' sugar

½ cup (50 g) unsweetened cocoa powder

½ cup (110 g) grated piloncillo (see page 274)

1 teaspoon kosher salt

1 teaspoon ground cinnamon

2 teaspoons pure vanilla extract

2 to 2½ cups (250 to 315 g) all-purpose flour

For the filling:

¾ cup (170 g) unsalted butter, at room temperature

2 cups (250 g) confectioners' sugar

Pinch of kosher salt

3 tablespoons Hibiscus Simple Syrup (page 261)

1 tablespoon whole milk or heavy cream

1 teaspoon pure vanilla extract

MAKES TWENTY 2-INCH (5-CM) COOKIES

To make the cookies, in a large bowl, using an electric mixer on low speed, beat together the butter and confectioners' sugar just until mixed, then increase the speed to medium and continue to beat until pale yellow and fluffy, stopping to scrape down the sides and along the bottom of the bowl to ensure an even mixture. Add the cocoa powder, piloncillo, salt, cinnamon, and vanilla and beat until well incorporated.

On low speed, add 2 cups (250 g) of the flour and beat until the mixture comes together in a dough similar to pie dough. You may need to add up to ½ cup (65 g) more flour to achieve a dough that holds together yet is relatively dry (you don't want the cookies to spread during baking). Transfer the dough to a clean work surface and shape into a thick disk. Wrap in plastic wrap and refrigerate for 20 to 30 minutes.

While the dough rests, make the filling. In a bowl, using an electric mixer on low speed, beat together the butter, confectioners' sugar, and salt just until mixed, then increase the speed to medium and continue to beat until pale yellow and fluffy, stopping once or twice to scrape down the sides and along the bottom of the bowl to ensure an even mixture. Add the hibiscus syrup, milk, and vanilla and beat until well blended. Cover and set aside to cool completely.

Preheat the oven to 375°F (190°C).

Have ready a large sheet pan. Unwrap the dough disk and place between two large sheets of parchment paper on a work surface. Roll out the dough ⅛ inch (3 mm) thick. (If you are a more experienced baker, you may want to use an embossed rolling pin.) Peel off the top sheet of parchment. Using a 2-inch (5-cm) round cookie cutter, cut out as many cookies as possible. Transfer the cookies to the sheet pan. Gather up the scraps, press into a disk, reroll, cut out more cookies, and add them to the pan.

Bake the cookies for 8 to 10 minutes, or until firm to the touch and fragrant. Transfer the cookies to a wire rack and let cool completely.

To assemble, spoon the filling into a piping bag fitted with a ½-inch (12-mm) plain tip. Turn half of the cookies bottom side up. Pipe about 1 tablespoon (or a little less) of the filling onto the center of each cookie bottom. Top with the remaining cookies, bottom side down. Store in an airtight container at room temperature for up to 1 week, in the refrigerator for up to 1 month, or in the freezer for up to 3 months.

BLOOD ORANGE MARGARITAS
WITH CHILE-SALT RIM

There are many stories about the origin of Mexico's most ubiquitous cocktail. One surrounds Acapulco socialite and tequila aficionado Margarita Sames, whose extravagant parties created quite a buzz in the late 1940s. Experimenting with her favorite spirit in hopes of creating a drink that would impress her guests, Margarita mixed tequila, lime juice, and Cointreau, successfully creating a cocktail that her party-going friends absolutely loved. From there, the word spread, and the margarita was born! Blood oranges add a beautiful color to this Mexican favorite. If you cannot find blood oranges, you can get a similar effect by using regular oranges and adding just a little beetroot powder.

INGREDIENTS

1 tablespoon kosher salt

1 tablespoon chile-lime salt, preferably Tajín Clásico Seasoning

1 lime wedge

2 fluid ounces (60 ml) silver tequila

1 fluid ounce (30 ml) Aperol

2 fluid ounces (60 ml) blood orange juice

1 fluid ounce (30 ml) fresh lime juice

1 fluid ounce (30 ml) simple syrup (see Note)

2 thin slices jalapeño chile

1 thin slice blood orange

MAKES 1 COCKTAIL

On a shallow saucer, mix together the salt and Tajín. Rub the rim of a cocktail glass with the lime wedge, then dip the rim in the salt-Tajín mixture to coat. (If you like, you can fill the glass half full of ice.) Set the glass aside.

Fill a cocktail shaker half full with ice. Add the tequila, Aperol, blood orange juice, lime juice, simple syrup, and jalapeño slices, cover, and shake vigorously until well chilled. Strain into the prepared glass, garnish with the orange slice, and serve.

NOTE To make simple syrup, combine equal parts sugar and water in a saucepan and heat over medium heat, stirring, until the sugar fully dissolves. Let cool, transfer to a tightly capped jar, and store in the refrigerator for up to 1 month.

HUCKLEBERRY MIMOSAS

Huckleberries are slightly tart and taste a bit like blueberries but with a hint of wildness. Bouchaine 2019 Brut Rosé, with its wild strawberry, raspberry, and brioche flavors and fine long-lasting bubbles, makes for a spectacular mimosa. Make a double recipe of the huckleberry syrup and save it for your next pancake breakfast. If you cannot find fresh huckleberries, frozen berries can be substituted.

INGREDIENTS

For the huckleberry syrup:

1 cup (145 g) huckleberries

1 cup (200 g) sugar

1 cup (240 ml) water

1 bottle (750 ml) Champagne, preferably Bouchaine 2019 Brut Rosé, or cava, prosecco, or other sparkling wine, chilled

3 cups (720 ml) fresh orange juice, chilled

MAKES 8 SERVINGS

To make the huckleberry syrup, in a saucepan, combine the huckleberries, sugar, and water over low heat and bring to a gentle simmer (do not allow it to boil), stirring to dissolve the sugar. Cook for 5 to 10 minutes, or until the mixture becomes a viscous syrup. Remove from the heat and let cool for 30 minutes, then strain through a fine-mesh sieve, pushing against the solids with the back of a spoon. Let cool completely, then refrigerate in an airtight container until chilled. The syrup will keep for up to 3 months in the refrigerator.

Line up 8 champagne flutes. Pour the Champagne into the flutes, dividing it evenly. Then pour in the orange juice, filling each flute to within ½ inch (12 mm) of the rim. Top off each glass with the huckleberry syrup. Serve at once.

FRESH APRICOT CHAMOY

In Mexico, the word *chamoy* is linked to everything from salted dried fruit (known as saladitos), candy, and sauce to seasoning powder and delivers a taste that is sour, sweet, and spicy all at once. At food stalls, you'll find chamoy-flavored paletas (ice pops) and raspados (shaved ice) as well as fruits and vegetables sprinkled or sauced with it. Food historian Rachel Laudan researched the origin of chamoy and found that it was adapted from see mui, salted dried apricots that were a favorite snack of the Cantonese immigrants who first settled in Mexico in large numbers in the 1880s. In the 1970s, the entry of a large commercial manufacturer propelled chamoy into national popularity. I like to use apricots from Frog Hollow Farm (see page 276) for my version, into which I incorporate Hibiscus Simple Syrup (see page 261) for an added "tang." Chamoy is extremely versatile and can be used in everything from a glaze for chicken or ribs to an accompaniment to salty cheeses on a cheese board. For a quick barbecue sauce, mix with ketchup to taste.

MAKES ABOUT THREE ½-PINT (240-ML) JARS

Preheat the broiler. Line a large sheet pan with aluminum foil.

Arrange the apricots, cut side up, on the prepared pan. Broil the apricots for 3 to 4 minutes, or until they are slightly charred on the surface. Remove from the oven and transfer to a food processor.

Add the piloncillo, hibiscus syrup, chipotle chiles and adobo sauce, lime zest and juice, tamarind paste, and salt to the processor and pulse until smooth.

Add the chamoy base to a heavy saucepan and cook over medium-high heat, stirring often, for 4 to 5 minutes, or until it comes to a simmer. Reduce the heat to medium and continue cooking, stirring occasionally, for 40 to 50 minutes (the timing depends on the juiciness of the apricots), or until the mixture reduces by half and resembles a syrup. Be careful when stirring as bubbles can burst and splatter. If you have a splatter screen, use it.

Remove from the heat and taste and adjust with salt and lime juice if needed. If the chamoy is still a bit chunky, let cool slightly, then blend in a blender until smooth.

Transfer the chamoy to clean, sterilized Mason jars, let cool, cap tightly, and store in the refrigerator for up to 3 months.

NOTE Follow best practices from a reputable source to sterilize Mason jars. For longer, shelf-stable storage, can the jars of chamoy using the water-bath method, following best practices from a reputable source.

INGREDIENTS

10 to 12 apricots (about 1 pound/ 455 g), halved and pitted

¼ cup (55 g) piloncillo (see page 274) or packed light brown sugar

¼ cup (60 ml) Hibiscus Simple Syrup (page 261)

2 to 4 chipotles in adobo sauce, plus 1 tablespoon adobo sauce

Grated zest and juice of 2 limes

1 tablespoon tamarind paste

1 teaspoon kosher salt

MAR

MAR

THE BOUNTY OF THE SEA

My absolute favorite ingredients are fresh finfish and shellfish. In the San Francisco Bay Area, we are blessed with amazing seafood and local fisherman who follow sustainable practices. I've shared some of my favorite recipes for everything from appetizers like ceviches and oysters to tacos, hearty stews, and soups. Some may be familiar favorites, like salmon and scallops, while other ingredients may be new to you, at least in terms of cooking them, like abalone and squid. I hope you'll be inspired to try some of those less familiar gifts from the sea; I promise your dinner guests will be delighted by the results.

According to the Monterey Bay Aquarium, "90 percent of fish populations are currently fished at, or beyond, their sustainable limits. Overfishing, habitat damage from [. . .] fishing methods, like dragging nets or dredges along the seafloor, can damage important habitats" with devastating effects, depleting sensitive species. In addition, turtles, sharks, seabirds, and marine mammals unintentionally caught by fishing gear, termed *bycatch*, are often discarded if fishermen aren't allowed to sell them.

"Farming seafood—known as aquaculture—can help reduce the pressure on wild fish stocks. In fact, more than 50 percent of the seafood we eat today is farmed. As the global human population grows, this number will continue to increase. But seafood is not always farmed in a responsible way, and these operations can damage the environment." —Monterey Bay Aquarium

So what should you buy? Hook-and-line fishing is one of the best methods of fishing with regards to sustainability, as it has little impact on the surrounding environment, plus the catch can be selective. This means any fish that is too small or not the right species can be thrown back without harm. In hook-and-line fishing, the fishing line is set in the water with baited hooks, using a rod and reel or longlines. Large-scale commercial operations use longline fishing, meaning a long length of fishing line (up to many miles long) with multiple branching lines, each with baited hooks.

PRAWN CEVICHE
WITH CHOCLO, GARNET YAMS, AND PEARS

The chewiness of choclo makes it the perfect foil for the fresh shrimp and soft, sweet Garnet yams in this dish. Choclo, aka Peruvian corn or Cuzco corn, is cultivated in the harsh climate and rugged terrain of the Andes and is integral to the cuisine and cultural identity of the region. A field corn, it has jumbo kernels that are starchier and chewier than sweet corn and that come in a variety of colors, from white, yellow, red, and purple to black. Look for choclo in Latin American markets.

MAKES 10 SERVINGS

Preheat the oven to 350°F (175°C).

To prepare the choclo, fill an 8-quart (7.5-L) pot three-fourths full with water and add the lime juice, sugar, and salt. Bring to a boil over high heat, add the choclo kernels, and boil for about 5 minutes, or until the kernels are tender. Drain and let cool completely. The choclo can be prepared up to 2 days in advance and stored in an airtight container in the refrigerator.

In a bowl, combine the yams, oil, and a big pinch of salt and toss and stir to coat evenly. Spread the yams on a small sheet pan and bake for 20 minutes, or until tender when pierced with a fork. Let cool completely.

Put the prawns into a large bowl, drizzle with the vinaigrette, and toss gently to coat evenly. Let stand for 10 minutes. The prawns will turn pink when ready (they "cook" in the acid from the vinaigrette). Do not leave in longer than ten minutes, as they will become rubbery.

Add the choclo, yams, and pears to the prawns. Season with salt.

Transfer to a serving platter, garnish with the cilantro and jalapeño, and serve at once.

Note: Make sure to use very fresh raw prawns for this recipe. They should not be previously frozen. If you cannot find prawns, fresh large or jumbo shrimp can be substituted.

AGUACHILE VS. CEVICHE Aguachile, which originated in the western Mexican coastal state of Sinaloa, can be described as Mexico's take on Peruvian ceviche. The classic version of this popular dish calls for pulverizing red onion, cucumber, and serranos or jalapeños with lime juice and/or water—this is the aguachile, or "chile water"—immersing fresh raw shrimp in the watery "bath," and then serving the dish with avocado slices and a tostada.

A key difference between aguachile and ceviche is that the seafood for ceviche is marinated for anywhere from 10 to 30 minutes before serving, while as soon as the seafood goes into the aguachile, the dish is served. This means you must seek out sushi-grade fish and raw shrimp that have not been previously frozen for aguachile.

INGREDIENTS

For the choclo:

Juice of 1 lime

1 tablespoon sugar

3 tablespoons kosher salt

1½ cups (190 g) frozen choclo (see page 273)

2 medium Garnet yams, peeled and diced into pieces the size of the choclo kernels

2 tablespoons olive oil

Kosher salt

2 pounds (910 g) fresh head-on raw prawns, peeled, deveined, and cut crosswise into slices ½ inch (12 mm) thick

1 cup (240 ml) Jalapeño-Yuzu Vinaigrette (page 268)

3 D'Anjou pears, peeled, cored, and cut into ¼-inch (6-mm) dice

Leaves from 1 bunch fresh cilantro, for garnish

Thinly sliced jalapeño, for garnish

AGUACHILE NEGRO
WITH WHITE SEA BASS, SUNGOLD TOMATOES, AND OPAL BASIL

To make this aguachile negro, you will need to visit your local fishmonger or specialty food market for squid ink, which is sold in small jars or packets. It adds both an exquisite color and distinctive briny flavor to the dish. You can use the leftover ink in pasta or risotto. If you cannot source California white sea bass, sub another semi-firm, white-fleshed ocean fish like striped bass, sole, or flounder.

INGREDIENTS

For the aguachile negro:

1 cup (240 ml) olive oil

1 cup (240 ml) lime juice

½ cup (120 ml) fresh orange juice

1 red onion, minced

1 English cucumber, peeled and cut into ¼-inch (6-mm) dice

1 serrano chile, minced, or to taste

1 tablespoon white soy sauce

1 teaspoon squid ink

¼ cup (10 g) chopped fresh cilantro

Kosher salt

1 pound (455 g) California white sea bass fillet, cut into ¼-inch (6-mm) dice

¼ cup (40 g) salted roasted peanuts

1 cup (145 g) Sungold or other cherry tomatoes, cut in half

Kosher salt

Leaves from 1 bunch fresh opal basil or sweet basil, for garnish

2 avocados, pitted, peeled, and cut into ¼-inch (6-mm), for garnish

MAKES 6 SERVINGS

To make the aguachile negro, in a large bowl, combine the oil, lime juice, orange juice, onion, cucumber, chile to taste, soy sauce, squid ink, and cilantro and stir well. Season with salt.

Add the sea bass to the aguachile and mix gently. Add the peanuts and tomatoes and mix gently again. Season with salt.

Divide the sea bass mixture evenly among six small bowls. Garnish with the basil and avocado and serve.

KONA KAMPACHI CRUDO
WITH GRAPEFRUIT AND JALAPEÑO-YUZU VINAIGRETTE

In 2008, *Fortune* magazine dubbed Kona kampachi "the wonder fish," and the description still holds. Solely produced by a Kona, Hawaii–based deepwater aquaculture company, this species of hamachi (yellowtail), or amberjack, is farmed sustainably, is not genetically engineered, is rich in omega-3 fatty acids, and, most importantly, has a wonderful taste and texture. The vinaigrette, which combines chile's heat and the sour-tart-floral juice of the yuzu, a round, yellow citrus fruit particularly popular with Japanese cooks, is an ideal partner for the buttery texture and mild flavor of the fish.

INGREDIENTS

2 Oro Blanco grapefruits

2 pounds (910 g) sushi-grade hamachi fillets, preferably Kona kampachi

Fine sea salt

2 cups (480 ml) Jalapeño-Yuzu Vinaigrette (page 268)

1 English cucumber, halved lengthwise, then thinly sliced into half-moons

1 cup (30 g) fresh micro cilantro or regular cilantro leaves

MAKES 10 SERVINGS

Using a sharp knife, cut a thin slice from the top and bottom of a grapefruit. (1) Stand the fruit on a flat end, and cut downward, following the curve of the fruit and removing the peel and white pith. (2, 3) Working over a bowl, make a cut on both sides of each segment to free it from the membrane, letting the segments drop into the bowl. (4, 5) Repeat with the second grapefruit.

Thinly slice the hamachi across the grain sashimi-style. Arrange the slices in a circle on a large plate and season with salt. Put the vinaigrette in a small bowl and place at the center of the circle.

Arrange the grapefruit segments on top of the fish, then arrange the cucumber slices on top of the citrus. Garnish with the cilantro and serve.

TEQUILA PAIRING Loco Blanco strikes the perfect balance between power and purity. Creamy and well-structured, the velvety mouthfeel lingers with a medium to long finish. With notes of agave, rosemary, and pears, the strength and character of Loco Blanco stands up to foods with fresh herbs, citrus, and even a bit of spice.

 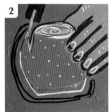 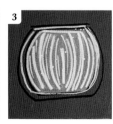 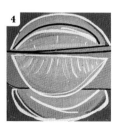 

NIÑO POBRE TACOS
WITH OYSTERS AND MEXICAN RÉMOULADE

Growing up with a single mom, our family lived in what is now called a food-insecure household. My mom's version of the storied New Orleans po'boy was a beautiful handmade tortilla smeared with tasty refritos that had been made from scratch: the beans were cooked in a clay pot and then smashed and fried with savory onions and garlic. Topped off with fresh salsa, my siblings and I all knew we were in for a delicious treat—a treat we never associated with poverty. This recipe is my take on the classic New Orleans po'boy, which is a "niño pobre" in Spanish. The original sandwich was born during the 1929 transit strike in New Orleans. The Martin brothers, Benny and Clovis, who had been streetcar conductors prior to opening their restaurant, started giving away free, inexpensive sandwiches to the striking workers, greeting them with, "Here comes another poor boy!" In time, that shout-out became the name of the sandwich itself.

MAKES 12 TACOS

Rinse the oysters in cold water, brushing away any dirt and other debris. To open each oyster, place the round side down on a folded kitchen towel. Holding the rounder end of the oyster with the towel, carefully yet firmly insert the tip of an oyster knife into the "hinge" at the tapered end. Wiggle the knife to begin loosening the shell until you hear a pop, then twist the knife to pry the shells apart. Gently slide the oyster knife along the top of the oyster, keeping it flat against the top shell, to sever the adductor muscle. Lift off the top shell. Separate the oyster from the bottom shell the same way, then transfer the oyster to a bowl. Repeat until all the oysters are shucked.

In a bowl, stir together the flour, garlic powder, onion powder, oregano, paprika, black pepper, dry mustard, and 1 teaspoon salt. Bury the oysters in the flour mixture.

In a second bowl, using a fork, stir together the egg and beer. Add the cornmeal and stir with the fork until you have a lump-free batter similar to a light pancake batter.

To deep-fry the oysters, pour the oil to a depth of 2 inches (5 cm) into a deep pot (no more than half full) and heat to 350°F (175°C). (Alternatively, heat a deep fryer.) Line a large plate or sheet pan with paper towels and set it near the stove.

When the oil is ready, working in batches to avoid crowding, remove the oysters from the flour mixture, tapping off the excess, then dip them in the egg-beer batter and add them to the hot oil. Fry, turning once, for about 1 to 2 minutes on each side, or until golden brown. Transfer to the paper towels to drain, season with salt, and keep warm. Repeat until all the oysters are fried.

To assemble, warm the tortillas on a hot comal or other pan. Spread the rémoulade on the tortillas and top with some coleslaw. Place 3 oysters on the slaw on each tortilla, top with more slaw, fold, and serve.

INGREDIENTS

36 oysters in the shell

½ cup (65 g) all-purpose flour

1 teaspoon garlic powder

1 teaspoon onion powder

1 teaspoon dried Mexican oregano

1 teaspoon sweet paprika

1 teaspoon freshly ground black pepper

½ teaspoon dry mustard

Kosher salt

1 large egg, beaten

¼ cup (60 ml) dark Mexican lager, preferably Modelo Negra

½ cup (90 g) fine yellow cornmeal

Canola oil, for deep-frying

12 (3-inch/7.5-cm) Homemade Tortillas (page 25), warm

½ cup (240 ml) Mexican Rémoulade (page 267)

½ cup (240 ml) Coleslaw (page 260)

NOTE To serve the tacos as a main course, make 5-inch (12-cm) tortillas and fill each one with 5 fried oysters.

FEATURED MENU:
NEW YEAR'S EVE

Chef's Story

When I was a child, the last day of the year in our house meant spending the whole day cooking. In Mexico and, in fact, in most Latin American cultures, it is customary to eat at midnight on New Year's Eve. Preparation for a spread of traditional favorites is time-consuming, and in my family, everyone pitched in, assembly line–style, to make tamales, my mom's famous tostadas de tinga de pollo, flan, and pozole. Prepping, munching, and chismeando (gossiping)—this was the party before the party! There were other rituals as well, such as eating twelve grapes at midnight, wishing with each grape for a great month in the year ahead.

An amusing Mexican tradition (although one we didn't practice in our home) is to wear colored underwear on New Year's Eve, with the color one chooses representing some desire for the coming year: red for love, yellow for good luck, green for improved finances, and white for peace.

Mesoamerican Calendars and the New Year

The Aztecs and Mayan both recognized the 365-day year, but their calendars were divided into eighteen months of twenty days each. This totaled 360 days, leaving five nameless days referred to as nemontemi, which were considered an unstable period of the year. At a time of fasting and abstinence, the only food permitted was tortillas, prepared in advance and only eaten once a day. There is some evidence that these may have been the last five days of the Mesoamerican calendar year and that the new year may have begun in February, but we do not know definitively when these ominous days fell. What we do know is that those five extra days were regarded with great trepidation among the Aztecs. They tore their clothing, destroyed their household idols and cooking tools, and waited nervously for New Year's morning. When dawn arrived, there was a great celebration, and new items were brought out to replace what had been destroyed during the previous days.

NEW YEAR'S EVE MENU

Huckleberry Mimosas 162

Caviar Tostones with Crema 180

Miyagi Oysters with Serrano-Cucumber Granita 183

Monterey Abalone Tostadas with Avocado and Salsa Arisbel 184

Molcajete Caesar Salad with Oil-Poached Trout 187

Roasted Black Sesame Mole Rib Eyes 237

Lime Paletas 152

Chestnut Cinco Leches Cake with Chocolate Dust 76

CAVIAR TOSTONES
WITH CREMA

Tostones are twice-fried and smashed plantain slices. Their crunchy texture makes them a perfect counterpoint to the caviar in this unusual presentation. For this dish, I use American sturgeon caviar from Tsar Nicoulai, which has farmed sustainably raised caviar in nearby Sacramento County for four decades.

INGREDIENTS

2 green (unripe) plantains

Light olive oil, for frying

1 tablespoon kosher salt

½ cup (120 ml) crema

2 ounces (55 g) American sturgeon caviar, preferably Tsar Nicoulai brand

MAKES 8 SERVINGS

Cut off both ends of the plantains. Using a paring knife, make a slit along the length of a plantain, being careful not to cut into the flesh, and then lift off and discard the peel. Repeat with the second plantain. Cut the plantains crosswise into rounds 1 inch (2.5 cm) thick.

Pour the oil to a depth of 1 to 2 inches (2.5 to 3 cm) into a large, deep skillet and heat over medium heat. When the oil is hot, using a slotted spoon, lower the plantain slices into the oil, making sure they do not overlap, and fry, turning once, for about 5 minutes, or until light golden brown. Using the slotted spoon, transfer them to a plate. Set the pan of oil aside.

Soaking the fried plantains in salted water before the second fry will ensure they will be crunchy on the outside while still moist and tender on the inside. Fill a medium bowl with water, stir in the salt, then add the fried plantains, submerging them in the water. Let sit very briefly, less than 20 seconds. Drain well and pat very dry, as excess moisture will make the oil splatter.

Working with one at a time, flatten each plantain slice in a tostonera (a wooden press) or tortilla press to about ¼ inch (6 mm) thick. Or you can flatten them with the flat base of a heavy cup.

Line a large plate with paper towels and set it near the stove. Reheat the oil over medium heat and fry the plantain slices, turning once, for about 5 minutes, or until golden yellow and crunchy on both sides. Transfer to the paper towels to drain and let cool completely.

To assemble, top each tostón with a dollop of crema and a generous portion of caviar.

WINE PAIRINGS Bouchaine 2022 Riesling, Estate Selection springs from the glass with apple, bright citrus, and lemongrass notes. It shows gorgeous texture with great intensity of flavors, finishing with a spicy lift.

Bouchaine 2022 Gewurztraminer, Estate Selection is a medium-bodied wine with crisp acidity. It has a beautiful perfume of lychee and rose petals followed by a full and dry palate of tropical and spice flavors with hints of white flowers and savory herbs.

MIYAGI OYSTERS
WITH SERRANO-CUCUMBER GRANITA

Plump, mild Miyagi oysters, which are grown along the coast of Marin County, pair perfectly with the cucumber granita, which both cools the palate and keeps the oysters chilled. It is always best to eat oysters the same day as purchase, or at least within a couple of days of purchase. Live oysters smell fresh, sweet, and briny and have tightly closed shells. Lightly tap any oyster with an open shell; if it snaps shut immediately, it's good.

MAKES 6 SERVINGS

Halve 2 of the cucumbers lengthwise, scoop out and discard the seeds, and cut it into chunks. If you prefer a less spicy granita, seed 1 serrano chile or use a jalapeño chile. In a blender, combine the cucumber chunks, chile, orange juice, lime juice, sugar, and salt and blend until smooth. Transfer to a bowl or jar,

Cut 4 of the mint leaves into chiffonade, add to the bowl or jar, and let steep for 30 minutes. This is your granita base. Once the mixture has steeped, strain it through a fine-mesh sieve into a shallow pan that will fit in the freezer.

Freeze the granita for 30 to 45 minutes, or until it just starts to freeze on the top and along the sides of the pan. Using a fork, scrape the partially frozen mixture, breaking up any large chunks into finer flakes. Return to the freezer for 30 to 45 minutes, then repeat the scraping process. Repeat the freezing and scraping steps three or four times, for a total of about 4 hours. The granita is ready when it is light and flaky and no liquid remains in the pan.

While the granita freezes, line a large sheet pan with crushed ice. Rinse the oysters in cold water, brushing away any dirt and other debris. To open each oyster, place the round side down on a folded kitchen towel. Holding the rounder end of the oyster with the towel, carefully yet firmly insert the tip of an oyster knife into the "hinge" at the tapered end. Wiggle the knife to begin loosening the shell until you hear a pop, then twist the knife to pry the shells apart. Gently slide the oyster knife along the top of the oyster, keeping it flat against the top shell, to sever the adductor muscle, then lift off the top shell. Separate the oyster from the bottom shell the same way, being careful to retain as much liquid as possible in the bottom shell. Clean up the edges of the shell and remove any debris, then transfer the oyster on its half shell to the bed of crushed ice. Once all the oysters are opened, refrigerate them until needed.

To prepare the garnishes, cut off about one third of the remaining cucumber, then peel, halve, seed, and cut into fine dice. Reserve the leftover cucumber for another use. Thinly slice the remaining chile. Cut the remaining 4 mint leaves into chiffonade. Ready the apples and shallot.

To assemble, remove the oysters from the refrigerator and place 2 oysters on each serving plate. Using a fork, scrape some of the granita over the top of each oyster. Garnish each serving with the chile, apples, shallot, and cucumber and serve at once.

INGREDIENTS

3 cucumbers, peeled

2 serrano or jalapeño chiles

¼ cup (60 ml) fresh orange juice

¼ cup (60 ml) fresh lime juice

1 tablespoon sugar

Pinch of kosher salt

8 large fresh mint leaves

Crushed ice, for the oysters

12 Miyagi oysters

2 Fuji apples, peeled, cored, and cut into fine dice

1 shallot, cut into fine dice

WINE PAIRING Bouchaine 2022 Riesling, Estate Selection springs from the glass with apple, bright citrus, and lemongrass notes. It shows gorgeous texture with great intensity of flavors, finishing with a spicy lift.

MONTEREY ABALONE TOSTADAS
WITH AVOCADO AND SALSA ARISBEL

Abalone are actually prehistoric sea creatures, unremarkable from the outside but prized on the inside. They are a staple of North American Indigenous culture and cuisine. Be sure the abalone you purchase is sustainably sourced and farm-raised, as opposed to wild-caught. Fresh abalone, though expensive and not always easy to find, is worth the effort. It is available online through the Monterey Abalone Company. I've given cleaning instructions below, but I highly recommend you ask your local fishmonger to clean the abalone for you. Frozen, cleaned abalones are an excellent alternative to fresh.

INGREDIENTS

8 live small abalones, 4 to 5 ounces (115 to 140 g) each, weighed in the shell (or substitute frozen)

2 tablespoons unsalted butter

1 yellow onion, thinly sliced

½ cup (120 ml) dry white wine

½ cup (120 ml) white wine vinegar

2 tablespoons sugar

Kosher salt

8 tostadas, homemade (page 28) or store-bought

1 cup (240 ml) Salsa Arisbel (page 266)

2 avocados, pitted, peeled, and sliced

1 lemon, cut in half

Cilantro blossoms, for garnish

MAKES 8 SERVINGS

Using a spoon, separate the abalones from the shells. Carefully remove the flap near the head, or mantle, and remove the innards. Rinse the abalone under cold tap water to remove any dark material, using a soft brush if needed. Discard the innards and head of the abalone. Wrap the cleaned abalone in plastic wrap and refrigerate overnight. This will help relax the meat.

The next day, place the abalone foot side down on a clean kitchen towel, then wrap the top of the abalone with the towel. Using the flat side of a mallet, gently pound the abalone 3 to 4 times until the abalone flattens slightly; use enough force to flatten the muscle but make sure not to disfigure it.

Turn the abalone foot side up, and cut it in a crisscross pattern about ⅛ inch (3 mm) deep and ⅛ inch (3 mm) between cuts.

In a large skillet, melt the butter over medium-high heat. Add the abalones and cook for about 2 minutes on the first side. Turn and cook for 1 minute on the other side, or until the abalone and the butter are golden brown, the flesh curls slightly and the abalone feels slightly firmer when gently pressed. Transfer to a plate and let cool completely.

Cut the cooled abalones into paper-thin slices, transfer to a platter, cover, and refrigerate until ready to serve.

To prepare the onion, add the wine, vinegar, sugar, and a pinch of salt to a small saucepan and bring to a simmer over medium heat. Add the onion slices and cook for 1 to 2 minutes, until slightly translucent. Remove from the heat, drain, and let cool.

To assemble, place a tostada on each serving plate. Lightly spread each tostada with the salsa. Shingle the avocado and abalone slices, one by one, on each tostada to create a mosaic. Evenly distribute some of the slices of onion in an attractive fashion. Garnish with a squeeze of lemon juice and a few cilantro blossoms and finish with a sprinkle of salt.

WINE PAIRING Bouchaine 2022 Gewurztraminer, Estate Selection is a medium-bodied wine with crisp acidity. It has a beautiful perfume of lychee and rose petals and a full, dry palate of tropical flavors with hints of white flowers and savory herbs.

MOLCAJETE CAESAR SALAD
WITH OIL-POACHED TROUT

According to the most commonly repeated account, the Caesar salad was invented in 1924 at Cardini's restaurant in Tijuana, Mexico, by chef Caesar Cardini. For my version of this wildly popular salad, I add trout fillets from family-owned Mt. Lassen Trout & Steelhead, which farms its fish in pristine spring waters at the base of the mountain. You don't have to use a molcajete to make your Caesar dressing, but it's more fun than the blender method!

MAKES 6 SERVINGS

To poach the trout, lay a roughly 10-inch (25-cm) square of cheesecloth on a work surface. Place the peppercorns, coriander seeds, bay leaf, thyme, basil, and árbol chile in the center, bring the corners together to form a pouch, and tie securely with kitchen string. This pouch is known as a bolsita in the Mexican kitchen.

In a medium saucepan, heat ½ cup (120 ml) of the oil blend. Add the garlic and shallot and heat for about 2 minutes to infuse the oil. Scoop out and discard the garlic and onion, then add the remaining oil blend, the bolsita, lemon zest and juice, and 1 tablespoon salt to the pan. Cook the oil for 1 to 2 minutes or until fragrant. Remove the pan from the heat and let the oil cool until it is cool to the touch. While the oil cools, preheat the oven to 180°F (82°C) or the lowest temperature your oven permits.

Divide the cooled oil between two 9 by 13-inch (22 by 33-cm) pans. Season the trout fillets on both sides with salt and immerse them in the oil in the pans. Place in the preheated oven and poach for 20 minutes. This timing will result in translucent, medium-rare flesh. If you prefer your fish cooked medium-well, leave it in the oven for 30 minutes. Remove the pan from the oven and let the fish rest in the oil for 10 minutes.

Carefully pour off 1½ cups (360 ml) of the oil without breaking up the trout. Reserve ¾ to 1 cup (180 to 240 ml) for the Caesar dressing and ½ cup (120 ml) for the croutons. Remove the trout from the remaining oil and let it cool completely.

To make the croutons, in a saucepan, heat the oil over medium heat for 2 to 3 minutes, or until the oil begins to form ripples. Add the bread pieces and toast, moving them constantly, for 3 to 5 minutes, or until evenly toasted and golden. Remove from the heat, add the garlic, cheese, and butter, and stir well, using the residual heat of the saucepan to melt the butter. Continue to stir until the croutons are evenly coated—not more than a minute—then scoop them out of the pan with a slotted spoon and let drain and cool on paper towels before using. You need 1 cup (35 g) croutons for the salad. Reserve the remainder for another use.

Make the Caesar dressing as directed, using the reserved poaching oil.

To assemble, cut the Little Gems in half lengthwise. Divide evenly among six salad plates, placing the halves cut side up. Drizzle each half with the dressing, dividing it evenly. Garnish with the croutons, anchovy fillets (if using; rinse in cold water and shake to dry if you want to reduce their saltiness), and poached trout. Finish with a sprinkling of cheese and egg whites (if using). Serve at once.

WINE PAIRING Bouchaine 2021 Estate Chardonnay has a succulent, crisp, and food-friendly flavor with notes of lemon and nectarine, finishing with minerality.

INGREDIENTS

For the trout:

1 tablespoon each black peppercorns and coriander seeds, dry roasted (see page 271)

1 bay leaf

1 fresh thyme sprig

1 bunch fresh basil

1 árbol chile, dry roasted (page 271)

2 quarts (2 L) oil blend of 90 percent canola oil and 10 percent olive oil (7¼ cups/1.9 L canola oil and ¾ cup/180 ml olive oil)

5 cloves garlic

1 small shallot, cut into thirds

Grated zest and juice of 2 lemons

Kosher salt

2 pounds (910 g) skin-on rainbow trout fillets, preferably Mt. Lassen

For the croutons:

½ cup (120 ml) poaching oil from the trout

3 to 4 Sourdough Teleras (page 69), crusts removed and torn into bite-size pieces

2 large cloves garlic, grated or minced

½ cup (50 g) crumbled queso Cotija

1 tablespoon salted butter

1 cup (240 ml) Molcajete Caesar Salad Dressing (page 268)

6 Little Gem lettuces

1 can (2 ounces/55 g) anchovy fillets in olive oil (optional)

Grated queso Cotija or Parmesan cheese, for finishing

Minced cooked egg whites, for garnish (optional)

PIEL DE SAPO MELON
AND SCALLOP AGUACHILE

Harvested in fall and early winter, the Piel de Sapo melon, also known as the Christmas or Santa Claus melon, has a green rind splotched with yellow and white to pale green flesh. If you cannot find one, a honeydew or cantaloupe can be substituted. Sea beans are not beans at all but, as the name suggests, grow wild in coastal areas and are a type of branching succulent that looks and crunches a bit like green beans. They have a salty flavor that tastes of the sea, making them a perfect ingredient in aguachile. You can use capers in their place, though the flavor profile will be different.

INGREDIENTS

For the aguachile:

½ cup (120 ml) melon juice

½ cup (120 ml) cucumber juice

¼ cup (60 ml) white soy sauce

2 tablespoons agave nectar

½ jalapeño chile, seeds and veins removed

Kosher salt

20 dry sea scallops

Kosher salt

1 Piel de Sapo melon, halved, seeded, peeled, and cut into ¼-inch (6-mm) cubes or into slices ½ inch (12 mm) thick

½ pound (225 g) sea beans, rinsed and cut into ¼-inch (6-mm) lengths, or 2 tablespoons capers

1 serrano chile, thinly sliced crosswise

MAKES 10 SERVINGS

To make the aguachile, in a blender, combine the melon juice, cucumber juice, soy sauce, agave nectar, and jalapeño and blend until smooth. Strain through a fine-mesh sieve into a measuring pitcher and season with salt.

Trim off the tough muscle on the side of each scallop, then cut each scallop horizontally into 3 uniform slices. Lay the slices on a large plate, season with salt, and let sit for 10 minutes to cure. Arrange 6 scallop slices (from 2 whole scallops) on each serving plate. Pour the aguachile over the scallop slices, dividing it evenly. Top with the melon pieces. Arrange the sea beans and the serrano chile slices over the melon. Serve at once.

Note: If you do not have a juicer to make the melon and cucumber juices, just peel and coarsely chop the melon and cucumber, purée in a blender, and then strain through a fine-mesh sieve to remove any pulp.

WET VS. DRY SCALLOPS Wet scallops are scallops that have been treated with a sodium tripolyphosphate (STPP) solution the moment they are harvested to preserve them, a practice that also inflates their weight. They are then usually frozen. Dry scallops (also known as day boat or diver scallops), in contrast, are never treated with chemicals. Consequently, wet scallops have significantly greater water weight, a springy texture, and a slightly soapy taste when cooked.

How can you tell if your scallops are wet or dry? Line a plate with a paper towel, put a scallop on the towel, and microwave the scallop for 15 seconds. If a ring of water is released onto the towel, you have purchased wet scallops. If there is no noticeable water, you have purchased dry scallops. If you find you have wet scallops, here's a trick to help cover up their soapy taste: soak the scallops in a mixture of 4 cups (960 ml) water, ¼ cup (60 ml) fresh lemon juice, and 2 tablespoons kosher salt for 30 minutes.

BRAISED SQUID AND GARBANZOS
IN SPICY TOMATO SAUCE

If your only experience with squid is as fried calamari, perhaps you think of squid as chewy and briny. In fact, it has a subtly sweet flavor, is not at all "fishy," and is prized for its soft, chewy texture. If you don't have access to fresh squid, no worries—squid freezes well and thaws quickly. Monterey Bay Aquarium's Seafood Watch classifies domestic squid as a "Good Alternative," (defined as "Buy, but be aware there are concerns with how they're caught, farmed or managed"). Do ask where your squid comes from: You are looking for domestic squid, which, fortunately, is available at most seafood markets. Even better, if you live on the coasts, you may be able to find local catch at farmers' markets or through CSFs (Community Supported Fishery programs, like CSAs for fish). It is best to avoid squid that is imported from India, Thailand, and China.

MAKES 4 SERVINGS

In a skillet, heat the oil over medium-high heat. Add the cascabel chiles and toast, turning as needed, for about 5 minutes, or until nicely colored on all sides. Remove the pan from the heat and transfer the chiles to a plate. Add the garlic and onion to the pan, stir to combine with the residual oil, and let sit for 5 minutes. Add the tomato paste, return the pan to medium heat, and cook, stirring often, for 5 minutes. Add the squid pieces and cook for 1 to 2 minutes, or until they shrink in appearance and the meat turns whiter and begins to slightly char in some spots. Pour in the wine and deglaze the pan, stirring to scrape up any browned bits from the pan bottom, then continue cooking until the wine is reduced by half. Remove from the heat.

Stem the cascabel chiles, add to a blender along with the Roma tomatoes, and purée until smooth.

In a saucepan, combine the squid mixture, puréed tomato mixture, and fennel and bring to a simmer over medium heat. Reduce the heat to medium-low and simmer gently, stirring occasionally, for about 30 minutes, or until the liquid has reduced by half. Add the garbanzos and olives and continue to cook until the beans and olives are heated through.

Stir in the lemon zest and juice. Season with salt, then garnish with the chopped basil. Serve with the teleras.

INGREDIENTS

1½ tablespoons olive oil

2 cascabel or guajillo chiles

2 cloves garlic, minced

½ yellow onion, diced

1½ tablespoons tomato paste

1½ pounds (680 g) cleaned squid, bodies cut into rings ½ inch (12 mm) wide and tentacles cut in half

1 cup (240 ml) dry white wine, preferably Sutter Home Sauvignon Blanc

5 Roma tomatoes, halved

½ fennel bulb, trimmed, cored, and diced

1 cup (160 g) cooked garbanzo beans

½ cup (75 g) pitted Castelvetrano or Manzanilla olives

Grated zest and juice of 1 lemon

Kosher salt

½ cup (20 g) chopped fresh basil leaves

Herbed Sourdough Teleras (page 69), split and grilled, for serving

BRANZINO WITH SHRIMP MOUSSE
AND CORN PICO DE GALLO

Whole branzino, a mild and flaky white fish, not only makes for a stunning presentation when stuffed with shrimp mousse, but the natural sweetness of the shrimp adds a beautiful flavor. The Squash Blossom and Maitake Rice Pilaf with Poblano Chile and Kale (page 137) makes an excellent side to this company-worthy main course. If you are wary of removing the bones and spine from each fish yourself, ask your fishmonger to do it for you. You can make the mousse and prep the fish, allowing it to dry in the refrigerator for a crispier finish, a day in advance.

INGREDIENTS

For the shrimp mousse:

1 to 1¼ pounds (455 to 570 g) shrimp, peeled and deveined

1 large egg

½ cup (120 ml) heavy cream

Grated zest and juice of 2 lemons

2 tablespoons chopped fresh chervil leaves

2 tablespoons chopped fresh dill leaves

1 tablespoon ground dried shrimp

2 cloves garlic, finely chopped

1 shallot, finely chopped

Kosher salt

8 whole branzinos, each about 1 pound (455 g), cleaned and all bones removed, with head and tail intact

Kosher salt

½ cup (120 ml) olive oil, or as needed

2 cloves garlic, crushed

2 cups (600 g) Corn Pico de Gallo (page 266)

MAKES 8 SERVINGS

To make the mousse, in a food processor, combine the shrimp, egg, cream, lemon zest and juice, chervil, dill, ground shrimp, garlic, shallot, and 1 tablespoon water and blend until well mixed and sticky but still a bit chunky. It should have an almost sausage-like texture. Season with salt. The mousse can be made up to a day ahead and stored in an airtight container in the refrigerator.

To prepare the fish for stuffing, first remove the spine and belly bones if they have not already been removed by your fishmonger. Open a fish and, using a sharp knife, cut along one side of the spine from the head end to the tail, being careful not to cut through the back. Using kitchen shears, snip the spine at the neck to release it. Then turn the fish 180 degrees and, starting at the tail end, cut along the opposite side of the spine the same way. Now, run the knife under the spine and lift it out, using the scissors as needed to free it. Rinse the fish under cool running water and pat dry. Repeat with the remaining fish.

If possible, place the fish on a plate and refrigerate uncovered overnight. This allows the skin and flesh to dry out a little for a crispier fry.

When ready to serve, season the inside of each fish with salt, then stuff each fish with 3 ounces (85 g) of the mousse, making sure to coat the flesh evenly from one end of the slit to the other. Close the fish and season the outside with salt.

Preheat a large skillet or grill pan over high heat. (If the pan is too small to accommodate all of the fish without crowding, use two pans.) When the pan is hot, add the oil as needed to coat the bottom. When the oil is hot, add the fish and cook for about 3 minutes, or until you have a nice sear on the underside. Flip the fish, add the garlic to the oil, and cook for about 5 minutes longer, or until seared on the second side and cooked through. To test for doneness, make a small incision in the flesh; it should appear opaque and flaky.

Transfer to individual plates, top with the corn pico de gallo and serve immediately.

WINE PAIRING Ceja Sauvignon Blanc Sonoma Coast has bold aromas of green apple, ripe pear, and apricot. Surprisingly round on the palette, flavors of nectarine and honeysuckle are complemented by refreshing acidity and clean minerality that lead into a long and complex finish of orange rind and pineapple guava.

KING SALMON POACHED IN ANCHO CHILE OLIVE OIL
WITH CASTELVETRANO OLIVES AND FENNEL PEPERONATA

So much of the difference between good food and great food is in the details: the technique you choose for prep and the extra steps you take that gets the most flavor out of your ingredients. Here, I share a foolproof way to make perfect salmon every time, using my preferred ingredients and techniques. Fish can be one of the most difficult things to get right because it is so delicate and easily overcooked. Slowly poaching salmon in olive oil in the oven at a low temperature means the fish will stay tender and never be overdone.

MAKES 4 SERVINGS

To make the peperonata, in a wide, shallow pan, heat the oil over medium heat. Add the onion and garlic and sweat, stirring occasionally, for 3 to 5 minutes, or until translucent. Add the red, yellow, and green bell peppers and fennel, reduce the heat to low, and cook, stirring occasionally, for 10 to 12 minutes, or until the vegetables begin to soften. Add the tomato paste, stir well, and cook, stirring often, for 10 to 12 minutes, or until the liquids reduce slightly and a sauce starts to form. Pour in the wine and deglaze the pan, stirring to scrape up any browned bits from the pan bottom, then continue to cook until the liquid is reduced by half. Pour in the stock, add the basil, and cook, stirring occasionally, until the liquid is reduced by half. Add the butter and stir constantly until the liquid emulsifies.

Remove from the heat, stir in the lemon zest and juice and season with salt. Set aside. The peperonata can be made up to 3 days in advance, cooled, and refrigerated in an airtight container; bring to room temperature before serving. (If you do not have the ancho-infused oil on hand for making it, use regular olive oil.)

To poach the salmon, preheat the oven to 180°F (82°C), or to the lowest temperature your oven permits. In a large skillet over medium-low heat, combine the ancho-infused oil, lime juice, salt, garlic, basil, and thyme and bring to a simmer over medium heat. Remove the pan from the heat and strain the oil through a fine-mesh sieve into a 9 by 13-inch (23 by 33-cm) baking dish. Let the oil cool until it is cool to the touch.

Arrange the salmon steaks in a single layer in the baking dish. They should be covered with oil. Place in the oven and poach for 10 to 15 minutes, or until medium-rare when tested with the tip of a knife. Carefully remove the salmon from the oil.

To assemble, divide the peperonata evenly among four dinner plates. Place a salmon steak atop each bed of peperonata. Sprinkle the almonds over the salmon and then finish with the olives. Serve at once.

ŌRA KING SALMON Ōra King have been awarded "green choice" by Monterey Bay Seafood Watch and is to salmon what Wagyu is to beef. With a naturally high oil content seen in the marbled fat lines—much like a great steak—these salmon are even individually numbered for traceability after being hand selected by a master.

INGREDIENTS

For the peperonata:

1½ tablespoons Ancho Chile Olive Oil (page 269)

½ yellow onion, cut into medium dice

2 cloves garlic, thinly sliced

1 red bell pepper, diced

1 yellow bell pepper, diced

1 green bell pepper, diced

½ fennel bulb, trimmed, cored, and cut into medium dice

1 tablespoon tomato paste

1 cup (240 ml) dry white wine

2 cups (480 ml) chicken stock or fish stock

1 fresh basil sprig

2 tablespoons unsalted butter

Grated zest and juice of ½ lemon

Kosher salt

For the salmon:

2 cups (480 ml) Ancho Chile Olive Oil (page 269)

3 tablespoons fresh lime juice

2 tablespoons kosher salt

3 cloves garlic

1 fresh basil sprig

1 fresh thyme sprig

4 salmon steaks (6 ounces/170 g each), preferably Ōra King

½ cup (50 g) sliced almonds, toasted

½ cup (75 g) thinly sliced, pitted Castelvetrano olives

CINCO CALAS ARROZ A LA ROBLES

Seafood and rice are a classic combination. For this recipe, I've adapted my mother's Sunday supper special, arroz a la Robles, turning a side dish into a main course. Be sure to seek out the best shellfish you can find. I like to use mussels from Penn Cove Shellfish in Washington, oysters from nearby Point Reyes, and Dungeness crab legs pulled from the water off Marin County.

INGREDIENTS

1½ cups (360 ml) fish stock

½ cup (120 ml) Spicy Shrimp Stock (page 270)

5 Roma tomatoes, cut into eighths

3 tablespoons olive oil

2 cups (400 g) Calrose rice or other medium-grain white rice such as Carolina rice

1 yellow onion, cut into small dice

1 clove garlic, grated or minced

1 tablespoon tomato paste

1 bay leaf

1 teaspoon kosher salt

1 pound (455 g) jumbo shrimp in the shell (11/15 count)

10 Dungeness crab legs (from live crabs; reserve and freeze bodies for another use)

1 pound (455 g) mussels, rinsed and any errant beards removed

1 pound (455 g) littleneck clams, rinsed

20 oysters (approximately 1 pound/455 g)

MAKES 10 SERVINGS

In a blender, combine the fish stock, shrimp stock, and tomatoes and blend until the tomatoes are liquefied. Set the "seafood-tomato water" aside. You should have about 5 cups (1.2 L).

In a large, wide, shallow pot, heat the oil over medium-high heat. Add the rice and toast, stirring occasionally, for 3 to 4 minutes. The rice will first turn translucent and then start to turn light brown. Add the onion and garlic and cook, stirring occasionally, for 2 to 4 minutes, or until aromatic. Add the tomato paste and cook, stirring occasionally, for 3 to 5 minutes, or until the rice is well-coated.

Pour in the seafood-tomato water, stir well, and bring to a simmer. Add the bay leaf and salt, stir one last time, taste the liquid, and adjust with salt if needed. Cover, reduce the heat to medium, and cook for 30 to 45 minutes, or until the liquid is absorbed and the rice is tender.

Reduce the heat to low. Insert the shrimp, crab legs, mussels, clams, and oysters (open side up) evenly over the top of the rice. Re-cover the pot tightly and cook for 7 to 10 minutes, or until the mussels and clams open and the crab legs, shrimp, and oysters are cooked.

Discard any mussels or clams that failed to open and serve at once.

HEIRLOOM TOMATO CIOPPINO
WITH CINCO MARES AND CHOCHOYOTES

San Francisco has a very special place in my heart. It is a city filled with innovators and has evolved into a culinary mecca, with talented chefs, world-class restaurateurs, and adventurous home cooks. Hospitality is at the forefront, and food is a large part of what brings millions of tourists to the Bay Area. But as innovative as San Francisco is, the locals never forget the classics brought to the city by immigrants. In the late 1800s, San Francisco's Italian immigrants created cioppino, a fish stew with a tomatoey broth that used the catch of the day. It is a dish I first tasted here and have cooked only here. Here, I highlight the flavor of heirloom tomatoes, both in the broth and for adding at the table; California's wealth of shellfish and fish; and my own immigrant's addition to the city's famed culinary stew, chochoyotes, small masa dumplings that float in the rich broth along with the seafood. For a hearty and easy soup, after you and your guests have eaten all the seafood, reheat any leftover cioppino base and serve with your favorite rustic bread.

MAKES 6 SERVINGS

To make the cioppino base, preheat the oven to 425°F (220°C). Arrange the tomatoes, cut side up, in a single layer in a baking dish. Drizzle with oil, sprinkle with salt, and roast for about 15 minutes, or until they begin to bubble and soften when gently pressed. Remove from the oven and set aside.

In a large pot, heat the oil over medium heat. Add the onion, leeks, fennel bulbs, garlic, and lemongrass and sweat, stirring occasionally, for 5 to 7 minutes, or until translucent. Add the basil and cook just until it wilts. Add the roasted tomatoes, bay leaf, and coriander and fennel seeds, stir well, and then stir in the tomato paste and saffron. Cook, stirring often, for 3 to 5 minutes, or until the tomatoes break down further and become aromatic.

Pour in the wine and deglaze the pot, stirring to scrape up any browned bits on the pot bottom.

Reduce the heat to medium-low and continue cooking, stirring occasionally, until the liquid is reduced by half. Watch closely so it does not burn. Add the shrimp stock and fish stock, raise the heat, and bring to a simmer, stirring occasionally. Reduce the heat to low and cook gently for about 2 hours, or until the vegetables are very soft.

Remove from the heat and season with the lemon juice to taste and salt. Strain through a chinois or a fine-mesh sieve lined with cheesecloth into a clean container. You should have about 3 quarts (2.8 L). Use half of this base for the cioppino and save the remaining base for the next time you make cioppino. It will keep in an airtight container in the refrigerator for up to 3 days or in the freezer for up to 3 months.

CONTINUED...

INGREDIENTS
For the cioppino base:

3 Early Girl or other heirloom tomatoes, cut in half'

Olive oil for drizzling, plus ¼ cup (60 ml)

Kosher salt

1 yellow onion, julienned

2 leeks, white and pale green parts, julienned

1 fennel bulb, cored and julienned

5 cloves garlic, thinly sliced

1 stalk lemongrass, tender inner portion only, roughly chopped into ¼-inch (6-mm) pieces

1 bunch fresh basil

1 fresh bay leaf

1½ teaspoons coriander seeds, dry roasted (see page 271)

1½ teaspoons fennel seeds, dry roasted (see page 271)

3½ cups (785 g) tomato paste

Pinch of saffron threads

3 cups (720 ml) dry white wine, preferably Sutter Home Sauvignon Blanc

2 cups (480 ml) Spicy Shrimp Stock (page 270)

2 quarts (2 L) fish stock or chicken stock

Fresh lemon juice, for seasoning

For the chochoyotes:

1 pound (455 g) store-bought fresh masa for tortillas (page 22) or Basic Masa from Masa Harina (page 24)

1 bunch fresh cilantro, finely chopped

2 tablespoons room-temperature lard, olive oil, or other fat

1 tablespoon kosher salt

For the cinco mares:

6 Dungeness crab legs, from live crabs (reserve and freeze bodies for another use)

½ pound (225 g) mussels, preferably from Penn Cove Seafood, rinsed and any errant beards removed (see Note)

½ pound (225 g) littleneck clams, rinsed

½ pound (225 g) jumbo shrimp (11/15 count), shelled and deveined

8 ounces (225 g) skinless black cod fillet, cut into large dice

1 cup (145 g) Sungold cherry tomatoes, cut in half, for garnish

1 cup (135 g) grape tomatoes, cut in half, for garnish

Leaves from 1 bunch fresh opal basil, torn, for garnish

While the cioppino base is simmering, make the chochoyotes. In a large bowl, combine the masa, cilantro, lard, and salt. Knead with your hands for about 5 minutes, or until all the ingredients are evenly mixed and a smooth has dough formed.

Dampen your hands with water and divide the dough into 1-ounce (28-g) portions (about the size of a half dollar), then roll each portion into to a ball. As you work, cover the balls with a damp kitchen towel to prevent them from drying out. Then, one at a time, use your thumb to press down in the center of each ball, making a large, deep dimple. (1)

To cook the cinco mares, bring the cioppino base to a full boil over high heat. Add the chochoyotes and continue at a full boil for 10 minutes. (2) Add the crab legs and continue boiling for 2 more minutes. Next, add the mussels, clams, shrimp, and black cod and cook for 5 additional minutes. To make sure the chochoyotes are ready, pull one out, cut it in half, and taste.

Remove from the heat. Ladle the cioppino into large individual bowls, discarding any mussels or clams that failed to open and including an equal number of chochoyotes in each serving. Serve the cherry and grape tomatoes and the opal basil on the side for diners to add to their bowls as desired.

NOTE Ask your fishmonger to make sure all the mussels are closed, and have them give you some crushed ice, enough to keep them cool. When you get home, check that all beards have been removed and rinse the mussels well in cold water. If you are not planning to use your mussels right away, keep them on crushed ice.

 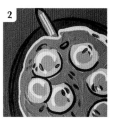

CAVIAR TOSTADITAS
WITH MEXICAN CHORIZO AND POTATO

With its slightly salty, mildly spicy flavor, chorizo and potatoes are a classic Mexican combination. Here, a dollop of caviar turns an everyday dish into a luxurious appetizer. The tostaditas add a nice crunch. I recommend Tsar Nicoulai's caviar brand because of their eco-certification and pioneering work in sustainability.

MAKES 16 TOSTADITAS; 8 SERVINGS

Divide the masa into 1-ounce (28-g) portions and shape into balls. Following the directions for tostaditas on page 28, press the balls and then cook the tortillas for 30 seconds on each side. Set aside.

In a saucepan, combine the potatoes with water to cover, place over medium heat, and bring to a simmer. Reduce the heat to medium-low and cook for about 15 minutes, or until fork-tender. Drain the potatoes, let cool until they can be handled, then peel and mash with a potato masher. Set aside.

If you are using chorizo in casings, remove and discard the casings. Place a skillet over medium-high heat and add the chorizo, breaking it up with a wooden spoon or spatula. Cook, stirring often, for 5 to 7 minutes, or until cooked through. Transfer the cooked chorizo and its rendered fat to the bowl with the potatoes, add the cheese, and mix well. Season with salt. Divide the potato-chorizo mixture into 16 equal portions and shape each portion into a patty slightly smaller than a tostadita. Let cool to room temperature.

To assemble, pour oil to a depth of ½ inch (12 mm) into a deep sauté pan and heat to 350°F (175°C). Line a large plate with paper towels and set it near the stove. When the oil is ready, working in batches to avoid crowding, add the tortillas and cook, turning once, for 30 seconds to 1 minute on each side, or until golden brown and crispy. Transfer to the paper towels to drain. Let cool to room temperature.

Place a potato-chorizo patty on each tostadita and top with a generous dollop of caviar. Serve at once.

INGREDIENTS

1 pound (455 g) store-bought fresh masa for tortillas (page 22) or Basic Masa from Masa Harina (page 24)

1 pound (455 g) Yukon Gold potatoes, unpeeled (see Note, page 87)

½ pound (225 g) Mexican chorizo, homemade (page 213) or store-bought

4 ounces (115 g) grated queso Cotija

1 teaspoon kosher salt

Vegetable or canola oil, for frying

2 ounces (55 g) American sturgeon caviar, preferably Tsar Nicoulai brand

SUMMER POZOLE
WITH SCALLOPS AND CORN

Pozole is a surprising dish, as this hot hominy favorite is served with an array of cold garnishes that most diners don't typically associate with a steaming bowl of stew. The garnishes are presented at the table in separate bowls, which guests add as they wish. They typically include shredded lettuce (cut with a knife, not torn), diced avocado, radish coins, Mexican oregano, diced onion, lime wedges, and ground dried piquín, ancho, or chipotle chile, or a combination.

INGREDIENTS

8 tomatillos, husks removed, rinsed, and coarsely chopped

½ Spanish white onion, cut into small dice

5 cloves garlic

1 serrano chile, stem and seeds removed

1 bunch fresh cilantro, roughly chopped

3 quarts (2.8 L) Corn Stock (page 269), seasoned with salt

2 cups (520 g) cooked hominy, homemade (page 261) or store-bought

3 cups (435 g) corn kernels (from about 6 large ears; see page 271)

Kosher salt

24 dry sea scallops

2 to 3 tablespoons olive oil

Freshly ground black pepper

½ cup (60 g) cut-up Blue Lake green beans, in ½-inch (12-mm) pieces

½ cup (60 g) cut-up wax beans, in ½-inch (12-mm) pieces

El Californio Fermented Salsa (page 264), Tostadas (page 28), and garnishes (see headnote), for serving

MAKES 8 SERVINGS

In a blender, combine the tomatillos, onion, garlic, serrano chile, and cilantro and blend until a chunky, salsa-like sauce forms. Set aside.

In a large saucepan, bring the corn stock to a simmer over medium heat. Add the hominy and corn kernels and cook, stirring occasionally, for 20 to 25 minutes, or until the hominy begins to crack. Add the tomatillo mixture, season with salt, and continue cooking until the mixture simmers again.

Preheat a large sauté pan or cast-iron skillet over medium-high heat. Line a large plate with paper towels and set it near the stove. While the pan heats, trim away the tough muscle on the side of each scallop, then dry the scallops well on both sides with paper towels. The drier the scallops, the better they will sear.

When the pan is hot, add 1 tablespoon of the oil and heat until ripples appear on the surface. Season the scallops on both sides with salt and pepper, then add as many scallops to the hot pan as will fit without crowding. Cook, turning once, for 1 to 2 minutes on each side, or just until they are a nice golden brown on both sides. Transfer the scallops to the paper towels to drain.

Carefully wipe out the pan with a paper towel. Then cook the remaining scallops the same way, heating 1 tablespoon of the oil in the pan before adding the scallops. Transfer to the paper towels.

Return the hominy mixture to a simmer, add the green and wax beans, and cook for 2 to 3 minutes, or until the beans are tender but still have a bit of a bite.

To assemble, divide the scallops evenly among eight rimmed soup or pasta bowls. Ladle in the pozole and serve at once, accompanied with the fermented salsa, tostadas, and garnishes alongside for diners to add to their bowls as they like.

TEQUILA PAIRING Loco Tequila's Loco Puro Corazon pairs beautifully with this lighter, slightly sweeter version of pozole. Unrivaled in its purity, elegance, and refinement, this tequila is extraordinarily smooth with ethereal aromatics and a rich, bright agave identity.

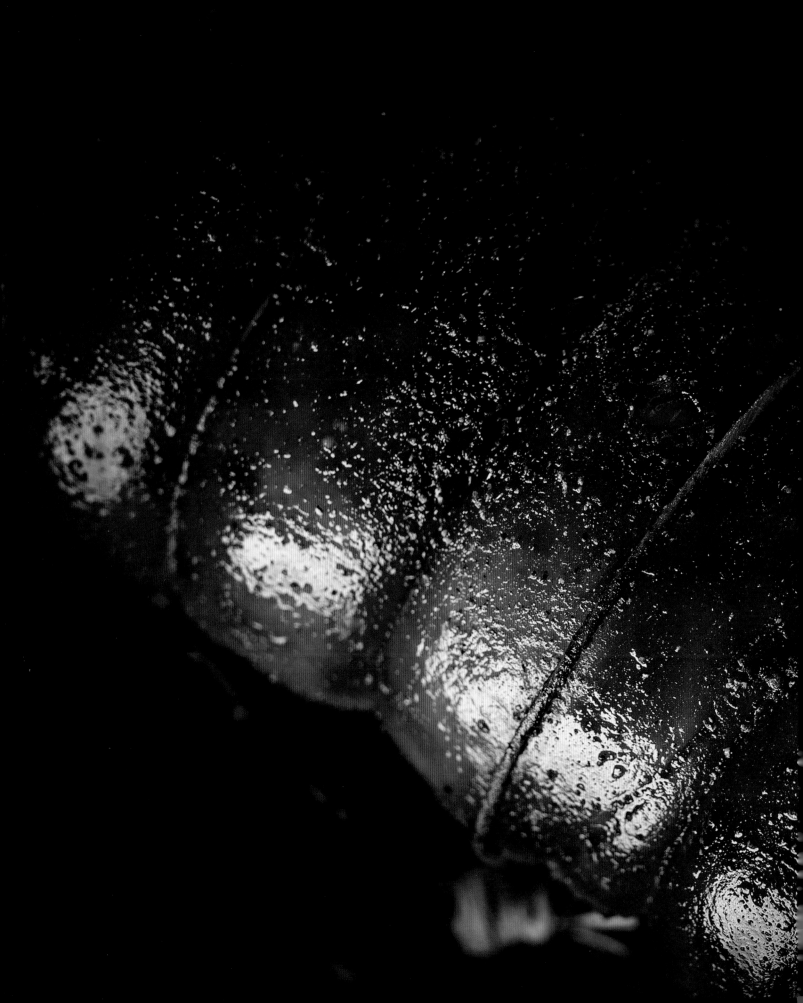

RANCHO

RANCHO

FROM RANCHOS TO REGENERATIVE RANCHING

California's ranchos were the precursors to today's cattle ranching industry. During the quarter century after Mexican independence in 1821, California was named a territory of the new nation of Mexico, and its Mexican residents were known as Californios.

An 1834 proclamation opened up the Church's extensive land holdings to colonization and as a result of the land grab that followed, over four hundred land grants were issued in just thirty years, a period romantically known as the "Days of the Dons," after the wealthy landowners and their famous hospitality and lavish lifestyles. Among their activities were elaborate fiestas often lasting several days (this is still not unusual in Mexico today, where weddings, even in the poorest villages, often last three days), bullfights, and huge rodeos. The private rancho grants were more than generous, creating expansive holdings and great wealth for their owners: the legal limit for a land grant was eleven square leagues, or about fifty thousand acres.

According to the proclamation, half of the property of the California missions was granted to the former "Mission Indians," Native Americans who had built, lived, and worked in the missions. Sadly, that promise was never fulfilled.

The ranchos transformed "Mexican California" and gave birth to a wholly new culture centered on animal husbandry. This focus provided goods for industries near and far, from tallow for soap in South America to hides for shoe manufacturers in New England. These huge cattle ranches dominated the economic landscape and attracted traders and settlers from all over the United States.

Today, there are approximately 38 million acres of private and public ranch lands in California. Most are family owned, and many have been in the hands of the same family for multiple generations.

Some of California's ranchers are focusing on regenerative ranching. This practice means going beyond organic, which means the animal was born and raised on certified organic pastures without chemicals in the grass or in the area where the animal was raised, and none of the feed was sprayed with synthetic pesticides. Another commonly used descriptor, "grass-fed," implies that the animals ate grass as opposed to feed. But meat being organic and grass-fed alone doesn't automatically make meat regenerative. While there are not yet any official guidelines from the USDA or FDA surrounding the term, regenerative meat is a general description for organic, grass-fed meat from ranchers who employ regenerative agricultural practices, the goals of which are to rebuild the organic matter in soil and restore degraded soil.

GRILLED RABBIT ADOBADO

Rabbit is a versatile and environmentally efficient meat that works well in stews, stir-fries, or grilled, as in this recipe, to really bring out its natural, slightly sweet side. It has a slightly stronger, meatier flavor than chicken, to which it is most often compared. Rabbits are no more difficult to cut up than a chicken, with anatomy that is pretty straightforward: front quarter, saddle, and hind end that give you two front legs, two to four pieces of saddle, and two hind legs. What's the saddle? Essentially, it is the loin, and in French gastronomy, is considered a "noble piece of meat," which means it's a prime cut, valued for its tenderness. I purchase rabbits from Devil's Gulch Ranch in Marin County (page 276) because they are free of hormones and antibiotics and are selectively bred for quality, to be large-framed, and to be meaty.

INGREDIENTS

2 young rabbits (2 to 3 pounds/910 g to 1.4 kg each), quartered

12-Hour Poultry Brine (page 270), chilled

Adobo Marinade (page 259)

Pickled Red Onions and Jalapeños (page 259), for serving

MAKES 8 SERVINGS

Add the rabbit pieces to the brine, making sure they are submerged in the liquid. Cover and refrigerate overnight.

Remove the rabbits from the brine and discard the brine. Dry the rabbits well, place in a clean container, add the marinade, and turn the pieces to coat evenly. Cover and refrigerate for about 3 hours.

Prepare a charcoal or gas grill for direct cooking over medium-high heat. Remove the rabbits from the marinade and wipe away any excess marinade.

When the grill is ready, place the rabbits on the grill directly over the fire and grill for 30 to 40 minutes, until a thermometer inserted into the thickest part of the meat away from bone registers 160°F (71°C), there are charred spots on the surface, and the meat begins to separate from the bones and feels firm when gently pressed.

Divide the rabbit evenly among eight dinner plates and serve at once, accompanied with the pickled onions and jalapeños.

WINE PAIRING Ceja Metzli Red Blend, Napa Valley represents the Aztec goddess of the moon. This rich, extroverted wine of cabernet sauvignon and Syrah brims with bright red fruit, black currant, plum, and toasted vanilla aromas.

CARNE APACHE LETTUCE CUPS
WITH CRISPY BODEGA RED POTATOES

Carne Apache is a traditional beef preparation typical to the Mexican state Michoacán. Usually made with lean ground beef, it is sort of a cross between steak tartare and ceviche. As with ceviche, the acid from the lime "cooks" the raw beef. The longer you leave the meat in the lime marinade, the more "well done" it will become. I prefer just a few minutes of "cook" time. While it is often served with a tostada or totopos (tortilla chips), I've updated the preparation using filet mignon or rib eye steak and served it in lettuce cups, with added crunch coming from crispy potatoes. The tomatillo-anchovy vinaigrette adds acid and umami, bringing everything together.

MAKES 4 SERVINGS

Put the beef into the freezer for about 20 minutes to make cutting it easier. Then, using a sharp chef's knife, cut the beef into ¼-inch (6-mm) cubes. Add the beef to a bowl, cover, and refrigerate until needed.

To make the vinaigrette, in a molcajete, add ½ teaspoon salt then, using the tejolote, work in the garlic and shallot to form a paste. Add the anchovy fillets, capers, and jalapeño and continue to mash the ingredients together to blend well. Add the tomatillos and continue to work the ingredients together with the tejolote to form a thickish sauce. Whisk in the olive oil until you have an emulsion, then fold in the cilantro. Stir in the lime juice. If a molcajete is not available, finely chop together the solid ingredients in the same order. Season lightly with more salt if needed, bearing in mind that the anchovy and capers are salty.

To make the potatoes, using a mandoline or the chef's knife, thinly slice the potatoes crosswise, transferring the slices to a bowl of water as you work. Let sit in the water for 30 minutes. Drain the potato slices well, arrange them in a single layer on paper towels, and let dry for 30 minutes.

Pour oil to a depth of 4 inches (10 cm) into a deep pot (no more than half full) or into a deep fryer and heat to 350° to 375°F (175° to 190°C). Line a sheet pan with paper towels and set it near the stove. When the oil is ready, working in batches to avoid crowding, add the potato slices and fry, turning once, for 5 to 6 minutes, or until golden brown. Using a slotted spoon, transfer the potatoes to the paper towels to drain. Season with salt while hot, then roughly chop.

For the lettuce cups, carefully remove 8 outer leaves from the lettuce heads, making sure they do not tear (the inner leaves are too small to hold the beef mixture). Place 2 lettuce cups on each individual plate.

Remove the beef from the refrigerator, add the vinaigrette and lime juice, and stir to coat the beef evenly. Taste the mixture and season with salt and more lime juice if needed. I prefer to do this just a few minutes before serving so the beef does not "overcook." Fold the corn kernels into the beef mixture.

Divide the corn-beef mixture evenly among the lettuce cups. Garnish with the crispy potatoes and serve at once.

INGREDIENTS

1 pound (455 g) filet mignon or rib eye

For the vinaigrette:

Kosher salt

1 clove garlic

1 small shallot, minced

2 anchovy fillets in olive oil

1 teaspoon chopped capers

1 jalapeño chile, minced

2 small tomatillos, husks removed, rinsed, and cut into quarters

½ cup (120 ml) extra-virgin olive oil

Leaves from 1 bunch fresh cilantro, roughly chopped

Juice of 3 limes

For the potatoes:

4 Bodega Red potatoes or russet potatoes (6 to 7 ounces/170 to 200 g each)

Canola oil, for deep-frying

Kosher salt

2 heads Little Gem or small heads butter lettuce

Juice of 2 limes

Kosher salt

Kernels from 2 ears yellow corn (see page 271)

BEEF CHEEK TACOS
WITH ÁRBOL SALSA

This recipe comes from chef Traci Des Jardins, who describes it this way: "This has become one of my favorite tacos, and tacos are my favorite food! My maternal grandfather was from near Hermosillo, and we would visit his family regularly when I was a child. On Sundays in Hermosillo, the specialty is tacos de cabeza. This might include lips, tongues, or brains—my favorite—though in my taste memory, the tacos had only the cheeks. I developed this recipe from my memories, making it my own Californian dish.

INGREDIENTS

2 pounds (910 g) beef cheeks, large sinew pieces removed

Kosher salt

Vegetable oil, for searing the cheeks

6 guajillo chiles, stems and seeds removed

1 Spanish white onion, cut in half

5 cloves garlic

1 tablespoon dried Mexican oregano

1 bay leaf

1 pound (455 g) tomatillos, husks removed and rinsed

4 árbol chiles, stems removed

1 tablespoon vinegar, such as distilled white, white wine, red wine, or cider

½ bunch fresh cilantro, finely chopped

12 to 18 (5- to 6-inch/12- to 15-cm) corn tortillas (page 25)

MAKES 12 TO 18 TACOS

To cook the beef cheeks, season them on both sides with salt. Coat the bottom of a large sauté pan with a little oil and heat the pan over medium-high heat. When the oil is hot, add the beef cheeks and sear, turning once, for 3 to 5 minutes on each side, or until well browned. Transfer to a plate and set aside.

One at a time, lightly toast the guajillos by moving them over a lit gas burner on your stovetop, or dry roasting them over a hot comal (see page 271), then transfer to a pressure cooker. Cut half of the onion in half and add it to the pressure cooker along with the garlic, oregano, bay leaf, beef cheeks, 1½ tablespoons salt, and 2 cups (480 ml) water. Top with the lid, seal in place, and bring up to high pressure. Reduce to medium pressure and cook for 45 minutes. Allow the pressure to reduce naturally, then remove the lid. Remove and discard the bay leaf, then transfer the beef cheeks, onion, garlic, guajillos, and cooking liquid to a heatproof bowl.

Alternatively, you can cook the beef cheeks on the stovetop. Sear as directed, then transfer the beef cheeks to a Dutch oven or other heavy pot with a lid and add all the ingredients that went into the pressure cooker. Bring to a simmer over medium-high heat, reduce the heat to low, cover, and cook at a gentle simmer for 5 hours. Check the water level now and again, and if it drops below 2 inches (5 cm) deep, add water.

To make the salsa, preheat the broiler. Place the tomatillos on a sheet pan and broil for about 5 minutes, or until blackened slightly on top. Turn the tomatillos over and broil for about 5 minutes longer, or until blackened on the second side. Transfer to a saucepan, add the onion, garlic, and chiles reserved from the cheeks, the árbol chiles, and ½ cup (120 ml) water, place over low-medium heat, and bring to a gentle simmer. Cover, reduce the heat to low, and cook for about 20 minutes, or until the sauce thickens slightly and turns a darker green. Remove from the heat and let cool.

In a blender, combine the tomatillo mixture, vinegar, and a pinch of salt and blend until smooth. Transfer to a bowl, taste, and adjust the salt if needed.

Dice the remaining onion half. If not freshly made, reheat the tortillas. If the beef cheeks have cooled, reheat them by returning them and their liquid to a pot on the stovetop over medium-low heat for 10 to 15 minutes. Break up the cheeks, using 2 forks to pull them apart into chunky shreds. (The beef cheeks can be braised up to a few days in advance and refrigerated. Reheat for 45 minutes.)

Using a slotted spoon, spoon the beef onto a platter, set it out on the table with the salsa, onion, cilantro, and warm tortillas, and invite guests to make their own tacos.

TRADITIONAL MEXICAN CHORIZO

Chorizo is surprisingly easy to make at home and freezes well. You can use it in bulk form in recipes (see pages 47, 199, and 229), shape it into patties, or, if you have a sausage stuffer attachment for your stand mixer, make your own chorizo sausages. If you are buying your ground pork from an upscale market, its fat content may be too low to make tasty sausages. You will need to either have your butcher grind pork mixed with fatback to order, or buy ground pork and grind the fatback yourself. You will need pork with 20 to 25 percent fat content.

MAKES ABOUT 2 ½ POUNDS (1.2 KG) CHORIZO

Dry roast the guajillo and ancho chiles on a comal as directed on page 271. Transfer the chiles to a bowl, add water to cover, and let rehydrate for 20 minutes.

Remove the chiles from the water, reserving the water, and squeeze out the excess moisture. Using a molcajete and tejolote, work the chiles until they form a thick paste. If needed, drizzle with a small amount of the chile water to loosen.

In a large bowl, combine the pork, chile paste, garlic, onion, vinegar, salt, oregano, coriander, paprika, black pepper, cumin, and cinnamon. Mix together with your hands until well blended.

Test for seasoning and salt by cooking a nugget of the chorizo in a small skillet, taste, and adjust the seasoning as needed.

Depending on the recipe, either cook the chorizo as is or form it into patties. The patties should be about ¼ inch (6 mm) thick but can be of any diameter you like. Or if you have a sausage stuffer attachment, stuff the bulk chorizo into casings. To cook the bulk chorizo, line a plate with paper towels and set it near the stove. Heat a skillet over medium heat, add the chorizo, and cook, stirring occasionally, for about 20 minutes, or until the fat is rendered and the meat is cooked through. Using a slotted spoon, transfer the chorizo to the paper towels.

Uncooked chorizo can be tightly wrapped and stored in the refrigerator for up to 5 days or in the freezer for up to 2 months.

TOLUCA GREEN CHORIZO This chorizo is a specialty of Toluca, Mexico, which lies about forty miles southwest of Mexico City. To make it, replace the guajillo and ancho chiles with 5 poblano chiles, peeled and seeded (see page 271), and 5 serrano chiles, stemmed, working them to a paste in a molcajete. Add 2 cups (80 g) finely chopped fresh cilantro and 2 cups (60 g) finely chopped spinach to the bowl with all the other ingredients.

INGREDIENTS

2 guajillo chiles, stems and seeds removed

3 ancho chiles, stems and seeds removed

2 ½ pounds (1.2 kg) 75 to 80 percent lean ground pork

3 cloves garlic, finely chopped

½ yellow onion, minced

1 ½ teaspoons distilled white vinegar

1 tablespoon kosher salt

1 tablespoon dried Mexican oregano

1 teaspoon ground coriander

½ teaspoon smoked paprika

½ teaspoon freshly ground black pepper

½ teaspoon ground cumin

½ teaspoon ground cinnamon

FEATURED MENU:
DÍA DE LA INDEPENDENCIA

Día de la Independencia—Mexican Independence Day—which commemorates the start of the Mexican War of Independence, falls on September 16, but the celebration begins late on the evening of September 15. That's when El Grito (the Battle Cry) de Independencia can be heard at midnight, accompanied by the ringing of church bells all across the country. This is Mexico's most important civic holiday, with schools, banks, and many businesses closed.

The Original "Secret" Grito

At the heart of the celebration is the story of a special Mexican hero, a Roman Catholic priest named Miguel Hidalgo y Costilla, from the small town of Dolores (now known as Dolores Hidalgo), near Guanajuato. Hidalgo led a group that included soldiers, civil servants, workers on landed estates, and more who sought independence from Spain.

On September 16, 1810, Hidalgo ordered the church bells to be rung and gathered his loyal followers, urging them to begin a revolt that they had long been secretly planning. The fight began with El Grito, a call to sedition and the initiation of their plot to reclaim their country from the Spanish. Although accounts vary on the exact language, this is a popular recreation of the words that sparked the revolution: "Long live Our Lady of Guadalupe! Death to bad government! Death to the gachupines!" (A gachupín was a native of Spain.). The revolutionaries carried a banner of the Virgin of Guadalupe as the emblem of their fight.

The Long Fight for Mexican Independence

Sometime on the afternoon of September 16, 1810, Hidalgo and his loyalists, armed with sticks and machetes, departed from the village of Dolores with a fighting force made up of Mexican-born Spaniards, Indigenous people, and mestizos (people of mixed Spanish and Indigenous lineage). As Hidalgo's army marched across Mexico, its numbers grew to nearly ninety thousand, with poor farmers and other Mexican civilians long frustrated with Spanish rule joining the insurgents. The Mexican Revolution would last for eleven years, a bloody and often politically complicated struggle. It culminated with the liberating army headed up by General Agustín de Iturbide riding victorious into Mexico City on September 27, 1821, and declaring Mexico's independence from Spain.

DÍA DE LA INDEPENDENCIA MENU

Crispy Pig Ear Salad with Mint, Black Mission Figs, and Frisée 216

Street Food–Style Corn on the Cob with Mexican Aioli 121

Grilled Squab with Pineapple Agridulce 219

Pepita-Crusted Rack of Lamb with Pomegranate Sikil P'aak–Style Sauce and Masa "Polenta" 220

Citrus-Cucumber Agua Frescas 223

Chocoflan with Strawberry-Hibiscus Sauce 157

CRISPY PIG EAR SALAD
WITH MINT AND BLACK MISSION FIGS

Mexicans are known for their "whole animal cooking," and nowhere is this more fully applied than to the whole pig. Orejas de cerdo (pig ears) are typically prepared in the style of carnitas, in a caldo of dark, sweetened pork lard used for frying seasoned cuts of pig. They can be served crispy, or bathed in salsa verde, which hydrates them, transforming the texture. I love pig ears in salad. Actually a delicacy (as there are only two ears per animal), these add a crunchy texture with an unexpected chewiness in place of croutons.

INGREDIENTS

For the pig ears:

6 pig ears

Kosher salt

1 leek, root end trimmed and cut in half

1 head garlic, top cut off

1 yellow onion, cut in half

2 cups (320 g) rice flour

2 cups (260 g) cornstarch

2 cups (480 ml) fresh orange juice

1 cup (240 ml) balsamic vinegar

¼ cup (60 ml) fresh lime juice

¼ cup (60 ml) soy sauce

¼ cup (50 g) sugar

1 teaspoon peeled and grated fresh ginger

1 jalapeño chile, minced

Canola oil, for deep-frying

3 heads frisée, core trimmed and cut in half lengthwise

5 heads Belgian endive, core removed and sliced crosswise ½ inch (12 mm) thick

¾ cup (180 ml) Balsamic Vinaigrette (page 267)

Kosher salt

8 Black Mission figs, trimmed and cut into quarters

Leaves from 1 bunch fresh mint, torn

2 serrano chiles, stems, veins, and seeds removed and thinly sliced crosswise (or use jalapeños for a milder result)

MAKES 6 SERVINGS

To prepare the pig ears, in a large pot, combine the pig ears with water to cover and bring to a boil over high heat. Reduce the heat to medium and cook for 1 to 2 minutes. Drain the ears and rinse under cold running water. Rinse out the pot, then return the ears to it. Add cold water to cover generously, along with 1 tablespoon salt, the leek, garlic, and onion, and return to the stovetop. Bring to a simmer over medium heat. Cover the pot, reduce the heat to low, and cook the ears for about 3 hours, or until tender when pierced with a knife tip and malleable. As the ears cook, check the water level from time to time and add more water if needed to keep them covered. Transfer the ears to a sheet pan and let cool completely. Discard the cooking liquid.

While the pig ears cool, in a shallow bowl, whisk together the rice flour, cornstarch, and 2 teaspoons salt and set aside. To prepare the glaze, in a saucepan, whisk together the orange juice, vinegar, lime juice, soy sauce, sugar, ginger, and jalapeño, mixing well. Place over medium-low heat and cook, whisking often, for about 20 minutes, or until the glaze is reduced by half and has a syrup-like consistency. Remove from the heat and set aside.

To deep-fry the pig ears, pour the oil to a depth of about 2 inches (5 cm) into a deep pot (no more than half full) and heat to 375°F (190°C). (Alternatively, heat a deep fryer.) Line a sheet pan with paper towels and set it near the stove.

While the oil heats, cut the ears into thin slices and toss the slices in the rice flour–cornstarch mixture, coating them evenly. When the oil is ready, working in batches to avoid crowding, remove the ear slices from the bowl, tapping off the excess flour mixture, and carefully add them to the oil. Be sure the pig ear slices are completely covered with oil. Fry for 5 to 6 minutes, or until they crisp up and turn a pale golden brown or honey color. Using a slotted spoon, transfer to the paper towels to drain and cool. Transfer the fried pig ears to a bowl, add a little of the glaze, and toss to coat well. Repeat until all the ears are fried and glazed, then taste and add more glaze to your liking.

To assemble, in a large bowl, combine the frisée halves and endive slices, drizzle with the vinaigrette, season with salt, and toss to coat the greens evenly. Divide the greens evenly among six salad bowls, then arrange the glazed pig ears on top. Garnish with the figs, mint, and serrano chiles and serve at once.

WINE PAIRING 2022 House of Brown Chardonnay is a juicy and bright medium-bodied wine with a silky, creamy texture and hints of honeydew.

GRILLED SQUAB
WITH PINEAPPLE AGRIDULCE

Squab just feels fancier than chicken, as dinner guests all get their own bird! Its smaller size also means it takes less time to cook. Squab has moist, dark meat and a slightly gamey flavor and is typically cooked until medium so the interior remains pale pink. Like duck, squab has a layer of fat (though less than duck) under the skin that liquefies during roasting, nicely basting the bird as it cooks. These squabs are first brined, then treated to a robust marinade before being grilled over a hot fire and served brushed with a Mexican sweet-and-sour sauce. You'll need to start them 2 days in advance.

MAKES 6 TO 12 SERVINGS

In a large stock pot, combine all the ingredients for the brine. Warm over medium heat, stirring, until the salt and sugar have dissolved. Let cool completely. Add the squabs to the brine, cover, and refrigerate overnight in the refrigerator.

Remove the squabs from the brine and discard the brine. In a large container or the stock pot, make the marinade according to the recipe on page 259, substituting ½ cup (85 g) fresh pineapple chunks for 2 of the Roma tomatoes and adding 1 cup (240 ml) pineapple juice. Add the squabs to the marinade and turn to coat evenly. Cover tightly and refrigerate overnight.

The next day, prepare a fire in a charcoal or gas grill for direct cooking over high heat.

While the grill heats, remove the squab from the marinade, wiping away the excess, and discard the marinade. Now, carefully spatchcock each squab: Place the squab breast side down. Using poultry shears, and starting from the neck end, cut along one side of the spine to the tail end. Then cut along the opposite side and lift the spine away. (You can save the spines for stock.) Turn the squab over and press down on the breastbone to flatten the bird. Tuck the wing tips under the drumettes. Sprinkle the squabs on both sides with salt.

Place the squabs, skin side down, directly over the fire and grill for 5 to 7 minutes, or until the skin is golden brown. Move the birds to a cooler area of the grill if the skin begins to char. Flip the squabs and cook for 5 to 7 minutes longer, or until a thermometer inserted into the thickest part of the breast away from bone registers 140°F (60°C) for medium. The meat should still be pink. Remove from the grill. If you prefer your meat more cooked, continue cooking for 3 to 5 minutes flipping halfway through to ensure even cooking.

To assemble, brush the hot squabs on both sides with the pineapple agridulce and divide evenly among dinner plates. Serve at once.

WINE PAIRING 2022 House of Brown Rosé is a vibrant and dynamic light-bodied wine with a silky texture and a delightfully subtle finish.

INGREDIENTS

For the brine:

8 quarts (7.5 L) water

½ cup (120 ml) fresh lemon juice

½ cup (120 ml) fresh orange juice

1 cup (140 g) kosher salt

½ cup (110 g) packed dark brown sugar

2 bay leaves

2 teaspoons dried thyme, or 5 sprigs of fresh thyme

2 teaspoons dried rosemary, or 3 sprigs of fresh rosemary

2 teaspoons crushed or minced garlic, or 3 whole cloves, peeled and crushed

3 strips lemon zest

12 squabs (each about 1 pound/455 g)

4 cups (960 ml) Adobo Marinade (page 259), made with ½ cup (85 g) fresh pineapple chunks and 1 cup (240 ml) pineapple juice (see method)

Kosher salt

2½ cups (600 ml) Pineapple Agridulce (page 262)

PEPITA-CRUSTED RACK OF LAMB WITH POMEGRANATE SIKIL P'AAK–STYLE SAUCE AND MASA "POLENTA"

Elysian Fields sells some of the finest lamb in the United States. The animals are grown on several family farms in Pennsylvania and Ohio, all of them operated according to a set of standards that ensures the lambs experience only the most humane treatment in an environmentally sustainable setting. Here, I pair this extraordinary meat with my riff on sikil p'aak, a Yucatecan pumpkin seed dip that I turn into a sauce flavored with pomegranate, a fruit that most likely arrived with the Spanish in the sixteenth century and is now used in many Mexican recipes. I serve the lamb and sauce with masa "polenta," my version of the traditional northern Italian accompaniment to meats, vegetables, and seafood.

INGREDIENTS

For the marinade:

1 cup (240 ml) plain Greek yogurt

2 tablespoons Dijon mustard

1 tablespoon olive oil

1 fresh rosemary sprig, finely chopped

Grated zest of 1 lemon

¼ teaspoon kosher salt

For the lamb:

2 racks of lamb

Kosher salt and freshly ground black pepper

Dijon mustard, for brushing

1 cup (130 g) toasted pepitas, chopped medium coarse

For the sikil p'aak sauce:

2 to 3 chipotle meco chiles or, for a milder sauce, chipotle morita chiles (see page 272)

1 cup (130 g) pepitas

½ teaspoon cumin seeds (optional)

1 red bell pepper

2 Roma tomatoes (about ½ pound/ 225 g)

2 Spanish white onions, thinly sliced

2 cloves garlic

¼ cup (60 ml) Seville or bitter orange juice, or a substitute (see page 272)

2 tablespoons pomegranate molasses

2 teaspoons kosher salt

MAKES 4 SERVINGS

To make the marinade, in a baking dish large enough to hold the lamb racks, combine the yogurt, mustard, oil, rosemary, lemon zest, and salt and mix well. Set the marinade aside.

Many meat counters sell lamb racks with the bones already "frenched," or you can ask the butcher to french the racks for you. When you get the racks home, scrape down the bones to remove any remaining membrane to ensure a "clean" look when the lamb is served. Using a sharp knife, score the fat side of each rack in a diamond pattern. Place the racks in the marinade. Flip the racks a few times to coat both sides, then place them fat side down to ensure good marinating. Cover the baking dish with plastic wrap and refrigerate for at least 3 hours or up to overnight. The longer the lamb marinates the better it will taste.

To make the sauce, dry roast the chipotle chiles on a comal as directed on page 271. Transfer the chiles to a bowl, add water to cover, and let rehydrate for 20 minutes. When they have rehydrated, transfer them to a blender and reserve the soaking water.

Dry roast the pepitas and transfer to a small plate. Then dry roast the cumin seeds, if using, just until they begin to turn golden brown and transfer them to the plate. When the pepitas and cumin seeds (if using) have cooled, add them to the blender.

Next, char, peel, stem, and seed the red pepper as directed on page 271. Cut the pepper in half, drop half into the blender, and reserve the remaining half for another use. Dry roast the tomatoes, onion slices, and garlic, using tongs to turn them so they char lightly on all sides and soften, then transfer them to the blender.

Add the Seville orange juice, pomegranate molasses, salt, and ¼ cup (60 ml) of the reserved chile soaking water and purée until smooth. The sauce should be velvety and have a thick but runny texture similar to maple syrup. Add more reserved soaking water if needed to achieve the correct consistency. Taste and adjust with salt and pomegranate molasses if needed. Set aside.

CONTINUED…

For the masa "polenta":

2 cups (480 ml) whole milk

1½ cups (195 g) yellow, red, or white masa harina, preferably Masienda brand

Kosher salt and freshly ground black pepper

2 tablespoons unsalted butter

¼ cup (25 g) grated Parmesan cheese or pulled and shredded queso Oaxaca (optional)

Roughly chopped fresh mint leaves, for garnish

Pomegranate arils (seeds), for garnish (optional)

Once the lamb has marinated, line a sheet pan with aluminum foil and top with a wire rack. Remove the lamb from the marinade, wipe off the excess marinade, and discard the marinade. Place the lamb fat side up on the wire rack and let sit at room temperature while the oven preheats.

Preheat the oven to 500°F (260°C).

When the oven is ready, season the lamb generously on both sides with salt and pepper. Keeping it fat side up, place it in the oven and roast for about 25 minutes, or until a thermometer inserted into the thickest part of the meat away from bone registers 125° to 130°F (52° to 55°C) for medium-rare. If you prefer your lamb cooked more, continue cooking to desired doneness.

While the lamb is roasting, make the masa "polenta." In a saucepan, whisk together 2 cups (480 ml) water, the milk, masa harina, and a pinch each of salt and pepper, making sure there are no lumps. Place the pan over medium heat and bring to a simmer. Cook, stirring or whisking frequently, for 10 or 15 minutes, or until thick and creamy. Lower the heat slightly if big bubbles are forming and bursting. The mixture should be as thick as pudding and hold its shape when scooped out. If needed, add a bit more masa harina to the pot until the desired consistency is achieved, making sure to stir well to dissolve any lumps. Stir in the butter and then, for extra creaminess, the cheese (if using). Taste and adjust with salt and pepper if needed.

When the lamb is ready, remove from the oven and lightly brush the fat side with mustard. Coat the mustard with the pepitas to create a crust, then loosely cover the racks with aluminum foil and let rest for about 5 minutes.

To assemble, working from the bone side, cut the racks into small chops of about 2 bones each. Serve half a rack of lamb (2 bones) to each diner. Spoon a generous amount of "polenta" onto each dinner plate, arrange the lamb on top, and spoon some sikil sauce over the lamb. Garnish with mint and pomegranate arils (if using) and serve at once.

WINE PAIRING 2021 Brown Estate Petite Sirah is bold, rich, and luxurious on the palate with full body, grippy tannins, and a layered reveal of fruit leather, triple-crème Brie, and baking spice.

CITRUS-CUCUMBER AGUA FRESCAS

According to Mexican folk history, Aztecs made aguas frescas using fruits gathered along the waterways of Tenochtitlán, which is now known as Mexico City. They then chilled their drinks with ice collected from Popocatépetl and Iztaccíhuatl, two dormant volcanoes that stand nearby.

MAKES 8 SERVINGS

In a blender, combine half of the cucumbers, 1 cup (240 ml) of the orange juice, ½ cup (120 ml) of the lime juice, and 2 cups (480 ml) water and blend until smooth. Strain through a fine-mesh sieve into a pitcher, pressing against the pulp with the back of spoon to extract as much liquid as possible. Repeat with the remaining cucumbers, orange juice, and lime juice and 2 cups (480 ml) water.

Add the agave nectar and sugar to the pitcher and stir until dissolved. Add and muddle the basil leaves. Cover and refrigerate until well chilled.

Serve over ice in tall glasses.

CITRUS-CUCUMBER COCKTAIL For a cocktail, add 1 fluid ounce (30 ml) tequila or mezcal to each glass.

INGREDIENTS

6 cucumbers, peeled, halved, seeded, and chopped

2 cups (480 ml) fresh orange juice

1 cup (240 ml) fresh lime juice

½ cup (120 ml) agave nectar

½ cup (100 g) sugar

1 bunch fresh basil, leaves picked

Ice cubes, for serving

AGRIDULCE CHICKEN WINGS
WITH VERDE GODDESS DRESSING

My two boys love chicken wings! I noticed that whenever we eat out there were hot wings, Asian wings, and Buffalo wings but no Mexican wings, so I developed this Mexican recipe for wings, and it is now a family favorite. Brining the wings first ensures the meat is flavorful and juicy, plus the breading will stick to the moist brined skin for an extra crispy finish. To keep the Mexican theme strong, I add ground pasilla chile to the coating to give it a little heat and cilantro and jalapeños to my version of green goddess dressing. These wings are also delicious cooked in an air fryer.

INGREDIENTS

For the brine:

½ cup (120 ml) fresh lemon juice

½ cup (120 ml) fresh orange juice

1 cup (140 g) kosher salt

½ cup (110 g) packed dark brown sugar

2 bay leaves

½ teaspoon dried thyme

½ teaspoon dried rosemary

½ teaspoon crushed or minced garlic

3 strips lemon zest

5 pounds (2.3 kg) chicken wings

2 cups (320 g) rice flour

2 cups (260 g) cornstarch

1 tablespoon ground pasilla chile, preferably Burlap & Barrel brand

Canola oil, for deep-frying

5 cups (1.2 L) Salsa Agridulce (page 262)

2 cups (480 ml) Verde Goddess Dressing (page 269)

MAKES 10 SERVINGS

To make the brine, in a large stockpot, combine 8 quarts (7.5 L) water, the lemon juice, orange juice, salt, brown sugar, bay leaves, thyme, rosemary, garlic, and lemon zest and bring to a simmer over medium-high heat, stirring to dissolve the salt and sugar. Remove from the heat and let cool completely.

Add the chicken wings to the cooled brine, making sure they are fully submerged, then cover and refrigerate for at least 8 hours or up to overnight.

When you are ready to begin cooking, remove the wings from the brine and discard the brine. In a bowl, whisk together the rice flour, cornstarch, and ground pasilla, mixing well. Transfer the flour mixture to a large paper bag. Add the wings to the bag, a few at a time, and shake to coat evenly. Pull the wings from the bag, shaking off the excess flour mixture, and set aside, not touching, on a large sheet pan.

Pour the oil to a depth of 1½ inches (4 cm) into a large, deep sauté pan or other large, wide, shallow pan and heat to 350°F (175°C). Set a large bowl next to the stove.

When the oil is ready, working in batches to avoid crowding, add the wings to the hot oil, making sure they are completely submerged, and fry for 8 to 10 minutes, or until golden brown. Using tongs, transfer the wings to the bowl and immediately coat with some of the salsa agridulce. Be sure to remove any bits of fried coating from the oil before frying the next batch of wings. If the oil starts to brown, discard the oil and start with fresh oil. Repeat until all the wings are fried and coated with the salsa.

To serve, divide the wings evenly among ten dinner plates. Drizzle with some of the goddess dressing and serve the remaining dressing on the side for dipping.

OXTAIL SOUP
WITH SUMMER SQUASH AND CABBAGE

This oxtail soup (caldo de colita de res) is truly a Mexican comfort food and can also be made with bone-in beef shanks. Both cuts are rich in collagen, a protein that contributes to healthy bones, skin, and muscles, making this soup as good for you as it is delicious. Oxtail is typically sold already cut into rounds. If you opt for beef shanks, you may need to ask the butcher to cut them into rounds 2 to 3 inches (5 to 7 cm) thick.

INGREDIENTS

3 pounds (1.4 kg) oxtail rounds or bone-in beef shank rounds, each about 2 to 3 inches (5 to 7 cm) thick

3 cloves garlic

1 yellow onion, cut into quarters

3 bay leaves

1 teaspoon dried Mexican oregano

1 tablespoon tomato paste

1 to 2 serrano chiles, stems removed

1 pound (455 g) fingerling potatoes

½ head green cabbage, cut into quarters

16 baby carrots

1 yellow summer squash, cut crosswise into 5 or 6 thick slices

1 zucchini, cut crosswise into 5 or 6 thick slices

2 ears yellow corn, each cut crosswise into quarters

Kosher salt

Fresh lime juice, for seasoning

1 cup (40 g) chopped fresh cilantro

Tostadas or corn tortillas (page 28), for serving

MAKES 4 SERVINGS

In a stockpot, combine the oxtail, 3 quarts (2.8 L) water, garlic, onion, bay leaves, oregano, and tomato paste and bring to a simmer over medium-high heat, skimming off any froth that rises to the surface. Adjust the heat to maintain a gentle simmer and cook, uncovered and skimming if needed, for 2 to 3 hours, or until the meat is fork-tender.

In a blender, combine the serrano chiles (use just one if you prefer a milder flavor) and some of the oxtail cooking liquid and blend until smooth. Add the mixture to the pot. Then add the potatoes, cabbage, carrots, summer squash, and zucchini and bring to a simmer. Reduce the heat to medium-low and cook for 20 to 30 minutes, or until the potatoes are fork-tender. Finally, add the corn, cover, and cook for 3 to 5 minutes, or until tender.

Remove from the heat and season with salt and lime juice. Ladle into bowls, garnish with the cilantro, and serve at once with tostadas.

WINTER PORK RIB "POZOLON" ROJO WITH CABBAGE, CHAYOTE, AND POTATOES

Here is a sort of Mexican take on corned beef and cabbage crossed with pozole. This hearty stew is great for family gatherings. This is similar to the Oxtail Soup with Summer Squash and Cabbage (opposite). Serve this with the same toppings suggested in the Summer Pozole with Scallops and Corn recipe (page 200): shredded lettuce, diced avocado, radish coins, Mexican oregano, diced onion, lime wedges, and ground dried piquín, ancho, or chipotle chile, or a combination.

MAKES 4 SERVINGS

In a stockpot, combine the pork ribs, 3 quarts (2.8 L) water, garlic, onion, bay leaves, oregano, and tomato paste and bring to a simmer over medium-high heat, skimming off any froth that rises to the surface. Adjust the heat to maintain a gentle simmer and cook uncovered, skimming if needed, for 2 to 3 hours, or until the meat is fork-tender.

While the ribs simmer, rehydrate the guajillo chiles in water for 20 minutes.

Drain the chiles. In a blender, combine the chiles and 2 cups (480 ml) of the cooking liquid from the braised ribs, and blend until smooth. Add the mixture to the pot with the ribs. Then add the potatoes, cabbage, carrots, and chayotes and bring to a simmer. Reduce the heat to medium-low and cook for 20 to 30 minutes, or until the potatoes are fork-tender. Finally, add the hominy, cover, and cook for 3 to 5 minutes, or until tender.

Transfer the ribs to a cutting board and pull the meat off the pork bones, discarding the bones and returning the meat to the pozole. Remove the pot from the heat and season with salt and lime juice. Ladle into bowls, garnish with the cilantro, and serve at once with tostadas.

INGREDIENTS

3 pounds (1.4 kg) pork ribs

3 cloves garlic

1 yellow onion, cut into quarters

3 bay leaves

1 teaspoon dried Mexican oregano

1 tablespoon tomato paste

6 guajillo chiles, stems and seeds removed, dry roasted (see page 271)

1 pound (455 g) fingerling potatoes

1/2 head green cabbage, cut into quarters

16 baby carrots

2 chayotes, peeled and cut into 1/2-inch (12-mm) cubes

2 cups (520 g) cooked hominy, homemade (page 261) or store-bought

Kosher salt

Fresh lime juice, for seasoning

1 cup (40 g) chopped fresh cilantro

Tostadas or corn tortillas (page 28), for serving

KALE SOUP
WITH TOLUCA GREEN CHORIZO ALBÓNDIGUITAS

Mini meatballs of green chorizo pair beautifully with kale in this Mexican soup that is reminiscent of Italy's classic zuppa di polpette. As filling as it is delicious, this recipe is high in protein, with cannellini beans and albóndiguitas (mini meatballs) and has plenty of fiber from the kale and vegetables. Make it into a complete meal by doubling up on the albóndiguitas in each serving. Serve with Sourdough Teleras (page 69) or warm corn tortillas (page 25).

MAKES 8 TO 10 SERVINGS

Sear the albóndiguitas as directed on page 238 and set aside.

In a large pot over medium-high heat, warm the oil. Add the carrots, onions, celery, jalapeño, and garlic and sweat, stirring occasionally, for 3 to 4 minutes, or until the vegetables begin to soften and turn light golden brown. Add the tomato paste, rosemary, thyme, and paprika, stir well, and cook, stirring often, for 1 to 2 minutes, or until the tomato paste turns dark and the herbs are aromatic. Next, add the puréed tomatoes, lower the heat to medium, and cook, stirring occasionally, for 4 to 6 minutes, or until reduced by half.

Pour in the stock, stir well, and bring to a simmer. Add the beans, reserved albóndiguitas, and kale and cook for 10 minutes. Add the zucchini and cook for about 5 minutes more, or until all the vegetables are tender.

Remove from the heat and season with salt. Ladle into bowls and serve at once with one lime half per guest.

INGREDIENTS

40 Toluca green chorizo albóndiguitas (see page 238)

¼ cup (60 ml) olive oil

3 carrots, peeled and diced

2 yellow onions, diced

5 celery stalks, diced

1 jalapeño chile, seeded and minced

10 cloves garlic

2 tablespoons tomato paste

1 tablespoon chopped fresh rosemary

1 tablespoon chopped fresh thyme

1 teaspoon smoked paprika

5 Roma tomatoes, cut in half and puréed in a blender

2½ quarts (2.4 L) chicken stock

3 cups (780 g) cooked cannellini beans (page 260)

2 bunches dinosaur (Tuscan) kale, stems and ribs removed and leaves coarsely chopped

3 zucchini, cut into large dice

Kosher salt

4 to 5 limes, halved

CARNITAS

In Mexico, a cazo de cobre is a special hand-hammered copper pot reserved for cooking special dishes, such as carnitas and calabaza en tacha (see my recipe for Calabaza en Tacha Flan, page 107). The town of Santa Clara del Cobre in the state of Michoacán is famous for its copper pots. There you can see artisans—almost always men—making these cauldrons exactly as they have been made for generations. As with so many of Mexico's culinary traditions, there is a practical reason why these copper vessels remain popular today: Copper is one of the most effective materials for the even transfer of heat, an important quality when cooking carnitas, one of Mexico's most iconic dishes. Carnitas are extremely versatile and can be used in soups, as a filling for tamales, or served as tacos or sandwiches. You can use either pork butt or pork ribs (see variation below) for this recipe.

INGREDIENTS

For the rub:

1 tablespoon dried Mexican oregano

1 tablespoon onion powder

1 tablespoon garlic powder

1 tablespoon packed dark brown sugar

1 teaspoon freshly ground black pepper

2 tablespoons kosher salt

For cooking the pork:

5 pounds (2.3 kg) boneless pork butt, cut into large pieces

2 cups (480 ml) fresh orange juice

1 cup (240 ml) fresh lime juice

¼ cup (55 g) lard or unsalted butter, plus more as needed

1 large yellow onion, cut into quarters

1 head garlic

1 bay leaf

2 árbol chiles

For serving:

Homemade corn tortillas (page 25), warmed

Salsa Borracha (page 263), El Californio Fermented Salsa (page 264), or your favorite salsa

¾ cup (95 g) minced Spanish white onion mixed with ½ cup (20 g) chopped fresh cilantro

MAKES 10 TO 15 SERVINGS

To make the rub, in a bowl, stir together all of the ingredients until well combined. Place the pork in a baking dish or roasting pan that is large enough to hold it and rub the mixture all over the pork pieces. Cover and refrigerate overnight.

The next day, preheat the oven to 300°F (150°C).

Transfer the pork and any juices to a cazo de cobre (see headnote) or a Dutch oven. Add the orange and lime juices, lard, onion, garlic, bay leaf, and árbol chiles, making sure the onion is distributed as evenly as possible to ensure even flavor distribution. Cover the pot with its lid or use aluminum foil wrapped tightly over the top. Braise in the oven for 4 to 5 hours, or until the meat is soft and tender and it easily pulls apart when using two forks.

Transfer the pork to a cutting board. Pull apart or shred the meat into large chunks. Season with salt to taste.

To give the carnitas a bit of crunch, preheat a large cast-iron pan over medium-high heat. Add enough lard to cover the bottom of the pan, then, in batches, add the carnitas and sear for 3 to 5 minutes on each side until the meat turns dark golden brown. Once ready, transfer to a serving bowl or platter. Season with salt to taste.

Serve the carnitas hot, in warm tortillas topped with salsa and the onion-cilantro mixture.

BABY BACK RIB CARNITAS Substitute 5 pounds (2.3 kg) baby back ribs for the pork butt.

CARNITAS LENTIL "STOUP"

A *stoup* is a fairly recent culinary term and is exactly what it sounds like: a cross between a soup and a stew. It is a perfect description of this hearty dish, for which I have also included a vegetarian variation. Lentils are an excellent source of plant-based protein, which makes either version of this stoup a healthy one-pot meal.

MAKES 8 TO 12 SERVINGS

In a large pot, heat the oil over medium heat. When the oil is hot, add the onions, carrots, leeks, garlic, and celery and stir to combine. Then add the thyme, cumin, curry powder, and tomato paste and mix well with the vegetables. Cook, stirring often, for 5 to 7 minutes, or until the vegetables begin to soften and the tomato paste darkens. Add the lentils, stock, and bay leaf, mix well, and bring to a simmer. Reduce the heat to low and cook, stirring occasionally, for 15 to 20 minutes, or until the lentils are tender but still have a bite.

Add the kale and carnitas, raise the heat to medium and bring to a simmer. Cook, lowering the heat if needed to maintain a simmer and stirring occasionally, for 10 to 15 minutes, or until the pork is heated through and the kale is tender.

Remove from the heat and season with salt and lime juice. Ladle into bowls and serve at once.

VEGETARIAN LENTIL "STOUP" For a vegetarian version of this soup, substitute vegetable stock for the chicken stock and omit the carnitas. Looking for a more unusual flavor combination? In Mexico, it is not uncommon to add chopped pineapple to lentil soup. For this recipe, I recommend stirring in ½ to 1 cup (85 to 165 g) chopped pineapple during the last 5 minutes of cooking.

INGREDIENTS

¼ cup (60 ml) olive oil, or ¼ cup (50 g) lard

2 yellow onions, diced

3 carrots, peeled and diced

2 leeks, white and tender green parts, diced

10 cloves garlic, minced

3 celery stalks, diced

Leaves from 10 fresh thyme sprigs, finely chopped

1 teaspoon ground cumin

1 teaspoon curry powder

3 tablespoons tomato paste

1 cup (200 g) black beluga lentils, picked over and rinsed

2 quarts (2 L) chicken stock

1 bay leaf

1 bunch dinosaur (Tuscan) kale, stems and ribs removed and leaves chopped

1 pound (455 g) carnitas, shredded (page 230)

Kosher salt

Fresh lime juice, for seasoning

BEEF TONGUE SALPICÓN
WITH MINT

The French cooking term *salpicon* refers to a combination of different minced ingredients bound together with a sauce, most typically used to stuff canapes. It is not clear how the word, or the recipe, migrated to Mexico. We know it had made it to the New World by the early nineteenth century, as *Novísimo arte de cocina*, a cookery book published in Mexico in 1831, includes salpicón de vaca (beef), a recipe it credits to late-medieval Spain. Today, some form of the dish is common across Latin America. In Mexico, the typical preparation is a shredded beef and potato salad, always served cold. For this recipe, I've chosen beef tongue because I love its tender texture and mild flavor.

INGREDIENTS

2 pounds (910 g) beef tongue

2 cloves garlic, crushed

½ Spanish white onion, cut into large chunks

2 to 3 chipotle meco chiles

1 teaspoon black peppercorns

Kosher salt

2 pounds (910 g) Bodega Red or other red potatoes, unpeeled and cut into ½-inch (12-mm) pieces

1 bunch green onions, white part only, sliced on the diagonal ¼ inch (6 mm) thick, or ½ cup (50 g) thinly sliced red onion

3 Early Girl or Roma tomatoes (6 ounces/171g total), preferably dry farmed, halved, seeded, and cut into ½-inch (12-mm) pieces

2 jalapeño chiles, seeds and veins removed and very thinly sliced crosswise

2 teaspoons minced fresh flat-leaf parsley

1½ to 2 cups (355 to 473 ml) Fig-Chipotle Vinaigrette (page 268), substituting fresh mint for the oregano

3 tablespoons fresh mint leaves (about 15), thinly sliced

4 medium avocados, pitted, peeled, and sliced

Freshly ground black pepper

Tostadas (page 28), for serving

MAKES 8 SERVINGS

In a large saucepan, combine the beef tongue, garlic, Spanish white onion, chipotle meco chiles, peppercorns, and 2 teaspoons salt and bring to a boil over medium-high heat. Reduce the heat to medium-low and simmer, occasionally skimming off any froth that forms on the surface, for 1½ to 2 hours, or until the tongues are tender when pierced with a knife tip.

Remove the pan from the heat and let the tongues cool in the cooking liquid just until they can be handled. Scoop the tongues out of the liquid and dry slightly with a kitchen towel. Reserve the cooking liquid. While the tongues are still warm, pull off and discard the skin and any bony parts. Set the tongues aside to cool.

Add the potatoes to the tongue cooking liquid, return the pan to medium-high heat, and bring to a boil. Reduce the heat to low and simmer for about 15 minutes, or until the potatoes are tender but still hold their shape; do not overcook. Drain the potatoes, discard the liquid (or strain and save for soup stock), and let the potatoes cool completely. Once cool, transfer the potatoes to a large bowl.

Cut the cooled tongues crosswise into slices ¼ inch (6 mm) thick or into medium dice, as you prefer. Add the tongues to the cooled potatoes along with green onions, tomatoes, jalapeño chiles, and parsley. Drizzle with the vinaigrette (you may not need all of it) and sprinkle with the mint and mix until all the ingredients are well combined, being careful not to break up the potatoes. Taste and adjust with more vinaigrette if needed. This is the salpicón.

To assemble, divide the avocado slices evenly among eight individual plates, then add a generous portion of the salpicón to each plate. Finish each serving with salt and pepper. Serve with tostadas.

WINE PAIRING Scalon Cellars 2018 Priority Red Blend is an energetic Bordeaux-style blend of Coombsville-grown cabernet sauvignon, merlot, and cabernet franc with notes of inky dark fruit, chocolate, licorice, and sweet spice.

MOLE XOCONOSTLE
WITH WAGYU BEEF

Moles are so special in Mexico that they are often served without any protein at all, accompanied by Frijoles de Olla (Clay Pot Beans, see page 260) and handmade tortillas. Even when served with a protein, the mole is the star of the dish. This is why I call this Mole Xoconostle with Wagyu Beef rather than the more expected Wagyu Beef with Mole Xoconostle. Xoconostle (pronounced choko-nose-leh) is a sour prickly pear cactus fruit, distinct from sweet prickly pears (or tunas, as they're called in Mexico). Their tangy, tart, citrus-like flavor is the perfect foil for Loco Tequila's Loco Ambar.

INGREDIENTS

For the mole:

4 green onions

5 cloves garlic

3 Roma tomatoes

2 cups (410 g) lard or clarified butter (page 269), plus more as needed

10 pasilla chiles, seeds and stems removed

10 guajillo chiles, seeds and stems removed

5 ancho chiles, seeds and stems removed

1 tablespoon raw hazelnuts

2 tablespoons raw almonds

2 tablespoons raw walnuts

2 tablespoons raw peanuts

¼ cup (35 g) raw pine nuts

10 pitted prunes

⅓ cup (50 g) raisins

5 dried xoconostle (dried prickly pears)

1 cinnamon stick (3 inches/7.5 cm)

1 star anise

1 banana, peeled

1 fresh hoja santa leaf or 1 fresh fennel frond

1 dried avocado leaf

⅓ Sourdough Telera roll (page 69) or other bread roll

1 corn tortilla, fried to create a tostada (page 28)

MAKES 8 SERVINGS

To make the mole, preheat the oven to 400°F (205°C).

Put the green onions, garlic, and tomatoes on a sheet pan and roast for 15 to 20 minutes, or until the tomatoes begin to bubble and collapse. Transfer the vegetables to a bowl and set aside.

In a large, deep sauté pan or other large, shallow, wide pot, melt 1 cup (205 g) of the lard over medium-low heat. When the fat is hot, add the pasilla, guajillo, and ancho chiles and bloom and toast, turning as needed, for 5 to 6 minutes, or until aromatic. Using a slotted spoon, transfer the chiles to the bowl with the roasted vegetables.

Add the hazelnuts, almonds, walnuts, and peanuts to the pan and toast, stirring occasionally, for 2 to 3 minutes, or until dark golden brown. Using the slotted spoon, transfer them to the bowl with the vegetables. Add the pine nuts to the pan and toast for 2 to 4 minutes, or until golden brown. Use the slotted spoon to transfer them to the bowl with the other ingredients. Finally, toast the sesame seeds. Watch them closely, and as soon as they start to jump, use the slotted spoon to transfer them to the bowl.

Add more lard if the pan seems dry, then add the prunes, raisins, and xoconostle and toast, stirring occasionally, for 2 to 5 minutes, or until the dried fruit starts to puff up. Using the slotted spoon, transfer them to the bowl.

Reduce the heat to low, add the cinnamon stick and star anise, and toast for about 1 minute, or until aromatic, then transfer to the bowl. Add the banana and toast, turning as needed, for 6 to 10 minutes, or until dark on all sides and gooey, then transfer to the bowl. Finally, add the hoja santa and avocado leaf to the pan and bloom for just 30 seconds, then transfer to the bowl.

Mix together the ingredients in the bowl, then transfer the mixture to a blender. You may need to blend the mole in two batches, depending on the size of your blender. Add the telera to the lard remaining in the pan and fry over medium-high heat, turning as needed, for 2 to 3 minutes, or until light golden brown, then add to blender along with the toasted tortilla. Blend the ingredients until a paste forms.

In a large cazuela or other wide, shallow, thick-bottomed pot, melt the remaining 1 cup (205 g) lard over medium-low heat. Add the mole paste and fry, stirring frequently, for 4 to 6 minutes, or until the color intensifies. Keep a splatter screen at hand as the mole base and lard tend to splatter.

Add the stock, sugar, and chocolate, stir well, and cook over medium-low heat, stirring occasionally, for 1 to 1½ hours, or until the mole has the consistency of a thick soup. Season with salt and remove from the heat. You should have about 2 quarts (2 L). Measure out about 1 quart (1 L) for this recipe. The remainder can be cooled and stored in an airtight container in the refrigerator for up to 2 weeks or in the freezer for up to 3 months.

Prepare a fire in a charcoal or gas grill for direct cooking over high heat. When the grill is ready, place the beef on the grill directly over the fire and grill, turning once, for 30 to 45 seconds on each side (for Wagyu beef, cooking time may be longer for other steaks), or until a thermometer inserted into the thickest part of the meat registers 125°F (52°C) for medium-rare, or until done to your liking. Remove from the grill and let rest for 5 to 10 minutes. While the beef rests, reheat the reserved mole and heat the tortillas on a preheated very hot comal or in a dry cast-iron pan.

To assemble, cut each piece of Wagyu in half. Put 2 tortillas on each of eight plates. Spoon ¼ cup (60 ml) of mole over each pair of tortillas. Place 1 piece of beef in the center of each tortilla. Finish with another ¼ cup (60 ml) of mole over both pieces of beef. Sprinkle with the black and white sesame seeds and garnish with the cilantro. Serve at once.

3 quarts (2.8 L) chicken stock

2 tablespoons sugar

1 Mexican chocolate tablet, preferably Rancho Gordo brand, coarsely chopped

Kosher salt

For the beef:

8 pieces Wagyu beef or NY strip steak, 4 ounces (115 g) each, or your preferred cut of beef

16 blue corn tortillas (page 24), or corn tortillas of choice

Black and white sesame seeds, toasted (see page 271), for garnish

2 cups (80 g) fresh micro cilantro or minced fresh regular cilantro

---

TEQUILA PAIRING Loco Ambar Tequila exhibits a measured complexity that is layered, elegant, and innovative. Bright, clean, and respectful of its Loco Blanco base, this limited production reposado is a sophisticated blend of four barrels, with notes of malt and roasted grains, nuts and sherry, and elegant vanilla and spice. The earthy tones of Loco Ambar pair well with charred or grilled foods, as well as dark chocolate and candied orange peel.

ROASTED BLACK SESAME MOLE RIB EYES

This Japanese mole is a tribute to my years at Cyrus in Geyserville, the first Michelin-starred restaurant I worked at and where I learned from Chef Douglas Keane about Japanese cuisine with its clean flavors and simple elegance. For this rich, dark mole, I use roasted sesame seeds, both black (kuro goma) and white (shiro goma), produced by Kuki, a Japanese company that has been in the sesame seed business since the 1880s. The seeds can be purchased in Japanese markets and online.

MAKES 8 TO 10 SERVINGS

To make the mole, in a large, shallow pot, heat the oil over medium-high heat. Add the guajillo chiles and toast and bloom, turning as needed, for 5 minutes, or until aromatic, making sure they don't burn. Then pull the chiles and set aside in a large bowl, leaving the oil in the pot. Reduce the heat to medium-low, add the green onion, garlic, and ginger and cook, stirring occasionally, for 2 to 4 minutes, or until aromatic. Using a slotted spoon, transfer to the bowl with the chiles. Add the peanuts to the same oil and toast, stirring occasionally, for 6 to 10 minutes, or until dark golden brown. Using the slotted spoon, transfer them to the bowl with the chiles and other seasonings.

Finally, reduce the heat to medium-low and add the white and black sesame seeds to the same oil. Watch them closely, and as soon as they start to jump, transfer them and the oil remaining in the pan to the bowl with the other ingredients.

Stir the ingredients in the bowl, mixing well, then transfer to a blender. Add the gochujang to the blender and blend until a paste forms. If the ingredients don't form a paste, don't worry, as the mole will be blended again at the end.

In a large cazuela or other wide, shallow pot, heat the lard over medium-low heat. Add the mole paste and fry, stirring, for 3 to 4 minutes, or until aromatic and toasted. Keep a splatter screen at hand as the mole base and lard tend to splatter. Add the stock, vinegar, soy sauce, and sugar and bring to a simmer. Reduce the heat to low and cook, stirring occasionally, for 1 to 1½ hours, or until it reaches the consistency of a thick pancake mix. Mole should coat the back of a wooden spoon.

Remove the pot from the heat, let cool for a few minutes, then transfer the mixture to a blender, add the chocolate, and blend until smooth. Add the lime juice and season with salt. You should have about 6 cups (1.4 L). Set aside until needed.

Prepare a wood-fired, charcoal, or gas grill for direct cooking over low heat. Salt the steaks on both sides. When the grill is ready, place the steaks directly over the fire and grill, turning once, for 5 to 10 minutes on each side for a rare to medium-rare finish. Transfer the steaks to a cutting board and let rest for 5 minutes. Reheat the mole.

To assemble, cut the steaks against the grain into slices 1 inch (2.5 cm) thick. Serve the meat either smothered in the mole or with the mole on the side. Garnish the mole with a mix of the white and black sesame seeds. Serve at once.

WINE PAIRING Bouchaine 2021 Pommard Clone Pinot Noir has medium to full-bodied notes of black cherries, dried herbs, and spices.

INGREDIENTS

For the roasted black sesame mole:

½ cup (120 ml) peanut oil

4 guajillo peppers, seeds and stems removed

6 tablespoons (25 g) thinly sliced green onion, white part only

2 tablespoons minced garlic

2 tablespoons peeled and minced fresh ginger

3 tablespoons peeled raw peanuts

3 tablespoons roasted white sesame seeds

3 tablespoons roasted black sesame seeds

¼ cup (90 g) gochujang (Korean chile paste)

½ cup (105 g) lard or clarified butter (page 269)

4 cups (960 ml) chicken stock or water

⅓ cup (75 ml) apple cider vinegar

2 tablespoons soy sauce

¼ cup (55 g) packed dark brown sugar

1 ounce (28 g) 70 percent cacao dark chocolate

Juice of 2 limes

Kosher salt

6 boneless rib eye steaks, 1 pound (455 g) each and 1 inch (2.5 cm) thick, preferably dry-aged 14 days

Kosher salt

Roasted white and black sesame seeds, for garnish

CHORIZO ALBÓNDIGAS

Meatballs stuffed with hard-boiled eggs can be found in cuisines around the world, from Morocco's kwari bilbeid in a spicy tomato sauce to India's nargisi kofta in curry to England's Scotch egg. In Mexico, meatballs are traditionally made with ground beef or pork or a combination and are almost never served without an egg in the center. In my variation of albóndigas, I mix in some of my homemade chorizo or Toluca green chorizo, which adds extra flavor to the meatballs. Here, I serve them in a shallow pool of tomato-chipotle soup. Albóndiguitas (little meatballs) for adding to soups and stews can be made with the same meat mixture (see variation below).

INGREDIENTS

1½ pounds (680 g) ground beef, preferably chuck

1 pound (455 g) traditional or Toluca green chorizo (page 213)

1 large egg, lightly beaten

1¼ cup (25 g) plain dried bread crumbs

6 hard-boiled eggs, peeled

Olive oil, for cooking

4 cups (960 ml) Tomato-Chipotle Stock (page 270)

½ cup (65 g) minced Spanish white onion mixed with ½ cup (20 g) chopped fresh cilantro

MAKES 6 LARGE ALBÓNDIGAS (6 SERVINGS)

In a large bowl, combine the ground beef, chorizo, raw egg, and bread crumbs and mix until all the ingredients are evenly blended.

Divide the meat mixture into 6 equal portions (6 to 7 ounces/170 to 200 g each). With a hard-boiled egg in the palm of your nondominant hand, use your dominant hand to wrap the egg with a portion of the meat mixture, enclosing the egg completely in an even layer of the mixture. Repeat with the remaining meat portions and eggs. Next, wrap each meatball with plastic wrap, twisting the top to seal it tightly closed. Place the wrapped meatballs in the freezer for 15 to 20 minutes. This step ensures the meatballs won't fall apart when you cook them.

Pour the oil to a depth of ½ inch (12 mm) into a large, wide saucepan and heat over medium-high heat. When the oil is hot, working in batches to avoid crowding, add the meatballs and sear, turning as needed, for about 1 minute on each side, or until nicely browned. When all the meatballs are browned, discard any oil remaining in the pan, return the pan to medium heat, and pour in the stock. Bring to a simmer, add the meatballs, and simmer for 15 to 20 minutes, or until the meatballs are cooked through.

To serve, cut each meatball in half to expose the beautiful hard-boiled egg in the center. Serve in rimmed soup bowls or pasta plates with a generous ladle of the soup. Garnish with the onion-cilantro mixture and serve at once.

CHORIZO ALBÓNDIGUITAS (MINI MEATBALLS) To make albóndiguitas, divide the meat mixture into 20 portions of about 2 ounces (55 g) each and shape each portion into a ball. (There is no need to wrap in plastic wrap and place in the freezer.) Pour enough oil into a large sauté pan to cover the bottom and heat over medium-high heat. When the oil is hot, add the meatballs and sear them, turning once, for about 30 seconds on each side, or until nicely browned. The meatballs are now ready to add to your favorite stock or soup, such as the Kale Soup with Toluca Green Chorizo Albóndiguitas (page 229). Just be sure to cook them at a boil for at least 10 minutes until they are cooked through.

If you wish to serve them as an appetizer, then continue cooking, turning occasionally, for 3 to 4 minutes longer, or until cooked through. Cut into one to check for doneness. Using a slotted spoon, transfer the albóndiguitas to a paper towel to drain any residual oil. Use them at your next cocktail party sprinkled with a little grated queso Cotija and served with the salsa of your choice. Albóndiguitas also freeze beautifully, cooked or raw.

MEXICAN "BOURGUIGNON" CHILE CON CARNE

This recipe is part of my repertoire of French-Mexican fusion cuisine known as la comida afrancesado. In this Mexican take on the French favorite, I've opted for a California pinot instead of a French burgundy for the requisite red wine. "Bourguignon" is also known as beef burgundy. The red wine and classic combination of pearl onions, mushrooms, and bacon lardons make it French, but the chiles and Mexican oregano, plus the option of thickening the stew with masa harina (in lieu of making a roux) make it Mexican.

MAKES 6 TO 8 SERVINGS

Dry roast the guajillo and ancho chiles on a comal, then rehydrate, as directed on page 271. Add the chiles to a blender along with the stock and blend until smooth. Set aside.

In a large Dutch oven or other large heavy pot, heat the oil over medium-high heat. Add the lardons to the pot and cook over medium heat, stirring occasionally, for about 2 minutes, or until they begin to render their fat and are browned. Using a slotted spoon, transfer the lardons to a bowl and set aside.

Working in batches to avoid crowding, add the short ribs to the pot and sear, turning once, for 3 to 4 minutes on each side, or until nicely browned. Transfer the seared short ribs to a plate and set aside, leaving the fat in the pot.

Add the onion, garlic, mushrooms, and carrots to the pot and cook, stirring occasionally, for about 3 minutes, or until they begin to soften. Add the tomato paste, masa harina, cumin, paprika, black pepper, and oregano and stir to combine. Pour in the wine, reduce the heat to medium, and deglaze the pot, stirring to scrape up any browned bits from the pot bottom, then cook for 1 minute.

Return the seared short ribs to the pot, then pour the chile stock over the short ribs. Add the bay leaf and salt and bring the mixture to a simmer. Reduce the heat to low, cover, and cook for about 3 hours, or until a knife slides easily in and out of the meat. Uncover, add the potatoes, and continue to cook, uncovered, for 10 to 15 minutes, or until the potatoes are fork-tender.

If you prefer a thicker sauce, spoon a little of the cooking liquid into a small bowl, stir in 1 tablespoon masa harina until dissolved, and then stir the mixture back into the pot and simmer until the sauce is thickened to your liking.

To serve, spoon the braise into individual bowls and finish with one or more of the suggested toppings. Serve at once.

NOTE To braise the short ribs in the oven, once the seared ribs are returned to the pot, you can finish cooking the meat in the covered pot in a preheated 300°F (150°C) oven for about 3 hours.

INGREDIENTS

1 dried guajillo chile, stems and seeds removed

1 dried ancho chile, stems and seeds removed

2 cups (480 ml) beef stock

2 tablespoons canola oil

6 slices thick-cut bacon, cut into lardons ¼ inch (6 mm) thick and 1 inch (2.5 cm) long

4 pounds (1.8 kg) boneless short ribs, cut into 2-inch (5-cm) pieces

1 pound (455 g) fresh pearl onions, blanched and peeled, or frozen pearl onions, or 1 yellow onion, finely diced

3 cloves garlic, finely chopped

½ pound (225 g) cremini mushrooms, cut into quarters lengthwise

10 baby carrots, peeled

2 tablespoons tomato paste

1 tablespoon yellow masa harina, preferably Masienda brand, plus more if needed

1 teaspoon ground cumin

1 teaspoon paprika

½ teaspoon freshly ground black pepper

½ teaspoon dried Mexican oregano

1 cup (240 ml) dry red wine

1 bay leaf

1 tablespoon coarse sea salt

8 fingerling potatoes

Shredded Monterey Jack cheese, crema, diced red onion, sliced green onions, chopped fresh cilantro, and/ or fresh lime juice, for topping

DUCK LEG QUESABIRRIA
WITH DUCK FAT TORTILLAS

Quesabirria was originally made with goat, but nowadays, it is more usual to find it made with beef. The birria part of the name refers to a smoky, tangy stew with a hint of sweetness and, of course, some heat. It is paired with cheese—the queso part of the name—in a folded tortilla, toasted on a hot comal, and accompanied with broth for dipping. In this recipe, I use Liberty Duck legs from Sonoma County Poultry, cook them birria-style, and then combine the meat with melty queso Oaxaca on homemade tortillas made with duck fat.

INGREDIENTS

3 tablespoons olive oil

6 duck legs, preferably Liberty Duck

4 guajillo peppers, seeds and stems removed

4 ancho chiles, seeds and stems removed

2 yellow onions, cut into medium dice

10 cloves garlic

6 Roma tomatoes, cut into quarters

2 quarts (2 L) duck stock or chicken stock

1 cup (240 ml) fresh orange juice

1 teaspoon cumin seeds, toasted and ground (see page 271)

1 teaspoon dried Mexican oregano

1 cinnamon stick (3 inches/7.5 cm)

Kosher salt

12 ounces (340 g) Basic Masa from Masa Harina (page 24), made with duck fat

12 ounces (340 g) queso Oaxaca, pulled into strips

1 bunch fresh cilantro, roughly chopped

MAKES 6 SERVINGS

Preheat an oven to 300°F (150°C).

In a large Dutch oven or other large pot, heat the oil over medium heat. When the oil is hot, working in batches if needed to avoid crowding, add the duck legs skin side down and sear for 5 to 7 minutes, or until the skin is golden brown. Flip the legs and sear on the meaty side for 3 to 5 minutes, or until golden brown. (You can press against the legs with a bacon press or metal spatula to make sure they make good contact with the pan.) Transfer the legs to a plate, leaving the fat in the pot. Add the guajillo and ancho chiles, onions, garlic, and tomatoes to the pot and cook, stirring occasionally, for 10 to 15 minutes, or until the vegetables are softened and golden brown. Pour in a little of the stock and deglaze the pot, stirring to scrape up any browned bits from the pot bottom. Remove the pot from the heat.

Using a slotted spoon, transfer the vegetables to a blender and blend until smooth. Return the puréed vegetables to the pot along with the duck legs, the remaining stock, the orange juice, cumin, oregano, and cinnamon and season with salt. Cover the pot, transfer to the oven, and braise the duck legs for 2 to 3 hours, or until the meat is tender and falls off the bone easily when gently pulled.

Remove the pot from the oven, transfer the duck legs to a plate, and let cool for an hour or so to room temperature. Strain the braising liquid into a small saucepan and set aside. When the legs are cool, remove and discard the skin and bones, then shred the meat and set aside to keep warm.

Using the masa made with duck fat, make and cook six tortillas according to the recipe on page 25. Each tortilla should be 5 to 6 inches (12 to 15 cm) in diameter.

To assemble, top a tortilla with about 3 ounces (85 g) of the shredded duck meat, 2 ounces (55 g) of the cheese, and a sprinkle of cilantro, then fold the tortilla in half. Place a dry comal or cast-iron skillet over medium-high heat. At the same time, heat the braising broth until hot. When the comal is hot, working in batches to avoid crowding, add the folded tortillas and cook for about 1 minute, or until golden brown and the cheese is melting. Flip and cook for about 30 seconds more, or until golden brown on the second side. It will help to use a bacon press to ensure good contact between the tortilla and the comal.

Serve the hot, filled tortillas in a basket, family-style. Ladle the warm braising broth into wide deep bowls, one for each diner to dunk the filled quesabirria tortillas into.

HUEVOS MOTULEÑOS
WITH SMOKED DUCK AND MUSHROOMS A LA CAZUELITA

Huevos motuleños—tortillas topped with beans, salsa, ham, cheese, and fried eggs—are named for the town of Motul, Yucatán, where an annual festival is held to celebrate the dish. In July 2018, an article in *Yucatán Magazine* put forth two different origin stories, both with a Lebanese connection. One credited Lebanese-Yucatec chef Jorge Siqueff, who, according to Evelia Sánchez, a Mayan cook from Motul, created it in the early 1920s to serve to Governor Felipe Carrillo Puerto, Diego Rivera, and other important figures of that time. The second account points to Carlos Saidén Isaac, another Yucatecan chef of Lebanese origin, who reported in 1990 that he and chef Olegario Katún created the dish for Governor Álvaro Torre Díaz, who served from 1926 to 1930.

The traditional method calls for fried eggs. I've reinterpreted the recipe with shirred eggs, which are easier to prepare for a crowd, as you just pop the ramekins into the oven.

MAKES 8 SERVINGS

Preheat the oven to 375°F (190°C).

In a small skillet, melt the butter over medium heat. Add the mushrooms and cook, stirring occasionally, for 2 to 3 minutes, or until they release their natural juices. Remove the skillet from the heat and let cool.

In a bowl, combine the duck breast, Jack cheese, Swiss chard, crema, and cooked mushrooms and stir until well mixed.

Grease eight ½-cup (120-ml) ramekins, using 1 tablespoon butter for each ramekin, and place them on a sheet pan. Cover the bottom of each greased ramekin with 1 tablespoon of the refried beans. Distribute the mushroom mixture evenly among the ramekins (a small ladle works well for this step). Crack an egg into each ramekin.

Transfer the sheet pan to the oven and bake the ramekins for 10 to 15 minutes, or until the white of the eggs is opaque and firm and the yolk remains soft and runny. Add more time if you prefer a firmer egg yolk.

Remove from the oven and top each ramekin with an equal amount of the salsa, queso fresco, and cilantro. Serve at once with the tortillas.

INGREDIENTS

3 tablespoons salted butter, plus ½ cup (115 g) at room temperature for the ramekins

½ cup (50 g) chopped lobster mushrooms

½ cup (30 g) chopped cremini mushrooms (see Note, page 54)

½ pound (225 g) smoked duck breast, preferably Liberty Duck brand, or Canadian bacon, cut into small dice

½ cup (55 g) shredded pepper Jack cheese

½ cup (75 g) chopped Swiss chard, blanched

¼ cup (60 ml) crema or sour cream

½ cup (130 g) refried beans (page 260)

8 extra-large eggs

½ cup (120 ml) Salsa a la Diabla (page 262)

8 ounces (225 g) queso fresco, crumbled

½ bunch fresh cilantro, minced

Corn tortillas (at least 2 per diner), warmed (page 25)

PORCHETTA STUFFED
WITH MEXICAN FORBIDDEN RICE AND CHORIZO

This recipe brings together elements of three great cuisines: Forbidden rice, a nutty, nutrient-rich purple-black variety with a chewy texture, has long been part of the Chinese diet. Porchetta, herb-scented rolled roasted pork with crackling skin, is a specialty of central Italy. Mexican adobo, a heady mixture of chiles, tomatoes, vinegar, and spices used as both a marinade and sauce, is widely paired with meats of all kinds. Here, I stuff rolled pork belly with the rice and adobo and then slowly roast it until it develops the hallmark crisp, flavorful skin of the Italian classic. You will need to start this recipe a full day before you plan to serve it, as the pork is brined before roasting.

INGREDIENTS

For the brined pork belly:

1 cup (240 ml) agave nectar

1 cup (240 ml) maple syrup

1 cup (140 g) kosher salt

1½ tablespoons fennel seeds, toasted (see page 271)

1½ tablespoons coriander seeds, toasted (see page 271) and crushed

1½ tablespoons black peppercorns, cracked

1½ teaspoons red chile flakes, toasted (see page 271)

2 gallons (8 L) ice

1 head garlic, cut in half and bruised

4 fresh sage sprigs, bruised

1 fresh rosemary sprig, bruised

1 bay leaf

1 rectangular slab skin-on pork belly, 5 to 6 pounds (2.3 to 2.7 kg)

For the black rice:

1 tablespoon olive oil

½ yellow onion, cut into small dice

2 cloves garlic, minced

1 cup (180 g) forbidden black rice

1½ teaspoons tomato paste

½ cup (120 ml) dry white wine

2 Roma tomatoes, puréed in a blender

3 cups (720 ml) chicken stock

Grated zest and juice of 1 lemon

Kosher salt

MAKES 8 TO 10 SERVINGS

To make the brined pork belly, in a large pot, combine 4 quarts (3.8 L) water, the agave nectar, maple syrup, salt, fennel seeds, coriander seeds, black peppercorns, and red chile flakes and stir to mix well. Place over high heat and bring to a boil, then remove the pot from the heat and add the ice to cool the brine quickly.

Once the brine is cold, add the garlic, sage, rosemary, and bay leaf. Then add the pork belly, cover, and refrigerate for 24 hours.

When the pork belly is ready to come out of the brine, make the rice. In a saucepan, heat the oil over medium heat. Add the onion and garlic and cook, stirring occasionally, for 2 to 3 minutes, or until the onion begins to soften. Add the rice and toast, stirring often, for 4 to 5 minutes, or until a nutty aroma can be detected. Add the tomato paste, stir to combine, and cook the rice and tomato paste, stirring, for 1 to 2 minutes. Pour in the wine and cook, stirring frequently, until the liquid is reduced by half. Stir in the puréed tomatoes and continue to cook, stirring, until reduced by half. Add 1 cup (240 ml) of the stock, reduce the heat to medium-low, and stir gently until almost all the liquid has been absorbed. Pour in 1 more cup (240 ml) of the stock and continue cooking, stirring gently, until almost all the liquid has been absorbed. Repeat the same step with the final 1 cup (240 ml) of stock. When all the liquid has been absorbed and the rice is tender, after 30 to 35 minutes, remove the pan from the heat and season the rice with the lemon zest and juice and salt. Some rice takes longer to cook; if needed add ½ cup (120 ml) extra of stock or water and cook until the rice is done. Transfer the cooked rice to a sheet pan, spread it out, and let cool to room temperature.

Preheat the oven to 400°F (205°C). Place a wire rack on a sheet pan.

CONTINUED...

For the porchetta:

2 cups (480 ml) Adobo Marinade (page 259)

1 pound (455 g) chorizo, homemade (page 213) or store-bought

Olive oil, for drizzling

Kosher salt

Remove the pork belly from the brine and dry well with a kitchen towel. Discard the brine.

To assemble the porchetta, lay the pork belly skin side down on a clean work surface. Spread a thin layer of the adobo marinade evenly over the top. Spread the cooled rice over the adobo layer. Now, arrange a tube-like line of the chorizo down the center of the rice layer, leaving 2 inches (5 cm) uncovered at each end of the pork belly and 1 inch (2.5 cm) uncovered along both sides. As you roll, the pork belly, the chorizo will squeeze out slightly, and these borders will keep it from escaping. Starting from a long side, roll up the pork belly, forming a snug roulade. Using kitchen twine, tie tightly at regular intervals along the length to secure the roll in place. Coat the outside of the rolled belly with a thin layer of adobo, then transfer the porchetta, seam side down, to the rack on the sheet pan.

Drizzle the porchetta with oil and sprinkle with salt. Roast for 1 hour, then adjust the oven control to 300°F (150°C) and continue to roast for 3 to 4 hours, or until a thermometer inserted into the center of the roll registers 160°F (71°C).

Remove from the oven and let rest for 30 minutes before clipping the twine and slicing.

WINE PAIRING Hoopes Vineyard Rosé is made predominantly from cabernet, giving it depth and texture. Punctuated with strawberry and lighter red fruit, this wine pairs well with the spices of the chorizo and chile, while also embracing the sweet aspects infused during the brining process.

CASSOULET WITH CABRITO, EYE OF THE GOAT BEANS, AND ALBÓNDIGUITAS

While not widely eaten in the US, goat is actually one of the most widely consumed meats in the world. This may be because goat has a reputation for having a strong, gamey flavor, but goats raised with care and fed well have a surprisingly mild taste. A successful cassoulet—one with a crusty top concealing creamy beans in a rich broth with duck, pork, or other protein—needs the right cooking vessel. French cooks use a cassole, an ovenproof clay pot with sloping sides and a broad top to ensure a crispy crust develops. Fortunately, some Mexican clay cazuelas have this shape. Or a large Dutch oven will work. In a departure from the French recipe, I use locally grown young goat (cabrito) for the protein. It comes from the family-owned Rossotti Ranch, which raises grass-fed goats and cattle in Sonoma and Marin Counties.

MAKES 6 TO 8 SERVINGS

If you are using chorizo in casings, remove and discard the casings. Divide the meat mixture into 6 to 8 portions and shape each portion into a ball. Cover and refrigerate until needed. If using andouille, cut them in half just before searing.

Preheat the oven to 300°F (150°C). While the oven preheats, into a molcajete and using a tejolote, work the onions, garlic, bell peppers, and cascabel and ancho chiles to a paste. Set the paste aside.

Place a cassole or other ovenproof vessel over medium-high heat and add the oil. Dry the goat leg well and season all over with salt. Add the goat leg to the hot oil and sear, turning once, until golden brown, 3 to 5 minutes on each side. Transfer to a plate.

Reduce the heat to medium and add the bacon and the albóndiguitas. Cook, stirring the bacon and turning the albóndiguitas as needed, for about 3 to 5 minutes, or until the bacon has rendered most of its fat and begins to crisp up and the albóndiguitas are seared on all sides. If using andouille sausages, turn to color on all sides.

Pour in the port and deglaze the pot, stirring to scrape up any browned bits from the pot bottom, then cook until the liquid is reduced by half. Add the broth, onion-chiles paste, paprika, and bay leaf and stir to mix well, then bring to a simmer and remove from the heat.

Place the seared goat leg in the center of the cassole and arrange the bacon and albóndiguitas or sausages evenly around it. Drain the beans and add them around the goat leg, distributing them evenly and making sure they are covered with the liquid. Cover the pot with a lid or aluminum foil and transfer to the oven. Braise for 3 to 4 hours, or until the goat meat shreds easily and the beans are tender. Most of the liquid should be absorbed and the top would look slightly dry and crackly.

When the cassoulet is ready, remove the cassole from the oven and break the almost-crusty top open with a spoon. Shred some of the leg meat and mix it in with the beans and albóndiguitas or sausages. Serve with tortillas alongside for sopping up the juices.

INGREDIENTS

1 pound (455 g) chorizo, homemade (page 213) or purchased, or 4 andouille sausages (about 12 ounces/340 g), cut in half

2 yellow onions, cut into large dice

10 cloves garlic, minced

5 red bell peppers, cut into large dice

5 cascabel chiles, dry roasted (see page 271), seeds and stems removed

3 ancho chiles, dry roasted (see page 271), seeds and stems removed

2 tablespoons canola oil

1 young goat leg, about 5 pounds (2.3 kg)

Kosher salt

1 pound (455 g) bacon, cut into large dice

1 cup (240 ml) port wine

4½ cups (1 L) chicken bone broth or chicken stock

2 teaspoons smoked paprika

1 bay leaf

2½ cups (465 g) dried Rancho Gordo Eye of the Goat beans, or dried flageolet or cannellini beans, soaked overnight in water to cover

Corn tortillas (page 25), for serving

OVEN-BRAISED PORK BELLY
WITH SWEET ONIONS, APPLES, AND MEXICAN CHOCOLATE

What makes an onion sweet? Sulfur is what gives onions their pungent, sharp flavor. Grown in sulfur-poor soil, sweet onions have half—or even less than half—the usual amount of sulfur, which means their natural sugars can shine. Any sweet onion variety, such as California Sweet, Vidalia, Walla Walla, or Maui, can be used for this recipe. This tender, flavorful pork belly can be diced and used as a taco filling along with a little of its braising liquid, cut into large dice for a casserole, or sliced and served with a side of my Marigold–White Sweet Potato Tortitas with Tomatillo Applesauce (page 103).

MAKES 10 TO 12 SERVINGS

To make the pork belly cure, in a small bowl, combine all the ingredients and mix well.

Lay the pork belly fat side up on a sheet pan. Using a sharp knife, score the fat side in a crisscross pattern, making finger-size diamonds. Spread the cure evenly over both sides of the pork belly. Cover the pan with plastic wrap and refrigerate for 24 hours.

After 24 hours, lightly rinse the pork belly with cool running water and pat dry with a kitchen towel. Preheat the oven to 300°F (150°C).

Place the pork belly, fat side up, in a large baking pan or dish. Surround the pork with the onions, apples, ancho chiles, fennel, lard, cider, and chocolate, distributing them evenly and making sure not to cover the fat side. Transfer the pan to the oven and braise, uncovered, for 4 to 6 hours, or until the meat is tender and the fat has turned crispy and golden brown.

Remove from the oven and let rest for 5 minutes, then cut and serve as suggested in the headnote or as you like.

WINE PAIRING Elusa 2019 Calistoga Cabernet Sauvignon is a vibrant wine with a savory finish, a nose of red currant and plum, and notes of tobacco and graphite.

INGREDIENTS

For the pork belly cure:

⅓ cup (45 g) kosher salt

3 tablespoons packed dark brown sugar

2 tablespoons granulated sugar

1 tablespoon grated Mexican chocolate, preferably Rancho Gordo brand

1 teaspoon pink curing salt no. 1

1 teaspoon freshly ground black pepper

1 teaspoon ground cinnamon

1 teaspoon fennel seeds

1 teaspoon sweet paprika

1 rectangular slab pork belly, 5 to 6 pounds (2.3 to 2.7 kg), skin removed

4 sweet onions, preferably California Sweet, cut into quarters with the core intact

3 Granny Smith apples, halved and cored

3 ancho chiles

2 fennel bulbs, tops removed and cut into sixths lengthwise

3 cups (615 g) lard, melted

3 cups (720 ml) apple cider

¼ cup (35 g) grated Mexican chocolate, preferably Rancho Gordo brand

FRIED CHICKEN TACOS
WITH SALSA VERDE CRUDA

If possible, seek out a source of heritage chicken—the poultry world equivalent of an heirloom vegetable—for this recipe. The meat of these older breeds has a deeper flavor and better texture than their more modern hybrid chicken kin. Marinating the chicken in a mixture of citrus juices, vinegar, garlic, and soy, and then dredging it in buttermilk, egg, and seasoned flour before deep-frying it to a crisp, golden finish brings out all that delicious flavor of these special birds. Have your tortillas and fixings all ready to go so the chicken is piping hot when you take that first bite of a taco.

MAKES 6 SERVINGS

In a bowl large enough to hold the chicken, combine the lime juice, vinegar, orange juice, soy sauce, and garlic and mix well.

Cut the chicken thighs into pieces about 1 inch (2.5 cm) long and ½ inch (12 mm) thick. Add to the bowl with the citrus juice mixture, turn to coat well, cover, and marinate in the refrigerator for 2 to 4 hours.

Line up three medium bowls. Pour the buttermilk into the first bowl. Crack the eggs into the second bowl and beat lightly with a fork until blended. Put the flour, salt, onion powder, garlic powder, and paprika into the third bowl and stir with a fork until well mixed.

Have ready a large plate or sheet pan. Remove the chicken from the marinade. One at a time, dip the chicken pieces into the buttermilk, allowing the excess to drip off, and then into the eggs, again letting the excess drip off. Lastly, dredge in the flour mixture, coating well and tapping off the excess. As the pieces are coated, set them aside on the plate.

To deep-fry the chicken, pour the oil to a depth of about 2 inches (5 cm) into a deep pot (no more than half full) and heat to 325° to 335°F (165° to 170°C). (Alternatively, heat a deep fryer.) Line a sheet pan with paper towels and set it near the stove.

When the oil is ready, working in batches to avoid crowding, add the chicken and fry, turning once halfway through the cooking time, for about 8 minutes, or until golden brown and cooked through. Using tongs or a slotted spoon, transfer the chicken to the paper towels to drain and season immediately with salt. Keep warm. The temperature of the oil is crucial. If the oil is too hot, the crust will darken too quickly and the meat will be undercooked. If the temperature is too low, the crust will be soggy. Always check the temperature of the oil before adding a batch of chicken.

Have the tortillas ready, reheating them right before serving if needed. To assemble each taco, spoon some curtido onto a tortilla, top with the crispy chicken, and finish with the salsa. Serve at once.

INGREDIENTS

½ cup (120 ml) fresh lime juice

½ cup (120 ml) rice vinegar

½ cup (120 ml) fresh orange juice

1½ teaspoons soy sauce

1 clove garlic, minced

6 boneless, skinless chicken thighs

2 cups (480 ml) buttermilk

4 large eggs

3 cups (375 g) all-purpose flour

1 tablespoon kosher salt

1 teaspoon onion powder

1 teaspoon garlic powder

1 teaspoon paprika

Canola oil, for deep-frying

6 to 12 corn tortillas (page 25)

¾ cup (165 g) Fennel Curtido (page 259)

¾ cup (180 ml) Salsa Verde Cruda (page 265)

FEATURED MENU:
NORTH AMERICAN THANKSGIVING

Thanksgiving memories for me are full of laughter, food, and music. My mother would start prepping the day before and finish cooking midday. She would have the refrigerator full and all the burners going on the stove. She would always give us a mordida (a bite) of whatever she was cooking, so my brother and I could check for flavor. It was amazing—and we knew we would have enough food to last for days. When we all sat down to eat the food she had made and she finally had time to sit down and eat, we would all have such a great time. Music would begin playing, and she would invite me to dance with her. I would stumble and step on her feet as she would guide me step-by-step to the music. This was my Thanksgiving as a child.

These days, I cook Thanksgiving dinner myself, and I like to get creative with it. In fact, serving an alternative to turkey is an easy way to be innovative and create a nontraditional meal. My North American Thanksgiving menu celebrates our geographic and culinary connections and features roasted quail instead of turkey, a Patatas Bravas Mexicanas with Crema and Cilantro (page 87) instead of mashed potatoes, and the sweet potatoes show up as one of my favorite childhood desserts, Camote en Leche with Candied Spiced Pecans (page 143). Paired with some outstanding wines from my friends at Hoopes Vineyards and finished with a Mexican version of Irish coffee, this feast is as memorable as it is delicious.

NORTH AMERICAN THANKSGIVING MENU

Poblano Vichyssoise with Huitlacoche Crème Fraîche and Toasted Hazelnuts 138

Roasted Stuffed Quail With Madeira-Quince Sauce and Tomato-Onion Confit 255

Broccolini and Spinach Tortitas with Fresh Salsa Verde with Peas and Mint 88

Patatas Bravas Mexicanas with Crema and Cilantro 87

Savory Herbed Teleras Bread Pudding 257

Camote en Leche with Candied Spiced Pecans 143

Mexican "Irish" Coffee 261

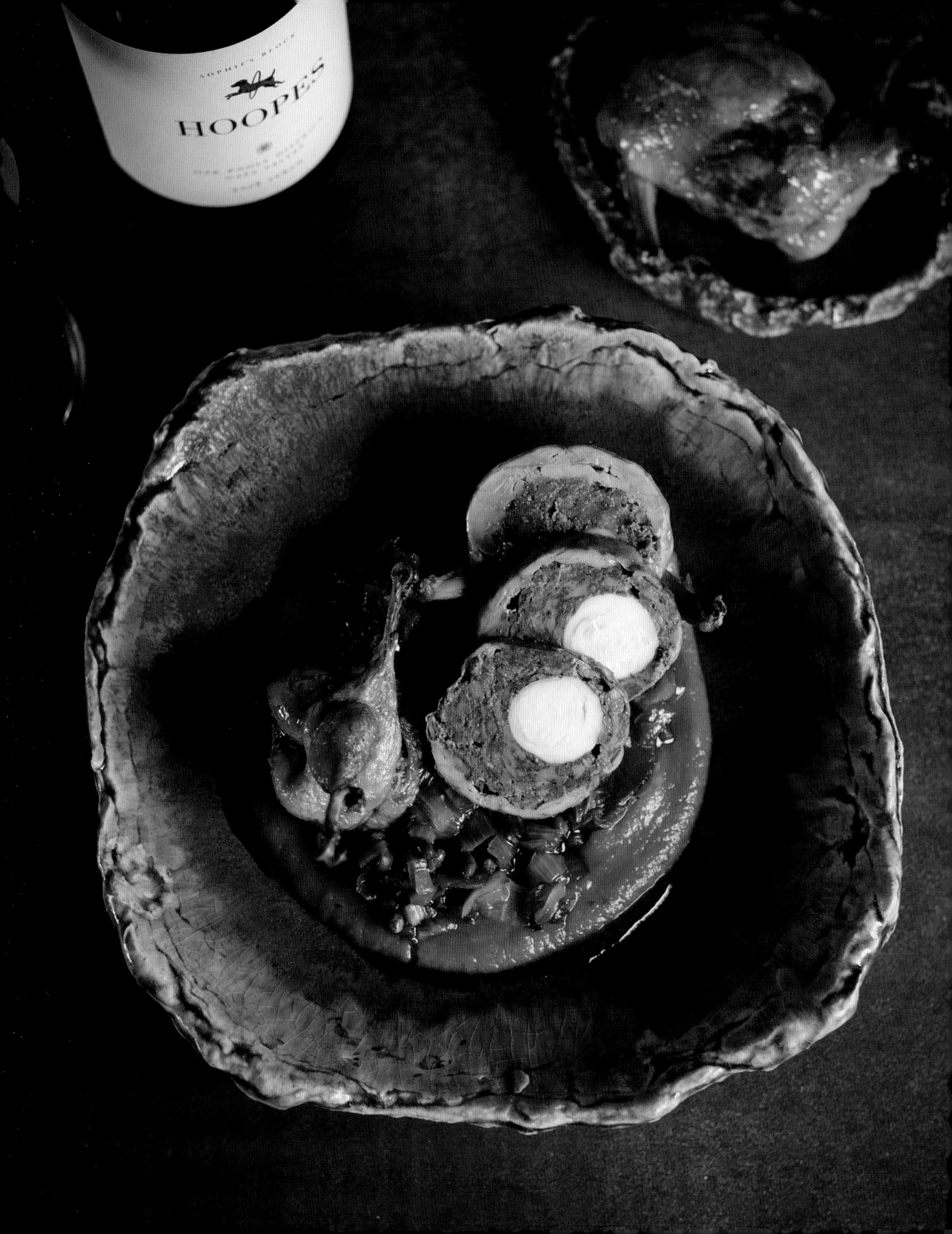
SOPHIE'S BLOCK
HOOPES

ROASTED STUFFED QUAIL
WITH MADEIRA-QUINCE SAUCE AND TOMATO-ONION CONFIT

Quail is typically more tender than chicken meat and is known for being very moist when prepared correctly. But because quail is much smaller than chicken, it's easier to overcook, so I brine the quail to ensure they come out perfectly. For fun—and because it makes a wonderful presentation—I've made this a double-quail dish, with a hard-boiled quail egg sealed inside the lamb meatball slipped into the cavity of each bird. The Madeira-quince sauce and the tomato-onion confit not only complement the quail, they play nicely off of each other and the lamb, adding a sweet tanginess to the finished dish—like cranberry sauce for turkey, a perfect pairing.

MAKES 12 SERVINGS

Add the quail to the poultry brine, making sure they are submerged in the brine. Cover and refrigerate for 4 to 6 hours (but no longer, or the birds will be too salty).

To make the tomato-onion confit, preheat the oven to 300°F (150°C). Bring a large pot of water to a boil over high heat. Prepare an ice bath and set aside. Cut a shallow X on the bottom of each tomato and set them aside. Once the water boils, add the tomatoes to the water in batches to avoid crowding, and cook for 20 to 30 seconds, just long enough to loosen the skin. Using a slotted spoon or kitchen spider, transfer the tomatoes to the ice batch. Gently peel the tomatoes by pulling the skin from the sides with the incision. Cut the tomatoes in half lengthwise and remove the seeds, making sure not to damage the tomatoes.

Line the tomatoes, cut side up, in a baking dish, and add a pinch of garlic and salt to each cavity. Drizzle the tomatoes with ½ cup (120 ml) olive oil and sprinkle with half of the thyme leaves. Cook for 1 hour, then gently flip the tomatoes and continue to cook for 45 to 50 minutes longer, or until the tomatoes are soft but not mushy and become a bit flat. Sprinkle the capers over the tomatoes and drizzle with ¼ cup (60 ml) olive oil. Continue cooking for 10 to 15 minutes, or until the capers are warm. Remove the baking dish from the oven and set aside.

Increase the oven temperature to 400°F (205°C). In another baking dish, combine the onions with the remaining ¼ cup (60 ml) olive oil and the remaining thyme leaves. Season with salt and plenty of pepper and toss to combine. Roast the onions for 20 to 25 minutes, stirring once halfway through cooking, until they are soft and take on a golden color. Stir in the vinegar and continue to cook for 5 minutes longer. Combine the onions with the tomato mixture and adjust the seasoning to taste. (Makes about 2 cups/400 g confit. The confit can be stored in the refrigerator for about 1 week or in the freezer for up to 2 months.)

To make the Madeira-quince sauce, fill a bowl with water and add the lemon juice. Lay a damp kitchen towel under your cutting board to prevent it from sliding as you cut the quinces. One at a time, wipe off the fuzzy exterior of each quince. Then, using

CONTINUED...

INGREDIENTS

For the quail:

12 quail, preferably semiboneless

12-Hour Poultry Brine (page 270)

2½ pounds (1.2 kg) ground lamb

1 raw egg, lightly beaten

2 tablespoons plain dried bread crumbs

1 clove garlic, finely chopped

2 tablespoons finely chopped fresh epazote or mint

12 hard-boiled quail eggs, peeled

Olive oil, for brushing

For the tomato-onion confit:

4 pounds (1.8 kg; about 10) ripe Roma tomatoes

5 cloves garlic, minced

Kosher salt and freshly ground pepper

1 cup (240 ml) extra-virgin olive oil

Leaves from 8 sprigs fresh thyme

½ cup (55 g) capers, drained

2 medium sweet onions, such as California Sweet, Vidalia, Walla Walla, or Maui, chopped

1 tablespoon balsamic vinegar

For the Madeira-quince sauce:

Juice of 1½ lemons

3 quinces (2½ to 3 pounds/1.2 to 1.4 kg) or very green (unripe) pears

6 tablespoons (85 g) unsalted butter

1 guajillo chile, stem and seeds removed

¾ cup (95 g) finely diced onion

3 fresh thyme sprigs

½ bay leaf

¾ cup (180 ml) Madeira wine or brandy

3 tablespoons grated piloncillo (see page 274) or more if needed

Kosher salt

For the albóndigas:

2½ pounds (1.2 kg) ground lamb

1 large egg, lightly beaten

¼ cup (25 g) unflavored bread crumbs

½ onion, chopped

1 clove minced garlic

2 tablespoons chopped epazote or fresh mint leaves

12 hard-boiled quail eggs, peeled

Light olive oil, for searing

a vegetable peeler, peel the quinces, cut them into quarters, and remove and discard the seeds. Cut the quinces into 1-inch (2.5-cm) pieces and add to the lemon water as you work to prevent oxidation. Set the bowl near the stove.

In a saucepan, melt the butter over medium heat. Add the guajillo chile and cook, turning once or twice, for about 1 minute, or until aromatic. Add the onion and stir to combine. Using a slotted spoon, transfer the quince pieces to the saucepan (discard the lemon water). Add the thyme, bay leaf, Madeira, ½ cup (120 ml) water, and the piloncillo to the pan and stir to combine with the fruit and onion. Reduce the heat to low, cover with a tight-fitting lid, and cook, stirring occasionally, for 45 to 60 minutes, or until the quince pieces are very soft when pierced with a fork. If the liquid reduces too much before the quinces are ready, add a bit more water.

Remove the pan from the heat and discard the thyme sprigs and bay leaf. Let cool slightly, then transfer the contents of the pan to a blender and blend until smooth. Season with salt. If the quinces were very tart, add a little more sugar. (The sauce can be stored in an airtight container in the refrigerator for up to 1 week.)

Remove the quail from the brine, pat dry with a towel, and set aside. Discard the brine.

To make the albóndigas, in a bowl, combine the ground lamb, egg, bread crumbs, onion, garlic, and epazote and mix until the ingredients are evenly blended. Divide the mixture into 12 equal portions. With a hard-boiled quail egg in the palm of your nondominant hand, use your dominant hand to wrap the egg with a portion of the meat mixture, enclosing the egg completely in an even layer of the mixture. Repeat with the remaining meat portions and eggs. Add enough olive oil to a sauté pan to cover the bottom and place over medium-high heat. When the oil is hot, add the albóndigas and cook, turning frequently, until the albóndigas are browned all over, 2 to 3 minutes. Stuff the cavity of each quail with an egg-stuffed albóndiga.

Preheat the oven to 425°F (220°C). Set a large wire rack on a sheet pan.

Truss the stuffed quail, using a section of kitchen twine about four times the length of the body. First, form a loop that you will fasten around the stub of the neck. Next, wrap the sides of the body, knotting the twine at the cavity and pulling it tight around the breast. The last step is to fasten the legs close to the rest of the bird by looping the twine around them, finishing with another knot, and tightening so the legs cross.

Brush the quail all over with oil. Set them, breast side up, on the rack on the sheet pan. Roast for 15 to 20 minutes, or until a thermometer inserted into the thickest part of a quail away from bone registers 145°F (63°C). Remove from the oven and let rest for 5 to 7 minutes for the internal juices to settle.

To assemble, using poultry shears, carefully cut each quail in half lengthwise. Then, using a sharp knife, cut each albóndiga in half, cutting through the quail egg so that an egg half rests in each albóndiga half. Serve with the Madeira-quince sauce and tomato-onion confit.

WINE PAIRINGS Hoopes Vineyard Syrah pairs well with spices, lighter proteins like quail, or mixed proteins. This wine has a beautiful orange essence, which plays well with the tomato and the quince.

Hoopes Vineyard Oakville Cabernet Sauvignon is the flagship of Hoopes Vineyard and the king of Napa wines. It pairs perfectly with the lamb stuffing.

SAVORY HERBED TELERAS BREAD PUDDING

Rajas (strips) of poblano chiles and onions are a classic pairing in Mexican cooking, and they often show up combined with crema as a simple, comforting side dish. Incorporating them into a bread pudding made with my herb-flecked sourdough teleras creates a memorable Thanksgiving side.

MAKES 12 SERVINGS

Bread pudding calls for stale bread, so you'll want to make and cube your teleras a day or two in advance. Alternatively, you can spread the cubes on one or two sheet pans and bake them in a preheated 350°F (175°C) for about 8 minutes, or until dry but not browned.

In a large pot, melt 1 cup (225 g) butter over medium-low heat. Add half of the onions and cook, stirring occasionally, until the volume reduces by half. Add the remaining onions and continue to cook over medium-low heat, stirring occasionally, for about 45 minutes, or until the onions turn golden brown. As the onions cook, you may need to add a few tablespoons of water to prevent them from burning. When the onions are ready, transfer them to a bowl, add the poblano chiles and a pinch of nutmeg, and stir to combine. Taste, adjust with more nutmeg if needed, and set aside.

In a large bowl, whisk together the eggs, half-and-half, salt, black pepper, thyme, oregano, epazote (if using), cayenne, cinnamon, and cloves until well blended. Add the telera cubes to the egg mixture and stir to moisten the bread evenly. Let soak for 30 to 35 minutes.

While the bread-custard mixture soaks, preheat the oven to 375°F (190°C). Grease two 9 by 13-inch (23 by 33-cm) baking dishes with the unsalted butter.

When the bread-custard mixture is ready, spread half of the onion-poblano mixture on the bottom of the prepared baking dish, making sure to distribute it evenly over the surface. Top with half of the bread-custard mixture, spreading it evenly. Next, spread two-thirds of the cheese over the bread-custard layer. Combine the remaining bread-custard mixture with the remaining onion-poblano mixture and pour evenly over the cheese mixture. Scatter the remaining cheese evenly over the top.

Bake for 40 to 45 minutes, or until the cheese is melted and begins to turn golden brown. The pudding is ready when it feels firm yet bouncy when gently pressed and no liquid is visible. Serve hot or warm.

INGREDIENTS

12 Herbed Sourdough Teleras (page 69), cut into 1-inch (2.5-cm) cubes

1 cup (225 g) salted butter, plus ¼ cup (55 g) at room temperature for the baking dish

6 large Spanish white onions (about 5 pounds/2.3 kg), thinly sliced

3 poblano chiles, charred, peeled, stemmed, and seeded (see page 271), then cut into strips ¼ inch (6 mm) wide

Freshly grated nutmeg, for seasoning

12 large eggs

2 quarts (2 L) half-and-half, whole milk, or a combination

1½ teaspoons kosher salt

1 teaspoon freshly ground black pepper

2 teaspoons fresh thyme leaves, coarsely chopped

2 teaspoons fresh Mexican oregano leaves, minced

1 tablespoon fresh epazote leaves, finely minced (optional)

2 teaspoons cayenne pepper

½ teaspoon ground cinnamon

¼ teaspoon ground cloves

1½ cups (170 g) "pulled" queso Oaxaca or grated Gruyère cheese

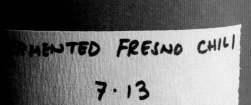
FERMENTED FRESNO CHILI

7·13

BASIC RECIPES

ADOBO MARINADE

MAKES ABOUT 1 CUP (240 ML)

2 guajillo chiles, stems and seeds removed

2 pasilla chiles, stems and seeds removed

2 ancho chiles, stems and seeds removed

6 cascabel chiles, stems and seeds removed

2 tablespoons olive oil

1 yellow onion, thinly sliced

6 cloves garlic

4 Roma tomatoes, cut in half

3 tablespoons tomato paste

1/3 cup (75 ml) apple cider vinegar

Juice of 3 limes

1 teaspoon ground cumin

Kosher salt

Dry roast the guajillo, pasilla, ancho, and cascabel chiles on a comal as directed on page 271. Transfer the chiles to a bowl, add water to cover, and let rehydrate for 20 minutes.

In a large skillet, heat the oil over medium-high heat. Add the onion and garlic and cook, stirring occasionally, for about 5 minutes, or until they turn translucent and just barely begin to brown. While the onion and garlic cook, put the tomatoes into a blender and blend on low speed for about 1 minute, or until puréed. When the onion and garlic are ready, add the puréed tomatoes and the tomato paste to the skillet, reduce the heat and simmer, stirring occasionally, for 10 to 15 minutes, or until fragrant and the flavors have infused. Remove the rehydrated chiles from the water, add to the skillet, and stir to mix well.

Remove from the heat and let cool for a few minutes, then transfer to the blender and blend on medium-high speed to a smooth purée. Season with the vinegar, lime juice, cumin, and salt. Store in an airtight container in the refrigerator for up to 1 week or in the freezer for up to 6 months.

FENNEL CURTIDO

MAKES 1 CUP (220 G), ABOUT 4 SERVINGS

1 carrot, peeled and shredded

1 yellow onion, thinly sliced

Leaves from 1 bunch fresh basil, cut into chiffonade

1 jalapeño chile, seeded and thinly sliced

1 teaspoon dried Mexican oregano

1/2 teaspoon kosher salt

1/4 to 1/2 cup (60 to 120 ml) apple cider vinegar

1 fennel bulb, tops removed and thinly sliced

In a large bowl, stir together the carrot, onion, basil, jalapeño, oregano, and salt, mixing well. Stir in 1/4 cup (60 ml) of the vinegar, then add the fennel and stir to combine. For a quick curtido, set aside at room temperature for 30 minutes before using. For a traditional, fermented curtido, pack the mixture into a large glass jar or other airtight glass container. Pour the remaining 1/4 cup (60 ml) vinegar into the jar or container to cover the vegetables, cover tightly, and set aside for up to 3 days at room temperature before serving. Toss the mixture one last time just before serving.

PICKLED RED ONIONS AND JALAPEÑOS

MAKES ABOUT 2 CUPS (475G)

2 carrots, peeled

2 red onions

5 jalapeño chiles, stems and seeds removed

2 cups (480 ml) white wine vinegar

1/4 cup (50 g) sugar

1 tablespoon coriander seeds, toasted (see page 271)

1 tablespoon kosher salt

Thinly slice the carrots, onions, and jalapeño chiles, making sure all the slices are about the same thickness. This will help to ensure the vegetables will be uniformly pickled.

In a saucepan, combine the vinegar, 1 cup (240 ml) water, sugar, and coriander seeds and bring to a simmer over medium-high heat, stirring to dissolve the sugar. Add the vegetables and return to a simmer, 3 to 5 minutes. Add the salt, stir to mix, and remove from the heat.

Let cool, then transfer to a jar, cap tightly, and store in the refrigerator for up to 2 months.

PICKLED RED ONIONS Omit the chiles. Serve with **Roasted Beets in Mole Rosada with Beet Chips (page 114).**

PICKLED RED ONIONS AND HABANEROS Substitute 2 habaneros for the jalapeños, seeds and stems removed, and very thinly sliced. Be sure to wear gloves when working with habaneros.

COLESLAW

MAKES ABOUT 4 CUPS (870 G)

½ head green cabbage, thinly sliced

1 small carrot, peeled and grated using the large holes of a box grater

2 tablespoons mayonnaise

2 tablespoons crème fraîche

1½ teaspoons apple cider vinegar

¼ teaspoon fresh orange juice

¼ teaspoon fresh lime juice

Kosher salt

In a large bowl, combine the cabbage and carrot and toss to mix. In a small bowl, stir together the mayonnaise, crème fraîche, vinegar, orange juice, and lime juice. Pour over the cabbage mixture and toss to coat evenly. Season with salt and toss again. Use immediately, or cover and refrigerate for no more than 1 day before serving.

FRIJOLES DE OLLA (CLAY POT BEANS)

MAKES ABOUT 3 CUPS (760 G); 6 TO 8 SERVINGS

1 cup (185 g) dried black beans or other dried beans of choice, such as pinto or cannellini

¼ Spanish white onion

1 large clove garlic

1 to 2 fresh epazote sprigs (optional)

Kosher salt

Pick over the beans, discarding any grit or other debris, then transfer to a bowl, add water to cover, and soak overnight.

The next day, drain and rinse the beans, then add them to a clay pot (olla) or saucepan. Be sure the pot is large enough to accommodate the beans as they expand. The dried beans should not rise above the bottom one-third of the pot. Add water to cover the beans by twice their depth.

Add the onion and garlic, place the pot over high heat and bring to a simmer. Reduce the heat to maintain a simmer and cook, uncovered and stirring occasionally, for about 2 hours, or until the beans are tender. If the water level drops (you always want your beans to be covered with water), add enough hot (never cold) water to cover the beans by at least 3 inches (7.5 cm).

Add 1 tablespoon of salt and continue cooking the beans over medium-low heat for 30 minutes to 1 hour more, or until the beans are tender but still have a slight "tooth." Add

the epazote during the last few minutes of cooking. Cooking time will vary depending on the size and condition of your beans. Beans that have spent a longer time on the grocery-store shelf will take longer to cook, and there is really no way to know how old the beans are. For the best results, buy beans in bulk, as they tend to be fresher. Also, larger quantities of beans can take longer to cook.

Once the beans are tender, taste for salt, adding up to another full tablespoon or more to taste (you will be able to taste the "bean water" to check this). It is important not to undersalt the beans. Remove the onion, garlic cloves, and epazote before serving.

Cooked beans spoil quickly. Let the beans cool for a while but refrigerate them within an hour or so of cooking. They will keep in an airtight container for up to 3 or 4 days. If you want to keep them for a bit longer, return them to the stovetop and bring to a boil, then let cool and refrigerate again. They will keep an additional day or so. However, beans freeze beautifully for up to 6 months.

NOTE Slow-cooked beans are the traditional bean dish of Mexico, served alongside fried or grilled meats, tacos, or other dishes. Cooking them in a clay pot (olla) adds a light but discernible earthy flavor. If you do not have an olla, a saucepan can be used in its place. Leftover beans can be turned into refried beans or into a smooth paste for filling tetelas (page 57), lining sopes (page 27), or other uses.

REFRITOS (REFRIED BEANS)

MAKES ABOUT 3 CUPS (760 G); 6 TO 12 SERVINGS

2 teaspoons lard or oil of choice

½ Spanish white onion, finely chopped

1 jalapeño chile, seeded and minced (optional)

1 small clove garlic, minced

3 cups (760 g) drained, cooked black beans (see Frijoles de Olla, left)

½ to 1 cup (120 to 240 ml) bean stock (see Note)

Kosher salt, as needed

In a skillet, heat the lard over medium heat. Add the onion and cook, stirring occasionally, for 2 to 3 minutes, or until lightly browned. Add the jalapeño chile (if using) and continue cooking for about 30 seconds, and then add the garlic and stir to mix well. Add the beans and heat, stirring, until the beans start to simmer. Remove from the heat.

Using a potato masher or the side of a wooden mallet, start to smash your beans, adding ½ cup (120 ml) of the bean stock, then adding more little by little as needed so your refritos are not dry. You are looking for the consistency of a thick pancake batter. Another option is to put the bean mixture and stock into a food processor and pulse to the desired consistency. I prefer to leave some beans whole or partially whole for more texture. Season with salt.

NOTE: The bean stock for these creamy refried black beans is the cooking liquid from cooking the beans in the Frijoles de Olla recipe (opposite). If you do not have enough stock, add more hot water as needed to the beans that are simmering, and cook for about 10 to 15 minutes, until the bean flavor has been infused.

BLACK BEAN PASTE Transfer the contents of the skillet to a blender and blend until you have a smooth purée, adding a little of the bean stock to loosen as needed. The consistency should be similar to that of hummus.

HOMINY (POZOLE)

MAKES ABOUT 3½ CUPS (910 G)

1 cup (225 g) dried prepared hominy, preferably Rancho Gordo brand
1 Spanish white or yellow onion, cut into quarters

Pick over the hominy for any grit, then rinse well, transfer to a bowl, add water to cover, and soak for 6 to 8 hours.

Drain the hominy, discarding the water. Fill a large pot with water, add the hominy and onion, and bring to a boil over medium-high heat. Reduce the heat to medium and cook at a gentle simmer, stirring occasionally, for about 2 hours. The hominy is done when the grains are tender but chewy and not chalky. Use a lid, if needed, to maintain a simmer and add more hot water as needed to keep the hominy covered as it cooks.

The hominy is best used right away. If necessary, store the hominy in its cooking liquid in an airtight container in the refrigerator for up to 5 days. Drain before using.

CAFÉ DE OLLA

MAKES 4 SERVINGS

½ cup (110 g) grated piloncillo (see page 274; optional)
1 cinnamon stick (3 inches/7.5 cm)
⅓ cup (40 g) freshly ground dark-roast Mexican coffee beans

In a clay pot (preferred) or saucepan, combine 3 cups (720 ml) water, the piloncillo (if using), and the cinnamon stick. Heat over medium-high heat for 5 to 10 minutes, or just until the piloncillo starts to dissolve. Add the coffee, stir well,

remove from the heat, and let steep, covered, for 10 minutes. Strain through a fine-mesh sieve into cups and serve hot.

MEXICAN "IRISH" COFFEE Preheat footed glass mugs by filling them with hot water and then pouring it out. Divide the hot coffee between the mugs, filling them three-fourths full. Add 3 tablespoons brandy, preferably Hoopes Vineyard, to each mug. Top with whipped cream and a dusting of ground Mexican cinnamon, then garnish with a cinnamon stick.

HIBISCUS SIMPLE SYRUP

MAKES ABOUT 1 CUP (240 ML)

½ cup (100 g) granulated sugar or ½ cup (120 ml) agave nectar
½ cup (110 g) grated piloncillo (see page 274) or packed light brown sugar
¾ cup (50 g) dried hibiscus flowers
½-inch (12-mm) piece fresh ginger, thinly sliced (optional)

In a saucepan, combine 2 cups (480 ml) water, the sugar, piloncillo, hibiscus flowers, and ginger (if using) and bring to a boil over medium-high heat, stirring to dissolve the sugars. Reduce the heat to medium and simmer for 10 to 15 minutes, or until reduced by half. Do not stir. Remove from the heat, let cool, and strain through a fine-mesh sieve into a glass jar. Cap tightly and store in the refrigerator for up to 3 months.

LAVENDER SYRUP Substitute ¾ cup (15 g) dried lavender for the hibiscus flowers.

STRAWBERRY-HIBISCUS SAUCE

MAKES ABOUT 1 CUP (240 ML)

½ cup (100 g) sugar
2 tablespoons dried hibiscus flowers
2 cups (290 g) strawberries, hulled
1½ teaspoons fresh lime juice
1 teaspoon kosher salt

In a saucepan, combine 1 cup (240 ml) water, the sugar, and hibiscus flowers, place over medium heat, and bring to a simmer, stirring until the sugar dissolves. Continue to cook, stirring, for 10 to 15 minutes, or until a syrup forms. Remove the syrup from the heat and strain through a fine-mesh sieve into a saucepan. Add the strawberries, place over medium-high heat, and cook, stirring often, for 20 to 30 minutes, or until a jam-like consistency forms. Remove from the heat and let cool to room temperature. Fold in the lime juice and salt.

SALSAS

Salsas are an indispensable condiment on any Mexican table, and recipes are as varied as the wide array of fresh and dried chiles they are made from. Textures range from a smooth purée to a chunky pico de gallo. Some salsas are best made in a molcajete, while others call for a blender. From sweet and sour (as in the Salsa Agridulce, below) to nutty (Salsa Macha "Chilango," page 265), I've offered salsa pairings with recipes throughout the book. As you explore this section, I'm sure you'll come up with your own favorites. There's really no wrong way to use them, so experiment and have fun!

SALSA AGRIDULCE

MAKES 1 CUP (240 ML)

5 guajillo chiles, stems and seeds removed

5 pasilla chiles, stems and seeds removed

$\frac{1}{2}$ cup (100 g) sugar

$\frac{1}{2}$ cup (120 ml) red wine vinegar

1 cup (240 ml) fresh orange juice

$\frac{1}{2}$ cup (115 g) unsalted butter, at room temperature

Juice of 2 limes

Kosher salt

In a bowl, combine the guajillo and pasilla chiles with water to cover and let rehydrate for 20 minutes.

In a sauté pan, combine the sugar and $\frac{1}{4}$ cup (60 ml) water and stir until the sugar is evenly moistened. Place over medium-low heat and bring to a simmer, stirring just until the sugar dissolves. Once the sugar has dissolved, immediately stop stirring (if you continue, the sugar will crystallize) and continue to cook for 6 to 8 minutes, or until the mixture turns from golden brown to dark brown.

Add the vinegar and deglaze the pan, stirring to scrape up any browned bits from the pan bottom. Pull the chiles from the water, squeeze out the excess moisture, and add them to the pan along with the orange juice. Cook over low heat, stirring occasionally, for about 30 minutes, or until slightly thickened, to the consistency of barbecue sauce.

Remove from the heat and let cool slightly. Add one-third of the chile mixture to a blender with one-third of the butter and blend until smooth. Transfer to a bowl. Repeat with the remaining chile mixture and butter in two batches and add to the bowl. Add the lime juice and season with salt. Store in an airtight container in the refrigerator for up to 5 days.

PINEAPPLE AGRIDULCE Substitute 1 small pineapple, peeled and crushed with its juices, for the orange juice.

SALSA A LA DIABLA

MAKES ABOUT 1 CUP (240 ML)

4 Roma tomatoes, cut in half

2 cloves garlic, not peeled

1 yellow onion, cut crosswise into slices $\frac{1}{2}$ inch (12 mm) thick

2 tablespoons olive oil

4 árbol chiles, stems removed

2 guajillo chiles, stems removed

Kosher salt

Preheat the oven to 350°F (175°C). Place the tomatoes, cut side up, on a sheet pan along with the garlic and onion slices and roast for about 25 minutes, or until the tomatoes appear collapsed and roasted. Remove the pan from the oven, let cool until the garlic cloves can be handled, and then peel the garlic. Add the tomatoes, onion, and garlic to a blender.

Meanwhile, in a skillet, heat the oil over medium heat. Add the árbol and guajillo chiles and toast, turning as needed, for 5 to 10 minutes, or until the chiles puff up and darken. Do not allow them to turn black. Remove from the heat, add $\frac{1}{4}$ cup (60 ml) water, cover, and let sit for 10 minutes. Transfer the chiles to the blender with the other ingredients and blend until smooth. Season with salt.

The salsa will keep in an airtight container in the refrigerator for up to 5 days or in the freezer for up to 3 months.

SALSA AL PASTOR

MAKE ABOUT 1 CUP (240 ML)

$\frac{1}{4}$ cup (60 ml) olive oil

2 guajillo chiles, stems and seeds removed

2 pasilla chiles, stems and seeds removed

1 homemade tortilla (page 25)

$\frac{1}{2}$ large Spanish white onion, roughly chopped

3 cloves garlic

$\frac{1}{2}$ pineapple, peeled, cored, and diced

$\frac{1}{4}$ cup (60 ml) fresh orange juice

$\frac{1}{4}$ cup (60 ml) champagne vinegar

1 teaspoon dried Mexican oregano

1 teaspoon ground cumin

2 tablespoons chopped fresh cilantro

2 teaspoons kosher salt

Fresh lime juice, for seasoning

In a large skillet, heat the oil over medium heat. Add the guajillo and pasilla chiles and toast, turning as needed, for 1 to 2 minutes, or until fragrant. Do not allow them to turn black. Transfer the chiles to a plate.

Add the tortilla to the pan and toast, turning as needed, for about 30 seconds on each side, or until pliable. Transfer to the plate with the chiles. Raise the heat to medium-high, add the onion and garlic, and cook, stirring often, for 5 to 7 minutes, or until fragrant and translucent. Remove from the heat and add to the plate.

In a blender, combine the chiles, tortilla, onion-garlic mixture, pineapple, orange juice, vinegar, oregano, cumin, cilantro, and salt and blend until smooth. Season with lime juice. Store in an airtight container in the refrigerator for up to 5 days or in the freezer for up to 3 months.

Note: Double or even triple the recipe and freeze it, then thaw when needed and add to leftover carnitas (page 230) for traditional tacos al pastor.

SALSA DE ANCHO CHILE BRAVA

MAKES ABOUT 3 CUPS (720 ML)

2 Roma tomatoes, cut into medium dice

3 cloves garlic, not peeled

1 large yellow onion, cut into medium dice

1 (14½-ounce/415-g) can tomatoes

1 tablespoon olive oil, plus ¼ cup (60 ml)

1 ancho chile, stem and seeds removed

1½ tablespoons sherry

1 tablespoon tomato paste

1½ teaspoons cayenne pepper

1½ teaspoons sweet paprika

Fresh lemon juice, for seasoning

Kosher salt

Preheat the oven to 350°F (175°C). Place the tomatoes, garlic, and onion on a sheet pan and roast for about 25 minutes, or until the tomatoes appear collapsed and roasted. Remove from the oven, let cool until the garlic cloves can be handled, and then peel the garlic. Add the tomatoes, onion, and garlic to a blender.

In a small skillet, heat 1 tablespoon of the oil over medium-high heat. Add the ancho chile and toast, turning as needed, for 1 to 2 minutes, or until it begins to brown, do not allow

to char. Remove from the heat, let cool, tear into small pieces, and add it to the blender.

Add the remaining ¼ cup (60 ml) oil, the sherry, tomato paste, cayenne, and paprika to the blender with the other ingredients and purée until smooth. Season with lemon juice and salt.

Store in an airtight container in the refrigerator for up to 3 days or in the freezer for up to 2 months.

SALSA BORRACHA (DRUNKEN SALSA)

MAKES ABOUT ¾ CUP (180 ML)

½ cup (120 ml) olive oil

4 pasilla chiles, stems and seeds removed

4 tomatillos, husks removed and rinsed

1 Roma tomato

1 yellow onion, cut into quarters

1 clove garlic

½ cup (120 ml) Mexican beer, preferably Negra Modelo

⅓ cup (75 ml) fresh orange juice

2 tablespoons fresh lime juice

Kosher salt

Preheat the oven to 400°F (205°C). Line a sheet pan with aluminum foil.

In a skillet, heat the oil over medium-high heat. Add the pasilla chiles and sauté for 1 to 2 minutes, or until they begin to brown; do not allow to char. Remove from the heat, transfer the chiles to a plate, and reserve the oil in the pan.

Place the tomatillos, tomato, onion, and garlic on the prepared sheet pan and roast for about 15 minutes, or until the tomatoes begin to collapse and bubble and the tomatillos are cooked all the way through when tested with a knife.

Transfer the roasted vegetables to a blender and blend until smooth. Then add the chiles and continue blending until all the ingredients are well mixed and smooth.

Return the skillet with the oil to medium-high heat. When the oil is hot, add the salsa, taking care to avoid splatter, then add the beer, orange juice, and lime juice and cook, stirring often, for about 5 minutes, or until thickened. Remove from the heat, let cool, and season with salt.

Store in an airtight container in the refrigerator for up to 3 days or in the freezer for up to 2 months.

SALSA CHILES DE ÁRBOL

MAKES ABOUT ½ CUP (120 ML)

5 árbol chiles, stems removed

½ teaspoon coarse sea salt

1 clove garlic

½ small shallot

5 Roma tomatoes

Juice of 1 lime, or more if needed

Kosher salt, if needed

Dry roast the árbol chiles on a comal as directed on page 271. Transfer the chiles to a bowl, add water to cover, and let rehydrate for 20 minutes.

Meanwhile, in a molcajete, combine the coarse salt, garlic, and shallot and work with a tejolote to a paste. Set aside.

Drain the chiles. In a saucepan, combine the chiles and tomatoes, add water to cover, and bring to a boil over high heat. Reduce the heat to medium-low and simmer for 10 minutes. Remove from the heat and let sit for 10 minutes. Use a slotted spoon to transfer the warm tomatoes and chiles to the molcajete in four batches, working in each batch well before adding the next, until a sauce forms. Season with lime juice and with kosher salt if needed.

Alternatively, to make the salsa in a blender, combine all the ingredients in a blender, substituting ½ teaspoon kosher salt for the coarse salt, and blend until smooth.

Store in an airtight container in the refrigerator for up to 3 days or in the freezer for up to 2 months.

EL CALIFORNIO FERMENTED SALSA

MAKES ABOUT 3 CUPS (720 ML)

5 cups (1.2 L) water

6¼ teaspoons (30 g) kosher salt (must be exact measure)

2½ pounds (1.2 kg) Fresno chiles, thinly sliced (see Note)

1 large carrot, peeled and thinly sliced

3 shallots, thinly sliced

5 cloves garlic, cut into quarters

Leaves of fresh herbs such as cilantro or basil (optional)

Honey, sugar, and/or kosher salt, for seasoning (optional)

In a saucepan bring the water to a boil, add the salt, and stir until dissolved. Remove from the heat.

While the brine is coming to a boil, combine the chiles, carrot, shallots, and garlic in a large bowl and toss to mix

evenly. Pack the vegetables into a sterilized 2-quart (2-L) Mason jar, or several smaller jars (see Note). Pour as much of the hot brine into the jar as will fit; the vegetables should be fully immersed in the liquid. Top the vegetables with a fermentation weight, a small ramekin, or other item to ensure they remain submerged. Cover the top of the jar with cheesecloth, then close loosely with a lid.

Place the jar in a cool, dark place for 5 to 7 days, or until the brine is cloudy (a sign that the vegetables are ready).

Drain the vegetables, reserving 1 cup (240 ml) of the brine. Transfer the vegetables and reserved brine to a blender and blend until smooth. Transfer the salsa to a bowl, taste, and add herbs, sweetener, and/or salt, if desired. Store in an airtight container in the refrigerator for up to 1 year.

NOTE Use best practices for sterilizing the jars. You can swap out the Fresno chiles for Thai, jalapeño, or Jimmy Nardello, which all work beautifully.

SALSA IRMA

MAKES ABOUT 2 CUPS (480 ML)

¼ teaspoon coarse sea salt

1 jalapeño chile, stem removed and seeded if desired (for a milder salsa), plus more if needed

1 small clove garlic

¼ shallot

10 small tomatillos, husks removed and rinsed

3 bunches fresh cilantro, roughly chopped

Juice of 2 limes

2 avocados

Kosher salt

In a molcajete, combine the coarse salt, jalapeño chile, garlic, and shallot and work with a tejolote until the chile breaks down. Add the tomatillos and work them together with the chile-garlic mixture until they are completely broken down and blended in well. You may need to transfer the mixture to a bowl at this point, depending on the size of your molcajete. Add the cilantro and lime juice and stir to combine. Finally, pit the avocados, scoop the flesh into a bowl, and mash with a fork, then mix into the tomatillo mixture. The salsa should be chunky. Alternatively, to make the salsa in a blender, combine all the ingredients in a blender, substituting kosher salt for the coarse salt, and blend until well mixed but still chunky. Taste and adjust with salt if needed. If you find the spice level too mild, mix in more minced jalapeño chile to your liking.

SALSA MACHA "CHILANGO"

MAKES ABOUT 2 CUPS (480 ML)

¼ cup (60 ml) olive oil

2 cloves garlic, crushed

2 tablespoons white sesame seeds

½ cup (75 g) raw peanuts

2 guajillo chiles and 2 pasilla chiles, stems and seeds removed and cut into small pieces with scissors

½ cup (120 ml) apple cider vinegar

½ cup (120 ml) fresh orange juice

Juice of 2 limes

1 teaspoon dried Mexican oregano

Kosher salt

In a saucepan, combine the oil, garlic, sesame seeds, and peanuts and sauté over medium-high heat. Cook for 5 minutes, stirring, until the garlic is lightly golden. Remove the pan from the heat and let the oil cool for 5 to 6 minutes.

Add the guajillo and pasilla chiles, vinegar, orange juice, lime juice, and oregano to the partially cooled oil, stir just to mix, and let sit for 5 minutes. Transfer to a blender and blend or pulse for about 30 seconds, or until well mixed but still chunky. Season with salt.

Store in an airtight container in the refrigerator for up to 2 weeks or in the freezer for up to 3 months.

SALSA VERDE CON CHILES DE ÁRBOL

MAKES ABOUT 2 CUPS (480 ML)

12 tomatillos, husks removed, rinsed, and coarsely chopped

1 small yellow onion, cut into eighths, plus 2 tablespoons diced onion

4 árbol chiles

3 cloves garlic

2 tablespoons olive oil

Fresh lime juice, for seasoning

Kosher salt

1 bunch fresh cilantro, coarsely chopped

In a small saucepan, combine the tomatillos, the onion in eighths, árbol chiles, and garlic with water to cover (about 1 cup/240 ml), bring to a simmer over medium heat, and simmer for 10 minutes. Remove from the heat and, using a slotted spoon, transfer the vegetables to a blender. Blend for a few seconds, just until you have a smooth purée. Reserve the water in the pan.

In another saucepan, heat the oil over medium heat. Add the blended salsa to the hot oil, being careful of splatter, and

cook, stirring occasionally, for about 10 minutes to infuse the flavors. Remove the pan from the heat, pour into a heatproof bowl, let cool, and season with lime juice and salt. Fold in the diced onion and cilantro. If the salsa is too thick, thin with a little of the reserved vegetable water.

Store in an airtight container in the refrigerator for up to 3 days or in the freezer for up to 2 months.

SALSA VERDE CRUDA

MAKES ABOUT ½ CUP (120 ML)

1 teaspoon coarse sea salt or kosher salt

1 clove garlic

½ shallot

2 jalapeño chiles, stems removed and seeded, if desired

6 tomatillos, husks removed and rinsed

1 avocado, pitted and peeled

1 bunch fresh cilantro, roughly chopped

Fresh lime juice, for seasoning

In a molcajete, combine the coarse salt, garlic, shallot, and jalapeño chiles and work with a tejolote until a paste forms. Add the tomatillos and avocado and work them with the paste until well mixed but still slightly chunky.

Alternatively, to make the salsa in a blender, combine the same ingredients in a blender, substituting kosher salt for the coarse salt, and pulse to create a slightly chunky salsa. Transfer to a bowl. Fold in the cilantro and season with lime juice. Taste and adjust with kosher salt, if needed.

SPICY CARROT SALSA

MAKES ABOUT 4 CUPS (960 ML)

1 yellow onion, cut in half

3 cloves garlic

2 large Roma tomato

6 tomatillos, husks removed and rinsed

4 cascabel chiles, stems and seeds removed

3 ancho chiles, stems and seeds removed

2 guajillo chiles, stems and seeds removed

3 cups (720 ml) fresh carrot juice

Kosher salt

Dry roast the onion, garlic, tomato, tomatillos, and cascabel, ancho, and guajillo chiles on a comal as directed on page 271 until roasted, charred, and aromatic.

In a saucepan over medium heat, combine the carrot juice

and roasted vegetables and bring to a simmer. Reduce the heat to medium-low and cook, stirring occasionally, for 20 to 25 minutes, or until the liquid has reduced by half and the vegetables are soft. Season with salt. Remove from the heat, cool for a few minutes, then transfer to a blender and blend until smooth. If too watery, simmer over medium-low heat until thickened. Store in an airtight container in the refrigerator for up to 3 days or freeze for up to 2 months.

VERDOLAGAS SALSA VERDE

MAKES 2 CUPS (480 ML)

1 teaspoon coarse sea salt

1 clove garlic

1 jalapeño chile, stem removed and seeded if desired

2 tomatillos, husks removed, rinsed, and cut into eighths

1 cup (45 g) purslane leaves or 1 cup (35 g) watercress or spinach

1 cup (30 g) fresh cilantro leaves

1 tablespoon red wine vinegar

Finely grated zest and juice of 2 limes

Kosher salt

In a molcajete, combine the coarse salt, garlic, and jalapeño chile and work well with a tejolote until a paste forms. Add the tomatillos, purslane, cilantro, vinegar, and lime zest and juice and work them with the paste until well mixed but still somewhat chunky. Season with kosher salt. Store in an airtight container in the refrigerator for up to 5 days.

CORN PICO DE GALLO

MAKES ABOUT 4 CUPS (960 ML)

2 tablespoons fresh lime juice

1 cup (240 ml) olive oil

Kernels from 4 ears yellow, white, or bicolored corn (see page 271)

½ cup (55 g) diced red onion

2 tablespoons chopped fresh basil

2 tablespoons chopped fresh cilantro

1 jalapeño chile, seeded if desired, and finely chopped

20 to 30 Sungold or other flavorful cherry tomatoes, cut in half, or 2 cups (360 g) large-diced Early Girl or other heirloom tomatoes

Kosher salt

In a bowl, using a balloon whisk, whisk the lime juice while slowly adding the olive oil to create an emulsion. Add the corn, red onion, basil, cilantro, and jalapeño and stir to combine. Fold in the tomatoes. Season with salt and toss lightly.

CLASSIC PICO DE GALLO Omit the corn.

FRESH SALSA VERDE WITH PEAS AND MINT

MAKES ABOUT 1½ CUPS (360 ML)

1 cup (145 g) fresh peas, blanched, or thawed frozen peas

¼ cup (60 ml) fresh lime juice

½ cup (120 ml) olive oil

2 tablespoons red wine vinegar

1 teaspoon honey

Leaves from 1 bunch fresh mint, minced

Leaves from 1 bunch fresh cilantro, minced

1 jalapeño chile, seeded and minced

1 small shallot, minced

1 clove garlic, minced

Kosher salt

In a blender, combine the peas, lime juice, oil, vinegar, and honey and blend until puréed. Pour the mixture into a bowl, add the mint, cilantro, jalapeño chile, shallot, and garlic, stir to mix well, and season with salt. Use immediately or within a few hours of preparation. If the salsa seems too thick, add more lime juice or a bit of cold water to thin it.

SALSA ARISBEL

MAKES 2 CUPS (480 ML)

2 tablespoons olive oil

2 to 5 árbol chiles, stems removed

2 Roma tomatoes, cut in half

1 yellow onion, cut into medium dice

3 cloves garlic

Kosher salt

Preheat the oven to 400°F (205°C).

In an ovenproof skillet large enough to accommodate all the ingredients, heat the oil over medium-high heat. Add the chiles to taste and toast, turning as needed, for 1 to 2 minutes, or until they begin to brown; do not allow them to char. Remove from the heat, add the tomatoes, onion, and garlic, and transfer to the oven. Roast for 10 to 15 minutes, or until the vegetables are slightly charred.

Transfer the contents of the skillet to a molcajete and work well with a tejolote until all ingredients are well blended. Season with salt. Store in an airtight container in the refrigerator for up to 3 days or in the freezer for up to 2 months.

MOJO VERDE

MAKES ABOUT 1½ CUPS (360 ML)

2 avocados, pitted and peeled
10 small tomatillos, husks removed, rinsed, and roughly chopped
3 bunches fresh cilantro, roughly chopped
½ cup (120 ml) olive oil
¼ cup (60 ml) crème fraîche
½ to 1 jalapeño chile, seeded, if desired
Juice of 2 limes
Kosher salt

In a blender, combine the avocados, tomatillos, cilantro, olive oil, crème fraîche, jalapeño to taste, and lime juice and blend until a chunky consistency forms. Depending on the size of your avocados and tomatillos, you may need to add more oil. Season with salt and set the sauce aside until serving. Serve at once.

TOMATILLO APPLESAUCE

MAKES 2 CUPS (480 ML)

2 cups (480 ml) apple cider
¾ cup (150 g) granulated sugar, plus more as needed
2 cinnamon sticks (3 inches/7.5 cm)
½ fresh sage sprig
1 tablespoon fresh lemon juice
2 Granny Smith apples (2 pounds/910 g) peeled, quartered, and cored
8 medium tomatillos, husks removed and rinsed

In a saucepan, combine the cider, sugar, cinnamon sticks, sage, and lemon juice and bring to a simmer over medium heat, stirring to dissolve the sugar. Add the apples, adjust the heat to maintain a gentle simmer, and poach for 25 to 30 minutes, or until just tender. Remove the pan from the heat, let the apples cool, transfer the apples and their liquid to a bowl, cover, and refrigerate until fully cooled.

Roast the tomatillos on a hot comal over medium-high heat until they start to turn color and small black patches appear, 3 to 5 minutes. Alternatively, roast them on a baking sheet in a 450°F (230°C) oven for 15 minutes. Let cool completely.

Strain the liquid from the apples and add them to a blender. Halve the tomatillos and add them to the blender, making sure not to add the tomatillo cooking liquid. Purée until you have an applesauce. Taste for sweetness and adjust to your taste.

MEXICAN RÉMOULADE

MAKES ABOUT 1½ CUPS (360 ML)

1 clove garlic, chopped
2 tablespoons fresh lemon juice
2 tablespoons Dijon mustard
1 large egg yolk
1 cup (240 ml) soybean oil
½ cup (80 g) drained cornichons
½ cup (20 g) each chopped fresh cilantro and parsley
½ avocado, pitted and peeled
1 jalapeño chile, seeded and sliced
Pinch of kosher salt

In a small food processor, combine the garlic, lemon juice, mustard, and egg yolk and pulse until smooth. With the processor running, slowly stream in the oil until the mixture emulsifies and thickens. Add the cornichons, cilantro, parsley, avocado, and jalapeño, and pulse just until they are finely chopped. Season with the salt. Store in an airtight container in the refrigerator for up to 2 months.

VINAIGRETTES AND DRESSINGS

Achieving the perfect balance of oil to acid, of sweet to salty to spice is the hallmark of a great vinaigrette or dressing. I've provided some of my favorites here, paired with recipes throughout the book. Don't be afraid to experiment, sub out fig butter or jam for a seasonal or favorite fruit, or try a pear or Champagne vinegar in place of red wine.

BALSAMIC VINAIGRETTE

MAKES ABOUT 1¼ CUPS (300 ML)

1 tablespoon honey
1 tablespoon Dijon mustard
¼ cup (60 ml) balsamic vinegar
1 cup (240 ml) extra-virgin olive oil
Kosher salt and freshly ground black pepper

In a bowl, whisk together the honey, mustard, and vinegar. Slowly drizzle in the oil while whisking continuously to form an emulsion. Season with salt and pepper. Store in an airtight container in the refrigerator for up to 3 days.

FIG-CHIPOTLE VINAIGRETTE

MAKES ABOUT 1½ CUPS (360 ML)

3 tablespoons fig butter or jam

1 tablespoon adobo sauce from canned chipotle chiles

½ teaspoon dried Mexican oregano

⅓ cup (75 ml) red wine vinegar, or to taste

1¼ cups (300 ml) extra-virgin olive oil

Kosher salt and freshly ground black pepper

In a bowl, whisk together the fig butter, adobo sauce, oregano, and vinegar. Slowly drizzle in the oil while whisking continuously to form an emulsion. Taste and add more vinegar as needed. Season with salt and pepper. Store in an airtight container in the refrigerator for up to 3 days.

JALAPEÑO-YUZU VINAIGRETTE

MAKES 2½ CUPS (600 ML)

6 tablespoons (90 ml) yuzu juice

2 tablespoons fresh lime juice

2 tablespoons honey

1 jalapeño chile, stem removed and seeded, if desired

1½ tablespoons Asian fish sauce, preferably Red Boat brand

1½ tablespoons yuzu kosho (yuzu-chile-salt paste)

1½ tablespoons peeled and grated fresh ginger

1¾ cups (420 ml) olive oil

Kosher salt

In a blender, combine the yuzu juice, lime juice, honey, jalapeño chile, fish sauce, yuzu kosho, and ginger. With the blender running on medium speed, slowly stream in the oil until the mixture emulsifies. Season with salt. Store in an airtight container in the refrigerator for up to 3 days.

MEZCAL VINAIGRETTE

MAKES 2½ CUPS (600 ML)

¼ cup (60 ml) red wine vinegar

2 tablespoons fresh orange juice

2 tablespoons mezcal

1 teaspoon sugar

2 cups (480 ml) blended oil (such as olive and canola), mild olive oil, or other light-flavored oil

Kosher salt and freshly ground black pepper

In a bowl, whisk together vinegar, orange juice, mezcal, and sugar until the sugar dissolves. Slowly drizzle in the oil while whisking continuously to form an emulsion. Season with salt and pepper. Store in an airtight container in the refrigerator for up to 3 days.

MOLCAJETE CAESAR SALAD DRESSING

MAKES ABOUT 2 CUPS (480 ML)

4 large eggs

Coarse sea salt or kosher salt

2 large cloves garlic

Juice of 1 lemon

4 to 6 anchovy fillets in olive oil, with oil from the can (optional)

2 teaspoons Dijon mustard

1 teaspoon Worcestershire sauce

¾ cup (180 ml) oil reserved from poaching the trout (see page 187), or ½ cup/120 ml if you are using oil from the anchovy can

4 to 6 tablespoons (25 to 40 g) grated queso Cotija or Parmesan

Freshly ground black pepper

First, pasteurize the eggs. Fill a bowl with cold water and set it near the stove. Put the eggs into a saucepan, add cold water to cover, place over high heat, and bring to a boil. As soon as the water boils, scoop out the eggs and plunge them into the bowl of cold water and carefully peel. If you have cooked your eggs perfectly, they will be just shy of soft-boiled. The yolks will go into the dressing. The whites should be firm enough to toss into your salad if you like.

In a molcajete, combine 2 teaspoons salt and the garlic and work together with a tejolote until a paste forms. Drizzle in the lemon juice, working it into the garlic paste. Work in the egg yolks, anchovies fillets (if using), mustard, and Worcestershire sauce until well mixed, then slowly drizzle in the poaching oil and the anchovy oil from the can (if using) while continuing to mix with the tejolote to form an emulsion. When the mixture is the consistency of runny mayonnaise, add the cheese and mix well. Season with pepper, then taste and adjust with more garlic, lemon juice, and salt if needed.

Alternatively, in a blender, combine the garlic, 2 teaspoons kosher salt, lemon juice, egg yolks, anchovies to taste (if using), mustard, and Worcestershire sauce and blend until a smooth paste forms. With the blender running on medium speed, slowly stream in the poaching oil and the anchovy oil (if using) to emulsify. When the mixture is the consistency of runny mayonnaise, add the cheese and blend briefly to mix well. Season with pepper, then taste and adjust with more garlic, lemon juice, and salt if needed. Store in an airtight container in the refrigerator for up to 3 days.

VERDE GODDESS DRESSING

MAKES ABOUT 3 CUPS (720 ML)

Leaves from 2 bunches fresh basil
2 bunches fresh cilantro
Leaves from 2 bunches fresh mint
Leaves from 2 bunches fresh flat-leaf parsley
1 cup (240 ml) plain, whole milk Greek yogurt
6 tablespoons (90 ml) red wine vinegar
3 tablespoons fresh lemon juice
1 tablespoon honey
½ to 1 clove garlic (to your taste), grated
1½ to 2 jalapeño chiles, stems removed
Kosher salt

In a food processor, combine the basil, cilantro, mint, parsley, yogurt, vinegar, lemon juice, honey, garlic, and jalapeño chile to taste and blend until smooth. Season with salt. Store in an airtight container in the refrigerator for up to 1 week.

ANCHO CHILE OLIVE OIL

MAKES 1 CUP (240 ML)

1 cup (240 ml) olive oil, preferably extra-virgin
4 ancho chiles

In a small saucepan, combine the oil and ancho chiles, making sure the chiles are completely submerged in the oil. Heat over medium-high heat until the oil barely begins to smoke (olive oil has a relatively low smoke point, so this will only take a few minutes). Remove from the heat and let the oil cool until you can safely work with it.

Pour the partially cooled oil and chiles into a molcajete and crush the chiles with a tejolote.

Transfer the crushed chiles and oil to a sterilized Mason jar. (You can choose to skip sterilizing the jar. Just be sure you store the infused oil in the refrigerator.) If you prefer a milder oil, strain the oil through a fine-mesh sieve into the jar. However, the unstrained infusion will mature over time, plus the crushed chile that settles at the bottom of the jar can be used as a condiment.

Cap the jar tightly and store at room temperature for up to 3 months.

CLARIFIED BUTTER

MAKES 1 CUP (225 G)

1 cup (225 g) unsalted butter

In a medium saucepan over medium-low heat, melt the butter. Let the butter simmer gently, making sure it never boils, for 15 to 20 minutes, or until it melts and the fats are separated from the solids. With a small ladle or spoon, skim the white foam that floats to the top, until it is completely removed. The clarified butter is ready when no more foam floats to the top and you can see the milk solids on the bottom of the pot. Strain the mixture through a fine-mesh sieve lined with a coffee filter and set over a bowl. Store the clarified butter in an airtight container in the refrigerator for up to 1 month.

STOCKS AND BRINES

For any dish that gets its flavor from stock or broth, be it arroz con pollo, paella, or my cioppino (page 197), the trick is to create a truly savory stock. Taste and taste again, adjust, cook some more, and taste again. I use salty brines to tenderize and add moisture to proteins before cooking.

CORN STOCK

MAKES 6 CUPS (1.4 L)

4 ears yellow, white, or bicolored corn
Kosher salt, if using for a savory recipe

Remove the corn kernels from the cobs (see page 271). Reserve the kernels for another use. Put the corncobs into a large pot, add 3 quarts (2.8 L) water, and bring to a boil over high heat. Cook, uncovered, for 30 to 45 minutes, or until white foams begins to rise to the top.

Remove from the heat, pull out and discard the corncobs, and strain the stock through a fine-mesh sieve. Season with salt if not using in a sweet preparation. Store the stock in an airtight container in the refrigerator for up to 5 days.

TOMATO-CHIPOTLE STOCK

MAKES 2 CUPS (480 ML)

2 tomatoes, coarsely chopped

½ Spanish white onion, chopped

1 clove garlic

3 chipotle chiles in adobo sauce

2 tablespoons olive oil

2 cups (480 ml) chicken or vegetable stock

3 fresh cilantro sprigs

In a blender, combine the tomatoes, onion, garlic, and chipotles and blend until puréed. Strain the purée through a fine-mesh sieve into a bowl.

In a saucepan, heat the oil over medium-high heat. Add the tomato mixture (have a splatter screen at hand, as the sauce will splatter when added to the hot oil), cover, and cook for 5 to 7 minutes, or until aromatic. Add the stock and cilantro, stir well, and bring to a boil. Simmer until reduced to 2 cups of stock. Remove from the heat. Remove the cilantro.

If not using immediately, cool, then store in an airtight container in the refrigerator for up to 1 week or in the freezer for up to 3 months.

SPICY SHRIMP STOCK

MAKES 4 CUPS (960 ML)

2 to 3 guajillo chiles

2 tablespoons olive or canola oil

½ cup (65 g) Spanish white onion, roughly chopped

¼ cup (25 g) roughly chopped celery (optional)

2 cloves garlic, crushed

Shells from 2 pounds (910 g) shrimp

1 ounce (28 g) dried shrimp (optional)

2 bay leaves

3 fresh thyme sprigs (optional)

Dry roast the guajillo chiles on a comal as directed on page 271 until they begin to take on color. They will char quickly, so watch closely. Set aside.

In a small Dutch oven, heat the oil over medium-low heat. Add the onion, celery (if using), and garlic and cook, stirring occasionally, for 10 to 15 minutes, or until the onion is translucent.

Add the shrimp shells, toss to coat with the vegetables, and cook, pressing down on the shells as you give them the occasional stir, for 2 to 3 minutes to release their flavor. Add

the chiles, dried shrimp (if using), bay leaves, thyme (if using), and 2 quarts (2 L) water, raise the heat to medium-high, and bring to a boil. Reduce the heat to a simmer and simmer, skimming off any foam that forms on the surface, for 45 minutes to 1 hour, or until reduced by half.

Remove from the heat and strain through a fine-mesh sieve. Store in an airtight container in the refrigerator for up to 2 days or in the freezer for up to 3 months.

12-HOUR POULTRY BRINE

MAKES ENOUGH BRINE FOR ABOUT 3 POUNDS (1.4 KG) OF CHICKEN OR OTHER POULTRY.

2 cups (480 ml) fresh lemon juice

2 cups (480 ml) fresh orange juice

2 cups (280 g) kosher salt

1 cup (220 g) packed light brown sugar

10 cloves garlic, crushed

3 bay leaves

1 fresh thyme sprig

1 fresh rosemary sprig

Peels of 5 lemons, removed with a vegetable peeler

In a large pot or other food-grade container, combine 2½ gallons (9.5 L) water, the lemon juice, orange juice, salt, brown sugar, garlic, bay leaves, thyme, rosemary, and lemon peels and stir to dissolve the salt and sugar. Follow the directions in individual recipes. Or to use the brine for your own recipe, submerge chicken or other poultry, whole or cut up, in the brine and refrigerate for 12 hours. Remove the poultry from the brine, discard the brine, and dry the poultry on a sheet pan or plate—well spaced if in pieces—in the refrigerator for 1 hour before cooking.

TECHNIQUES

WORKING WITH CHILES AND SWEET PEPPERS

PEELING AND SEEDING FRESH CHILES AND PEPPERS

This technique is most often used for poblano chile peppers and can also be applied to sweet peppers. Heat a comal or dry cast-iron skillet over high heat. Add the pepper and heat, turning frequently with tongs, until the skin is charred black and blistered on all sides. Or, if you have a gas stove, use tongs to hold the pepper over the flame (I usually set it right on the grate) until charred black and blistered on all sides. Immediately slip the peppers into a plastic bag, close the bag tightly, and allow the peppers to sweat and cool for 5 to 10 minutes. In the Mexican kitchen, this technique is known as *sudar* (to sweat).

Remove the cooled peppers from the bag and use your fingers to peel away the blackened skin. Don't worry if not every tiny bit is removed. If you will be stuffing the pepper, cut a short (2 to 3 inches/5 to 7.5 cm long) lengthwise slit along one side, being careful not to tear the walls of the pepper and keeping the stem intact, then carefully remove the seeds. Alternatively, if you prefer to stuff your pepper from the top rather than the side, remove the very top portion and stem. If you will be using the flesh of the pepper, slit it open lengthwise, lay it flat on a work surface, and cut around the stem end. Remove the stem, seeds, and veins and cut the flesh as directed in individual recipes.

DEVEINING AND SEEDING LARGE DRIED CHILES

This technique is most commonly used when preparing chiles to make a dish adobado style.

First, bloom the chiles by dry roasting them on a blistering-hot comal as directed in the next column, taking care not to burn them. (For certain salsas and moles, you will be instructed in the recipe to burn the chiles. Burning the chiles reduces the spice level and changes their flavor.) Then soak the chiles in water to cover until softened, about 20 minutes. When a chile is pliable, gently pull the stem from the top. The veins will often come out along with the stem. If not, break the chile open and remove the veins and seeds.

SEEDING AND DEVEINING ÁRBOL CHILES

These chiles are small, so deveining and seeding them is more easily done without first soaking them. Just break off the stem, break open the chile, shake out the seeds, and carefully cut away the veins.

TOSTAR (DRY-ROASTING)

This is often the very first step in preparing a Mexican dish. It is how I char the dried chiles and bloom the spices I use in my moles. Oils were not introduced to Mexico until the arrival of the Europeans, so the Aztecs used this dry-heat method to seal in the flavor of—and get the most flavor out of—chiles, tomatoes (red or green), and tomatillos, primarily for salsas.

Rinse and dry the chiles, then roast them on a very hot comal or dry cast-iron skillet over high heat, turning as needed. A bacon press or large metal spatula can be used to make sure all parts of the chile are touching the hot surface. Remove them from the heat before they begin to change color (unless a recipe specifies otherwise). If they darken too much, their flavor can become bitter.

For tomatoes and tomatillos (remove the husks and rinse the tomatillos before putting them on the comal), dry roast, turning as needed to color all sides, until their skins are charred. Leaving the charred skin on adds a smoky, more intense flavor that is often favored in salsas.

For skin-on garlic cloves, dry roast just until some charred spots appear and the cloves soften a little. This makes the skins easier to slip off and produces a sweeter flavor, desirable in some recipes, than raw garlic.

Some spice seeds—such as cumin, coriander, fennel, and sesame seeds—are dry roasted on a hot comal to heighten their flavor. Dry roast them just until fragrant, watching carefully so as to not burn them.

REMOVING CORN KERNELS

Remove the husk and silk from a corn ear, then lay the ear flat on a large cutting board. You want your cutting board to be substantially larger than the length of the corn so any flyaway kernels land on the board. Using a sharp knife and positioning the knife as close to the cob as possible, cut straight between the kernels and the cob along the top of the ear. Rotate the ear a quarter turn and cut again. Repeat two more times until all the kernels are removed.

GLOSSARY

ADOBO

The word *adobo* comes from the Spanish "adobar" which means "to marinate" in English. It shows up nearly every place the Spanish colonized, and its meaning varies through the Spanish diaspora. In Mexico, it is a basic marinade that can be used for almost any protein. It is even the term used to describe the sauce in canned chipotles.

ANTOJITOS

Literally translated as "little cravings," antojitos are small-bite street foods, usually made with some kind of masa, such as tacos, sopes, tostadas, tamales, and gorditas. The term also includes elote (grilled corn on the cob, slathered with sauce; page 121) and fresh fruit with "chile y limon."

AVOCADO LEAVES, DRIED MEXICAN

Harvested from *Persia americana var. drymifolia*, the native Mexican avocado, these deep green leaves are widely available in Mexico, where they are as common as bay leaves are in the US. When bloomed or crushed, they release a faint anise-like aroma. Look for packages of the dried leaves in Latin American markets. Do not be tempted to use leaves from other avocado trees, such as the Hass or Fuerte, as the leaves are considered toxic.

BITTER OR SEVILLE ORANGE

A hybrid citrus fruit with a flavor that is sour, somewhat like a lemon, these oranges still have a warm, orange flavor; it's not so bitter that you wouldn't eat it. You can substitute equal parts of lime and orange juice.

CANCHA

Cancha is a Peruvian crispy toasted corn snack available in Latin American markets. (In Spain, the same snack is known as quicos.) You can also purchase the large dried corn kernels and make cancha at home just as you would popcorn. Place a large heavy skillet over medium heat and heat 2 tablespoons of olive oil. Add the corn kernels and shake the pan from time to time to move the kernels around in the pan. As soon as they start to pop, cover the pan loosely with a lid and continue to cook, stirring often, until the kernels are no longer popping and they are golden brown. The timing will depend on how many kernels you are toasting. Transfer to a plate lined with paper towels to drain and season while hot with kosher salt. They are good warm or at room temperature and will keep in an airtight container at room temperature for several days.

CANELA OR CEYLON CINNAMON (MEXICAN CINNAMON)

Sometimes called "true cinnamon," canela—also known as Ceylon cinnamon—has a softer bark and a less astringent or pungent flavor than other types of cinnamon. It is most widely used in Mexican cuisine, where it more common as an ingredient in savory dishes.

CAZUELAS AND OLLAS

These hand-thrown and often hand-decorated Mexican clay cooking vessels impart a subtle but perceptible earthy flavor to foods. Both are round, but a cazuela is wide and shallow, usually with 4 inch (10 cm) sides and about 16 inches (40.5 cm) wide as this aligns with the size of the "quemadores," or burners of a typical colonial-era tiled Mexican stove. They are primarily used for moles and guisados (stews). Ollas, on the other hand, are used to make beans, caldos (soups), and coffee, and hence are deeper. (An olla used for beans and soups is never used for coffee.) These range in size from small, squat clay pots to large, taller, and wider ollas. A well-made cazuela or olla is one with a bottom that is not too thin, so food cooks without burning. Clay pots must be cured before use: rub the outside bottom of the pot (the side that will be directly on the fire) with garlic and/or heat milk in the pot until the milk is scalding hot. Never use either pot in the oven. If using with an electric stove, you will need a diffuser.

CHIQUIHUITE

A basket found on every Mexican table at mealtime, the chiquihuite (pronounced cheeky-wheety) is traditionally made from palm leaves and is usually lined with a beautifully hand-embroidered table linen made especially for the purpose. For everyday use, some Mexican households use a dedicated kitchen towel. It is used to keep tortillas warm as they come off the comal.

CHILES

Anaheim (fresh, aka California chiles) Mostly used in the United States for chiles rellenos (although poblanos are more common for this preparation), the Anaheim is green and about 6 inches (15 cm) long, with mild to medium heat (1,000 to 2,500 on the Scoville scale).

Ancho (dried) A popular choice for salsas, moles, and stews, the ancho (a dried poblano) is brownish red and about 4 inches (10 cm) long, with mild heat (1,000 to 2,000 on the Scoville scale).

Árbol (dried, aka rat's tail) Used primarily in sauces and as a garnish, the small, slim árbol is about

3 inches (7.5 cm) long and bright red, with serious heat (15,000 to 30,000 on the Scoville scale).

Cascabel (dried, aka bola) Mostly used in salsas, the small, round cascabel is brown to red and has medium heat (3,000 on the Scoville scale).

Chipotle (dried or canned) Used in stews and soups for its sweet, smoky flavor, the chipotle (a dried, smoked jalapeño) is dark red to dusky brown and 3 to 4 inches (7.5 to 10 cm) long, with medium to hot heat (10,000 to 50,000 on the Scoville scale). They are also sold canned in an adobo sauce of tomato, garlic, vinegar, and spices. Use the adobo from the can as a quick and easy way to spice up mayonnaise, vinaigrettes, and sauces. I've used two different types of dried chipotles in my recipes: the chipotle meco has a more intense flavor as a result of smoking for a longer time, while the morita has a milder, fruitier flavor.

Fresno The hint of sweetness, resulting from the thinner walls of these fresh, bright red chiles, makes them more versatile than red jalapeños, for which they are sometimes mistaken. They were originally cultivated in Fresno County, California (2,500 to 10,000 on the Scoville scale).

Guajillo (dried) Good for salsas, moles, and stews, the guajillo has thin, smooth, shiny red to dark red skin and is about 5 inches (12 cm) long, with medium heat (5,000 on the Scoville scale).

Güero (fresh) Used in yellow moles, stews, and in escabeche, the tapered, pale yellow güero (güero is slang for a fair-skinned Mexican!) is about 4 inches (10 cm) long and mild (500 on the Scoville scale).

Habanero (fresh or dried) Used in salsas and in escabeche, the small, lantern-shaped habanero is bright yellow to orange and extremely hot (100,000 to 350,000 on the Scoville scale).

Jalapeño (fresh or canned or jarred in vinegar) The proper name of this most ubiquitous of Mexican chiles is jalapeño, but they were first named cuaresmeño, after Cuaresma or Lent, the season in which they were originally harvested. Fresh jalapeños are used in salsas and guacamole; stuffed (see page 194); and in stews and escabeche. They are dark green or red and have a medium kick (2,500 to 5,000 on the Scoville scale). Vinegar-packed jalapeños are great in sandwiches as a garnish.

Jimmy Nardello (fresh, aka Sweet Italian Frying pepper) Originally from southern Italy, this chef's favorite takes its name from heirloom seed saver Jimmy Nardello, who brought the seeds for these long, slim, curved peppers from Italy when he immigrated to Connecticut in 1887. The best flavor is found in fully ripened, bright red peppers. They have no heat (0 to 100 on the Scoville scale).

Pasilla (dried) A popular addition to moles and other sauces, the pasilla is deep brown and about 6 inches (15 cm) long, with mild heat (500 to 1,000 on the Scoville scale).

Piquin (dried, aka pequín) Primarily used ground as a garnish, the small, oval piquin is bright red and about ¾ inch (2 cm) long, with a fiery heat (50,000 to 75,000 on the Scoville scale).

Poblano (fresh) Used for stuffing and for making rajas (strips), the poblano is dark green and about 3 inches (7.5 cm) long, with mild to medium heat (1,000 to 2,500 on the Scoville scale).

Serrano (fresh or canned or jarred in vinegar) Fresh serranos are used in salsas, especially guacamole, if you like it a little hotter than what a jalapeño can deliver, and in escabeche. They are small and cylindrical (1 to 2 inches/2.5 to 5 cm long), bright green to scarlet when ripe, and medium to hot (7,000 to 25,000 on the Scoville scale).

CHOCLO

Choclo is a form of corn popular in Peru, Columbia, and Central America. It has bigger kernels, is a little starchier, and less sweet than what we know as "sweet corn."

CHOCOLATE, GROUND

Dandelion, a San Francisco–based chocolate manufactory, produces Ground Chef's Chocolate by coarsely grinding its 70 percent Camino Verde, Ecuador origin chocolate, which it describes as having "deep, fudgy notes" (see page 276). If you cannot purchase this product, pulse any high-quality 70 percent cacao dark chocolate in a blender or spice grinder to a coarse grind, being careful not to overgrind to a paste.

COMAL

A round disk made of cast iron, aluminum, or even clay, a comal is used to cook and heat tortillas and to dry roast chiles, tomatillos, garlic, and spices. Always used over a medium-high to high flame, you can tell if your comal is ready when the metal is hot and the heat can be sensed when placing a hand over it. If you do not have a comal, use a dry cast-iron skillet (or a nonstick pan, though you won't get that nice little char that sometimes appears on tortillas).

CORN HUSKS

Before using, soak corn husks in warm water to soften, which usually takes around 30 minutes. Shake off any excess water and pat them dry with a paper towel. (Any husks you don't use can be dried and used another time.) Dry them in a warm oven, or you can even hang them with clothespins.

DRIED SHRIMP AND GROUND DRIED SHRIMP

Dried shrimp are popular additions to tortitas de camarón (shrimp patties), tamales, rice, bean and potato dishes. They can be found in different sizes, from ½ inch to 3 inches (12 mm to 7.5 cm) long. For the best quality, select dried shrimp that are almost flat and nearly colorless. Lightly cooked, salted, and sun-dried, they have a concentrated salty shrimp flavor. Look for them in Mexican grocery stores. I do not recommend buying dried shrimp powder online. Instead, make your own. To make ground dried shrimp, pulverize dried shrimp in a spice grinder or blender until reduced to a powder, being careful not to form a paste.

EPAZOTE

This pungent herb grows wild nearly everywhere in Mexico, even between the cracks in sidewalks. You'll see it popping up along highways and sidewalks in the American Southwest too. Epazote has a distinctive flavor—bright, peppery, lemony, and mint-like—and is frequently added to beans (due to its gas-inhibiting properties) toward the end of cooking, as it doesn't "cook" well and tends to take on a spicier flavor if cooked too long. Epazote is also a welcome addition to quesadillas, adding both texture and flavor. Always use fresh epazote if at all possible; available year-round at most Mexican markets.

HOJA SANTA

Literally "sacred leaf," hoja santa (aka Mexican pepperleaf) can be used fresh or dried. Fresh is preferred, but it can be hard to source. If you have space, you can try growing your own. The leaves are used to wrap food, such as fish, infusing it with their complex, root beer–like flavor (hoja santa has the same oils as the sassafras tree, used to make root beer) and with notes of anise, mint, and tarragon. Dried leaves, used in some moles and sauces, are brittle and need to be bloomed to bring out their flavor.

HOMINY, DRIED

Also known as pozole, hominy is whole kernels of dried field corn that have been nixtamalized. It is most commonly used in Mexican cooking to make pozole, a hearty stew.

MASA HARINA

Corn flour ground from nixtamalized corn, masa harina is the basis of many masa products, including tortillas and tamales. Popular commercial brands, such as Maseca, contain preservatives. I highly recommend Masienda-brand masa harina, which is available in red, white, blue, and yellow varieties, all the colors coming from natural pigments of the corn. For Masienda brand masa harina, see page 276.

MEXICAN OREGANO

Mexican oregano (*Lippia graveolens*) is a member of the Verbenaceae family (as is lemon verbena), while Mediterranean oregano is a member of the Lamiaceae or mint family, which puts them far apart on the flavor scale. Mexican oregano has a citrusy, earthy flavor and mild anise notes that allow it to pair well with hoja santa, cumin, chiles, and garlic in moles, guisados (stews), and salsas. If you cannot source fresh Mexican oregano, marjoram along with a little fresh cilantro (for the citrus notes) makes a better substitute than Mediterranean oregano.

MOLCAJETE AND TEJOLOTE

This Mexican molcajete (mortar) and tejolote (pestle) set releases more flavor from herbs and spices than when they are puréed in a blender. The word *molcajete* derives from the Nahuatl word *molli*, which means "seasoning" or "sauce," and *caxitl*, which means "bowl." Tejolote is also from two Nahuatl words, *tetl*, or "stone," and *xolotl*, or "doll." Usually made from porous volcanic rock, the best molcajetes are made of basalt with the lowest possible sand content. In order to achieve a coarser texture, which is needed for grinding, the basalt is mixed with granite, feldspar, and quartz, creating a hard, rough surface.

Your molcajete and tejolote require curing. First, rinse well with water (no soap). Next, use the pestle to grind small amounts of rice several times until the resulting gray sand and grit are ground away. Rinse again and let the molcajete and tejolote air-dry before using.

MOLINILLO

This hollow wooden stirrer is similar to a whisk in function but far more beautiful. It is traditionally paired with a simple pitcher for making Mexican hot chocolate. Method: rapidly rotate the handle between your palms, and its smooth pestle bottom will soften and grind the chocolate as it dissolves in hot milk or water, creating a frothy finish.

NOPALES AND NOPALITOS

Nopales, or cactus paddles, can be grilled whole or cut up for adding to salads, stews, and other dishes. Most

Mexican markets and some well-stocked supermarkets sell nopalitos, cactus paddles that have been diced, with their spines (stickers) already removed. If you have bought paddles with spines, it is not difficult to remove them. Grab the base of the paddle with your nondominant hand and, using a sharp knife or vegetable peeler and working away from the base, cut off all the spines and any bulging areas on both sides. Then trim away the base and the hard edges of the paddle. Now use the paddle whole or cut into pieces as you like.

PEPITAS

Pepitas are pumpkin seeds, but not all pumpkin seeds are pepitas. Thin skinned and green, pepitas come from specific pumpkin varieties that produce hull-free seeds. They have a mild, sweet flavor and are rich in oil, which make them perfect for adding smoothness and flavor to moles and pipianes (pepita-based sauces, mole's seed-based cousins). They also add a delightful crunch to salads, even better when toasted first.

PILONCILLO

This slightly smoky, caramelly unrefined sugar is sold in hard cones in most Mexican markets and some well-stocked grocery stores. Just like brown sugar, there two types, lighter (blanco) and darker (oscuro). Either type can be used in the recipes in this book, though the darkest cones will have the richest flavor. The cone size varies from 1 inch (2.5 cm) tall, weighing about ¾ ounce (21 g) to 3 inches (7 cm) tall, weighing about 9 ounces (255 g).

Granulated piloncillo is available online and has the advantage of being easy to measure and is a great time-saver. Piloncillo can be used in everything from moles and other savory sauces to desserts—or simply to sweeten coffee. To work with piloncillo cones, use a cheese grater to grate the amount you need for a recipe. Or, if you need a relatively large amount, slip the piloncillo into a heavy-duty plastic bag and pound it with a meat mallet.

PINOLE

Rich in fiber, complex carbohydrates, and antioxidants, pinole is the superfood you have probably never heard of. Pinole is not made from nixtamalized corn; rather, the corn is lightly toasted and ground to make a fine powder, which is mixed with a small amount of piloncillo and cinnamon. I recommend Napa Valley–based Rancho Gordo Pinole made from ground heirloom blue corn in Mexico.

POZOLE

This term does double duty, as Spanish for both hominy (see entry) and for a hot stew. The stew is always served with a selection of garnishes, presented in separate bowls, which each guest adds as they wish. These include shredded lettuce (cut with a knife, not torn), diced avocado, radish coins, Mexican oregano, diced onion, lime wedges, and ground dried piquín, ancho, or chipotle chile, or a combination.

QUESO PANELA

This fresh, mild cow's milk cheese is also known as queso canasta. It can be crumbled (or fried) and holds its shape when heated as it does not melt. Look for it in Mexican markets and well-stocked supermarkets.

SQUASH BLOSSOMS

Also called zucchini flowers, squash blossoms can be found in farmers' market at the height of the summer squash season. Select flowers that are bright in color and not wilted. To prepare them for cooking, gently open each flower to reveal the stamen or pistil. You can remove these with your fingers or culinary tweezers. Rinse with cold water, making sure the flow is gentle. Then place on a paper towel and top with a second paper towel to absorb the water.

XOCONOSTLE

The fruit of a particular variety of cactus, xoconostle (pronounced choko-nose-leh) is sour and citrusy, unlike its better-known cousin, the sweet prickly pear cactus fruit. You can purchase the fruits through Rancho Gordo's website, where they are available sweetened and dried, salty and dried, or plain and dried, ready for rehydrating and very close to the elusive fresh version. They will need to soak in water for a couple of hours, then you can add them to salsas, stews, or other dishes. Or for braised dishes, you can skip the soak and rehydrate them in the dish as it cooks.

OUR PURVEYORS

DANDELION CHOCOLATE

Todd Masonis started making chocolate in his garage in 2010, setting out to source single-origin cocoa beans from around the world to bring it to market in the form of bean-to-bar chocolate made from just two ingredients: cocoa beans and cane sugar. Today, Dandelion Chocolate has locations in San Francisco, Las Vegas, New York City, and Tokyo. The company prides itself on working with producers "who make good beans but also people who share similar values around transparency, accountability, and are looking to maintain long-term partnerships." dandelionchocolate.com

DEVIL'S GULCH RANCH

Mark Pasternak and his wife, Myriam, own and run Devil's Gulch Ranch, located in Marin County, California. When they started the company, the only rabbit meat available in California was shipped in from out of state. Devil's Gulch Ranch was born when the Pasternaks entertained a chef friend from San Francisco, serving a rabbit dinner—a dinner that impressed him so that, very soon, orders started coming in—from Chez Panisse, then later from the likes of French Laundry and State Bird Provisions. devilsgulchranch.com

FROG HOLLOW FARM

Located in Brentwood, CA, Frog Hollow Farm is home to thousands of organic fruit trees—peach, nectarine, cherry, apricot, plum, pluot, pear, olive, persimmon, quince, apple, Meyer lemon, blood orange, and more—on its 280 acres. The fruit is picked tree-ripe, which ensures maximum flavor and nutritional value. Frog Hollow Farm is renowned for its stone fruits, which both home and professional cooks in the San Francisco Bay Area and beyond are quick to snap up for making everything from empanada fillings to salads to ice cream. froghollow.com

FULL BELLY FARM

Located in northern California's Capay Valley, Full Belly Farm is committed to sustainability and respect in all aspects of their business, from the way they treat the soil to providing stable year-round, rather than seasonal, employment for their farm workers, to supporting local food systems, and a strong local food economy. Their products are available at select retail stores nationwide and ship via their website. fullbellyfarm.com

LIBERTY DUCKS

Jim Reichardt, a fourth-generation duck farmer, founded Sonoma County Poultry in 1992 in Sonoma County, CA, where the temperate climate lends itself to raising ducks year-round in an open environment with minimal intrusion. Liberty Ducks are raised without antibiotics or hormones. Their products ship nationally via their website and can be found at select retail stores all across California. libertyducks.com

MASIENDA

Using heirloom corn and single-origin ingredients sourced from Mexico, Masienda produces the masa harina that I recommend for all my masa-based recipes. They also sell cookware for making tortillas, tamales, and salsa, such as tortilla presses and molcajetes. Their products are available online via their website or at Whole Foods and gourmet retailers. masienda.com

NBC POTTERY GALLERY & STUDIO

Located in the mountains above St. Helena, California, Nikki Ballere Callnan (NBC) and her husband, Will, specialize in custom-made wares with an organic edge and rustic flare. They draw inspiration from the raw, flexible nature of the clay itself and from the rugged beauty of the surrounding Napa Valley. Their pieces are in service at many fine restaurants, including Auro in Napa Valley, as well as resorts, wineries, and private collections across the country. nbcpottery.com

RANCHO GORDO

Founder Steve Sando has focused his business on supporting small producers in Mexico and "products indigenous to the Americas" since the inception, long before he became known as the "Bean King." The company is best known for their heirloom beans, as well as their pinole, Mexican chocolate, pozole, dried chiles, spices, and more. A testament to Steve's commitment to Mexico's small farmers, the Rancho Gordo–Xoxoc project is a cooperative effort to make sure indigenous crops in Mexico have a market and are sold at a fair price. ranchogordo.com

TSAR NICOLAI CAVIAR

Since 1984, Tsar Nicolai has been a pioneer of eco-certified caviar, incorporating innovative production practices that are rooted in the California ethos and are at the forefront of technological advances for sustainable farming. Their over twenty handcrafted, small-batch products are free of growth hormones, GMOs, and synthetic preservatives. tsarnicoulai.com

WINEMAKERS

BROWN ESTATE VINEYARDS

In 1980, Dr. Bassett Brown and his wife, Marcela, immigrants from Jamaica and Panama, respectively, purchased an abandoned walnut orchard in the eastern hills of the Napa Valley. In 1983, they began planting vineyards and, for nearly ten years, sold fruit to established winemakers in the region. In 1995, their children, Deneen, David, and Coral, founded Brown Estate. Regarded as one of California's premier zinfandel producers, Brown Estate is Napa Valley's only Black-owned estate winery. In 2018, the siblings created their House of Brown sister label, offering a palate-driven, certified sustainable, vegan-friendly lineup of chardonnay, rosé, and red blends. brownestate.com and houseofbrown.wine

BOUCHAINE

Originally planted in the 1880s, Bouchaine is the oldest continuously operating winery in Carneros, a region located in the southern tip of Napa Valley. Founded in 1981, their focus is crafting wines with the elegance of Burgundy, the exuberance of California, and the terroir of Carneros. Specializing in small-lot productions, they make over twenty award-winning wines. bouchaine.com

CEJA VINEYARDS

Ceja Vineyards is a family-owned winery founded by Mexican American immigrants Amelia, Pedro, Armando, and Martha Ceja. In 1983, Amelia, with Pedro, his brother, and their parents, purchased their first property in the Napa Valley and planted their first grapes in the Carneros American Viticultural Area (AVA) in 1986. They later cofounded Ceja Vineyards. In 1999, Amelia Morán Ceja became the first Mexican American woman ever to be elected president of a winery. Celebrated winemaker Armando Ceja, a graduate of the Viticulture and Enology program at UC Davis, creates a limited collection of wines that are complex and memorable. cejavineyards.com

ELUSA WINERY

Napa Valley's Elusa Winery embodies winemaker Thomas Rivers Brown's impeccable craftsmanship and long-standing relationships with Calistoga's most premier growers. Their small-lot wines are all crafted from vineyards within a four-mile radius. Winemaker Jonathan Walden works closely with Thomas Rivers Brown to showcase unique expressions of Calistoga terroir with precision and focus. elusawinery.com

HOOPES VINEYARD

Founded by Spencer Hoopes in 1981, today, the family business is led by his daughter and second-generation proprietor, Lindsay Hoopes. Honoring her heritage and her father's love of farming and winemaking philosophy, Lindsay has adopted regenerative agricultural practices and biodiverse farming initiatives, founded a rescue sanctuary for animals, worked with environmental groups for organic and sustainability certification, and created a hub for young wine fans to immerse themselves in wine culture. hoopesvineyard.com

LOCO TEQUILA

Loco Tequila was born out of a passion to create one of the purest possible spirits in the world. Their Hacienda La Providencia and its 250-acre agave plantation is situated in the birthplace of tequila production, yielding rare distillates of significant heritage and distinctive terroir. Artisanally crafted in limited quantities, their process begins by hand selecting perfectly ripened agaves, then shaving each piña to its white flesh to eliminate all bitterness, before slowly cooking it in traditional ovens. Sweet juices are extracted with an ancient stone wheel, fermented with their proprietary hundred-year-old yeast strains, then double distilled in small copper pots. loco-tequila.com

SCALON CELLARS

As a young man, Jesus Espinoza arrived from Mexico and worked as a day laborer in Napa planting grapevines. Over thirty years later, he is the owner of those same grapes. In 2005, Cruz Calderon started construction of the prestigious wine cave at Caldwell Vineyard, where Jesus worked as vineyard manager. In 2010, the two men forged their friendship, and Scalon Cellars was born within the cave that Cruz constructed and using the fruit from the vines Jesus planted. In 2014, Napa Valley's hundred-point winemaker Julien Fayard joined the Scalon team. Julien's practices as a winemaker employ traditional, low-manipulation winemaking methods, always preceded by carefully considered viticultural decisions, a process that leads to the creation of esteemed traditional wines. scaloncellars.com

INDEX

CONTRIBUTORS

ROGELIO GARCIA, a Michelin-starred chef and previous contestant on *Top Chef*, is currently the executive chef at Auro—named one of the best new restaurants in America by *Esquire* magazine—and TRUSS Restaurant + Bar at Four Seasons Resort Napa Valley. He was formerly the executive chef at Luce, Traci Des Jardins' Commissary, and Spruce; chef de partie at the French Laundry; and a featured chef at the famed James Beard Foundation House. He resides in the Napa Valley.

ANDRÉA LAWSON GRAY is a private chef, cookbook author, and food writer. For the past fifteen years, she has prepared meals in the kitchens of San Francisco, Paris, and Puerto Rico. She founded Private Chefs of the SF Bay in 2013. Lawson Gray has a long and distinguished career in branding and marketing, working with Fortune 500 companies. She resides in the San Francisco Bay Area.

JOHN TROXELL is a highly sought-after food and lifestyle photographer who specializes in storytelling and brand-building images that capture emotion. His work has been published in *Food & Wine* and *Robb Report*. He is based in Los Angeles, California.

Chef Rogelio Garcia,
pictured with his sons,
Daniel and Christian.

ACKNOWLEDGMENTS

Rogelio Garcia

A heartfelt thank you to my mother, Irma Robles, for all her perseverance and love: She was able to accomplish so many things in her life. I am so proud of her for doing her best with the cards she was dealt. My sons have been my strength and motivation to continue to become a better chef and person. They mean the world to me. I'm so proud of the amazing young men they have become. I love you both, Daniel and Christian. My brother, Alfonso, and my sister, Arisbel, we grew up together and have seen many things, but you guys are always there to listen and support my crazy ideas.

To my writer, Andréa, thank you. We met in 2017, when she was putting together a charity dinner for DACA recipients who couldn't afford the application fee. Andréa reached out to me, and we did a dinner at Jardiniere, along with two other chefs. We raised upwards of $10,000 that night. We became friends after that; her guidance and support has helped me in so many ways. This book is her vision as much as it is mine; thank you, Andréa, for working countless hours and dealing with me through the process.

An enormous thank you to Mexico. I can't wait for the day we meet again, to listen to your breath of good food. I was born in your heart and will carry you everywhere I go. You are the heart of this book. I have always felt lost not being able to fully explore you.

To the Napa Valley wine country, farmers, fishermen, chefs, and colleagues: You have shown me so much support through my career. Thank you for always being there. I found a home in one of the most iconic and beautiful parts of the world.

Thank you to the dedicated kitchen staff at Auro for having my back and believing in the dream, as well as the service staff, who are so committed to giving the most amazing service to all of our guests.

I want to thank everyone who has given me guidance, support, and love through my career. If we met when I was fifteen or later, or if we haven't even met yet, thank you. Thank you to all the chefs I have had the privilege of working alongside. All I needed was an opportunity.

A huge thank you to Aldana Iturri, who was such a help in putting this book together. I know you had long days and I can't thank you enough.

A huge thank you to Nikki Ballere Callnan at NBC Pottery for allowing me to plate my culinary creations on her outstanding dishware. I can't think of a more perfect way to show off my recipes.

And last but not least, my immense gratitude goes out to the many folks who made this book a reality: photographer John Troxell, whose stunning photography brought my food to life; the team at Cameron + Company, including publisher Chris Gruener, creative director Iain Morris, managing editor Jan Hughes, and editorial assistant Krista Keplinger. This book would not be here without the tireless efforts of project editor Kim Laidlaw, who made everything shine, and the beauty that designer Ali Zeigler brought to the project.

Andréa Lawson Gray

First and always, I want to thank my three amazing children, Andre, Armand, and Cienna Gray, for believing in me, encouraging me, and listening to me rant. To Aldana Iturri: Your diligence, attention to detail, and endless patience in testing and retesting recipes was invaluable. To my editor, Kim Laidlaw: Your vision as you helped organize and reorganize the chapters and recipes and deft hand at editing my writing is so appreciated. This book would not be what it is without you.

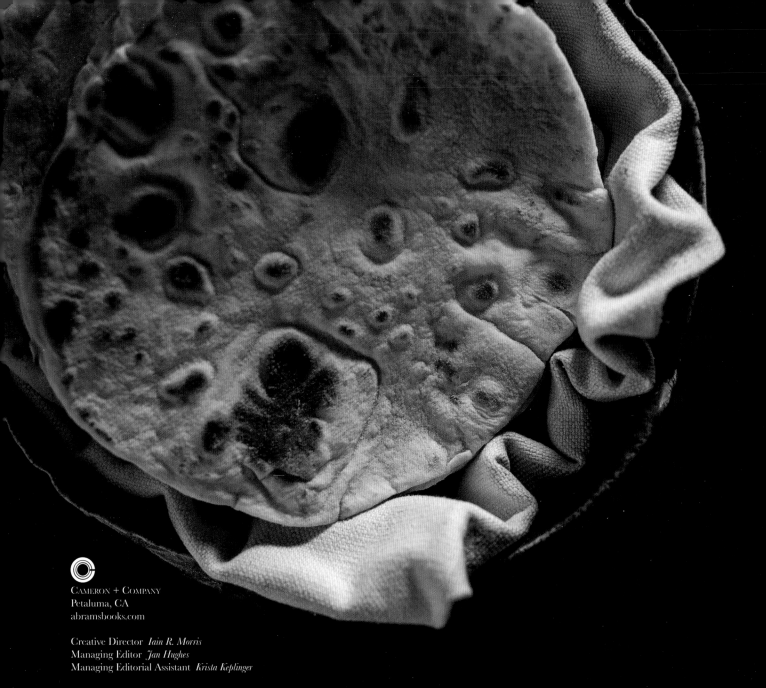

CAMERON + COMPANY
Petaluma, CA
abramsbooks.com

Creative Director *Iain R. Morris*
Managing Editor *Jan Hughes*
Managing Editorial Assistant *Krista Keplinger*

Designer *Ali Zeigler*
Executive Editor *Kim Laidlaw*
Copy Editor *Sharon Silva*
Proofreader *Amy Treadwell*
Indexer *Ken Della Penta*

Text copyright © 2024 by Rogelio Garcia
Photographs copyright © 2024 John Troxell

Published in 2024 by Cameron + Company,
an imprint of ABRAMS. All rights reserved.

No portion of this book may be reproduced, stored in
a retrieval system, or transmitted in any form or by any
means, mechanical, electronic, photocopying, recording,
or otherwise, without written permission from the publisher.

Library of Congress Control Number: 2023947513
ISBN: 978-1-949480-33-7

10 9 8 7 6 5 4 3 2 1

Printed in China

ABOUT THE COVER
Huaraches with Chorizo and Queso Panela (page 47)

The broken plate from Nikki and William Callnan of Napa-based NBC Pottery is a nod to a fascinating bit of Mexican history. The Aztec and Maya calendars both divided the year into eighteen "feasts" of twenty days (veintenas), which comes to 360 days. The year ended with five nameless days, referred to as nemontemi (there is some evidence that every four years, this was extended to six days, as with our "leap year"). Considered ominous or unlucky, accounts note that domestic utensils were destroyed and clothing torn as people waited anxiously for the first dawn of the new year, at which time, there was great rejoicing, and new items were brought out to replace those destroyed the night before. Thought to be the last five days of the Mesoamerican calendar year, it is not known precisely when these unstable days fell. There is some evidence that the end of the year occurred during our month of February. Remnants of this tradition survive in a Oaxacan holiday custom where buñuelos (see page 151) are served on cracked pottery, which are then smashed on the ground